First World War
and Army of Occupation
War Diary
France, Belgium and Germany

31 DIVISION
Headquarters, Branches and Services
Commander Royal Engineers
1 March 1916 - 23 March 1919

WO95/2348/2

The Naval & Military Press Ltd
www.nmarchive.com
Published in association with The National Archives

Published by

The Naval & Military Press Ltd

Unit 10 Ridgewood Industrial Park,

Uckfield, East Sussex,

TN22 5QE England

Tel: +44 (0) 1825 749494

www.naval-military-press.com

www.nmarchive.com

This diary has been reprinted in facsimile from the original. Any imperfections are inevitably reproduced and the quality may fall short of modern type and cartographic standards.

© **Crown Copyright**
Images reproduced by permission of The National Archives, London, England, 2015.

Contents

Document type	Place/Title	Date From	Date To
Heading	WO95/2348-2		
Heading	31st Division Divl Engineers C.R.E. Mar 1916-Mar 1919		
Heading	War Diary Headquarters 31st Divisional R.E. From 1.3.16 to 31.3.16 Volumn 3.		
War Diary	Kantara	01/03/1916	10/03/1916
War Diary	Hallencourt	11/03/1916	12/03/1916
War Diary	CRE's Move Order in accordance with 31st Divn. Order No. 10.	31/03/1916	31/03/1916
War Diary	Hallancourt.	13/03/1916	27/03/1916
War Diary	On the move	28/03/1916	29/03/1916
War Diary	Bus	30/03/1916	31/03/1916
Heading	War Diary of C.R.E. 31st Division From 1.4.16 to 30.4.16 Volume 4.		
War Diary	Bus	01/04/1916	30/04/1916
Heading	War Diary of Headquarters 31st Division Engineers From 1.5.16 to 31.5.16 Volume 5.		
War Diary	Bus	01/05/1916	29/05/1916
War Diary	War Diary of 31st Divisional Engineers From 1.6.16 to 30.6.16 Volume VI.		
War Diary	Bus	04/06/1916	30/06/1916
War Diary	Work Done During Month.	01/07/1916	01/07/1916
Operation(al) Order(s)	Operation Order No. 1 by Lt Col. J F Machem Commanding 31 Divisional Engineers.	25/06/1916	25/06/1916
Heading	War Diary of Headquarters 31st Divisional Engineers. From 1-7-16 to 31-7-16 Volume VIII		
War Diary	Bus-Les-Artois	01/07/1916	11/07/1916
War Diary	St. Venant	14/07/1916	24/07/1916
Heading	War Diary Of Headquarters: 31st Divisional Engineers From 1-8-16 to 31-8-16 (Volume VIII)		
War Diary	Lestrem	07/08/1916	29/08/1916
Miscellaneous	Fld Qrs 31st Div	24/08/1916	24/08/1916
Miscellaneous	R.A: O.P's		
Miscellaneous	Keeps		
Heading	War Diary Headquarters 31st Divisional Engineers September 1916 Vol 9.		
War Diary	Lestrem	01/09/1916	29/09/1916
Miscellaneous	War Diary of Headquarters, 31st Divisional Engineers. From 1/10/16 to 31/10/16. Volume X.		
War Diary	Locon	01/10/1916	08/10/1916
War Diary	Marieux	09/10/1916	09/10/1916
War Diary	Authie	17/10/1916	27/10/1916
War Diary	War Diary Headquarters R.E. 31st Division November 1916. Volume XI.		
War Diary	Authie	01/11/1916	23/11/1916
War Diary	Couin	30/11/1916	30/11/1916
Heading	War Diary of Headquarters, 31st Divisional Engineers. From 1st December. 1916 to 31st December. 1916. Volume XII.		
War Diary	Couin	01/12/1916	29/12/1916

Heading	War Diary of Headquarters, 31st Divisional Engineers. From 1/1/17 to 31/1/17 Volume XIII.		
War Diary	Couin	01/01/1917	28/01/1917
Heading	War Diary of 31st Divisional Engineers from 1-2-17 to 28-2-17 Vol XIII.		
War Diary	Bernaville	01/02/1917	20/02/1917
War Diary	Coigneux	21/02/1917	28/02/1917
Operation(al) Order(s)	31st Divisional Engineers Order No. 3.	26/02/1917	26/02/1917
Heading	War Diary of Headquarters, 31st Divisional Engineers. From 1/3/17 to 31/3/17. Volume XV.		
War Diary	Coigneux	01/03/1917	01/03/1917
War Diary	Couin	04/03/1917	31/03/1917
War Diary	War Diary of Headquarters 31st Div R.E. April 1st to April 30th 1917. Vol. XVI.		
War Diary	St Venant	02/04/1917	08/04/1917
War Diary	Lannoy	08/04/1917	11/04/1917
War Diary	Bruay	11/04/1917	13/04/1917
War Diary	Ourton	15/04/1917	30/04/1917
Heading	War Diary of Headquarters, 31st Divisional Engineers. From 1st May 1917 to 30th May 1917. Volume XVII.		
War Diary	Roclincourt G.4.a.6.3.	01/05/1917	30/05/1917
Heading	War Diary of Headquarters, 31st Divisional Engineers. From 1/11/17 to 30/11/17 Volume XXIII.		
War Diary	Roclincourt	01/11/1917	30/11/1917
Heading	War Diary of Headquarters, 31st Divisional Engineers. From 1/12/17 to 31/12/17. Volume XXIV.		
War Diary	Roclincourt	01/12/1917	31/12/1917
Operation(al) Order(s)	31st Divisional Engineers Operation Order No. 19.	05/12/1917	05/12/1917
Operation(al) Order(s)	31st Divisional Engineers Operation Order No. 20.	06/12/1917	06/12/1917
Operation(al) Order(s)	31st Divisional Engineers. Operation Order No 21.	16/12/1917	16/12/1917
Heading	War Diary of Headquarters, 31st Divisional Engineers. From 1/1/18 to 31/1/18. Volume XXV.		
War Diary	Roclincourt	01/01/1918	31/01/1918
War Diary	A.29.a.12.	01/10/1917	01/10/1917
War Diary	Roclincourt	01/10/1917	30/10/1917
Heading	War Diary of Headquarters., 31st Div. Engineers. October 1st. 1917 to October 31st. 1917. Volume XXII.		
War Diary	Roclincourt	06/09/1917	23/09/1917
Heading	War Diary of Headquarters, 31st Divisional Engineers. From 1/9/17 to 30/9/17. Volume XXI.		
War Diary	Fort George	14/08/1917	30/08/1917
War Diary	Fort George	01/08/1917	13/08/1917
Heading	War Diary of Headquarters, 31st Divisional Engineers. From August 1st. 1917 to August 31st. 1917. Volume XX.		
War Diary	ACQ	04/07/1917	26/07/1917
Heading	War Diary of Headquarters., 31st Divisional Engineers. July 1st. 1917. to July 31st. 1917. Volume XIX.		
War Diary	Roclincourt G.5.b.3.8.	25/06/1917	30/06/1917
War Diary	Roclincourt G.5.b.3.8.	01/06/1917	22/06/1917
Heading	War Diary of 31st Divisional Engineers. From June 1st.1917. to June 30th. 1917. Volume XVIII.		
Heading	War Diary of Headquarters, 31st Divisional Engineers. From 1/2/18 to 28/2/18. Volume XXVI.		
War Diary	Roclincourt	04/02/1918	27/02/1918

Type	Description	From	To
Heading	31st Divisional Engineers War Diary C.R.E. 31st Division March 1918.		
Heading	War Diary of Headquarters, 31st Divisional Engineers. From 1/3/18 to 31/3/18. Volume XXVII.		
War Diary	Maroeuil	01/03/1918	23/03/1918
War Diary	Ayette	24/03/1918	31/03/1918
Heading	31st Divisional Engineers C.R.E. 31st Division April 1918.		
Heading	War Diary of Headquarters, 31st Divisional Engineers. From 1/4/18 to 30/4/18. Volume XXVIII.		
War Diary		01/04/1918	30/04/1918
Heading	War Diary of Headquarters, 31st Divisional Engineers, From 1/5/18 to 31/5/18. Volume XXIX.		
War Diary	Hondeghem	01/05/1918	24/05/1918
War Diary	Wardrecques	25/05/1918	31/05/1918
Operation(al) Order(s)	31st Divisional Engineers. Operation Order No. 30.	09/05/1918	09/05/1918
Heading	War Diary of Headquarters, 31st Divisional Engineers. From June 1st 1918 to June 30th, 1918 Volume XXX.		
War Diary	Wardrecques	01/06/1918	14/06/1918
War Diary	Eblinghem	15/06/1918	16/06/1918
War Diary	Wardrecques	17/06/1918	29/06/1918
Miscellaneous	R.E. Instructions No. 1.	16/06/1918	16/06/1918
Miscellaneous	R.E. Instructions No. 2.	17/06/1918	17/06/1918
Miscellaneous	R.E. Instructions No. 3. Orders in case of attack.	20/06/1918	20/06/1918
Miscellaneous	Corrigenda.	23/06/1918	23/06/1918
Miscellaneous	R.E. Instructions No. 4.	23/06/1918	23/06/1918
Miscellaneous	Table "A".		
Miscellaneous	R.E. Instructions No. 5. Forestry Dump.	23/06/1918	23/06/1918
Miscellaneous	R.E. Instructions No. 6.	23/06/1918	23/06/1918
Miscellaneous	R.E. Instructions No. 7.	26/06/1918	26/06/1918
Miscellaneous	R.E. Instructions No. 8.	30/06/1918	30/06/1918
Miscellaneous	R.E. Instructions No. 8.		
Miscellaneous	C.R.E's Instructions No 2. Stable Management. etc.	15/06/1918	15/06/1918
Operation(al) Order(s)	Operation Order No 31. 31st Divisional Engineers.	16/06/1918	16/06/1918
Operation(al) Order(s)	31st Divisional Engineers. Operation Order No. 32.	20/06/1918	20/06/1918
Miscellaneous	Table "A".		
Heading	War Diary of Headquarters, 31st Div. Engineers. From 1/7/18 to 31/7/18. Volume XXXI.		
War Diary	Wallon-Cappel	01/07/1918	31/07/1918
Miscellaneous	Report on Part Taken By 31st Div. R.E. And Pioneers In Operations of June 28th, 1918, East of Nieppe Forest.	28/06/1918	28/06/1918
Miscellaneous	R.E. Instructions No. 9.	31/07/1918	31/07/1918
Map	Beaulieu Fm. Map 'A'.		
Operation(al) Order(s)	R.E. Instructions No 9.	08/07/1918	08/07/1918
Miscellaneous	R.E. Instructions No 9. Demolitions in Divisional Area. General Instructions.	05/07/1918	05/07/1918
Miscellaneous	Demolitions. Right Brigade Area.		
Miscellaneous	Demolitions. Left Brigade Area.		
Map			
Miscellaneous	R.E. Instructions No. 10.	09/07/1918	09/07/1918
Miscellaneous	Addendum to R.E. Instructions No. 11.	20/07/1918	20/07/1918
Miscellaneous	R.E. Instructions No. 11.	15/07/1918	15/07/1918
Miscellaneous	R.E. Instructions No. 12.	22/07/1918	22/07/1918
Miscellaneous	Distributions		
Miscellaneous	R.E. Instructions No. 13.	31/07/1918	31/07/1918

Heading	War Diary of Headquarters, 31st Divisional Engineers. From 1/8/18 to 31/8/18 Volume XXXII.		
War Diary	Meadow Camp V. 30.c.0.5	01/08/1918	18/08/1918
War Diary	Renescure	23/08/1916	25/08/1916
War Diary	St. Sylvestre Capel	26/08/1918	30/08/1918
War Diary	Proude House	31/08/1918	31/08/1918
Operation(al) Order(s)	31st Divisional Engineers. Operation Order No. 33.	21/08/1918	21/08/1918
Miscellaneous	R.E. Instructions No. 3. Notes on Sandbags a Revetments Builts of Same.	02/08/1918	02/08/1918
Miscellaneous	C.R.E.'s Circular No 4. Notes on Large and Small English Shelters and Erection of Same.		
Miscellaneous	Large Elephant Steel Shelter		
Miscellaneous	Small English Shelters.		
Miscellaneous	Quantities for One Shelter Of 5 Sectors.	05/08/1918	05/08/1918
Miscellaneous		28/08/1918	28/08/1918
Miscellaneous	R.E. Instructions No 17.		
Miscellaneous	R.E. Instructions No. 16.	18/08/1918	18/08/1918
Miscellaneous	R.E. Instructions No. 15.	13/08/1918	13/08/1918
Miscellaneous		10/08/1918	10/08/1918
Miscellaneous	R.E. Instructions No. 14.		
Miscellaneous	Table "A".		
Miscellaneous	Table "B".		
Heading	War Diary of Headquarters, 31st Divisional Engineers. From Sept. 1st to Sept. 30th, 1918. Volume XXXIII.		
War Diary	Prove Houve W.4.d.1.8. (Sheet 27)	01/09/1918	04/09/1918
War Diary	Gough House (S.30.a.1.4)	05/09/1918	05/09/1918
War Diary	Prude House W.4.d.1.8.	06/09/1918	25/09/1918
War Diary	Caestre	26/09/1918	30/09/1918
Miscellaneous	R.E. Instructions No. 18.	01/09/1918	01/09/1918
Miscellaneous	R.E. Instructions No. 19.	02/09/1918	02/09/1918
Miscellaneous	R.E. Instructions No 20.	03/09/1918	03/09/1918
Operation(al) Order(s)	31st Divisional Engineers. Operation Order No. 34.	03/09/1918	03/09/1918
Miscellaneous	R.E. Instructions No 21.	06/09/1918	06/09/1918
Miscellaneous	R.E. Instructions No 22.	06/09/1918	06/09/1918
Miscellaneous	R.E. Instructions No 23.	07/09/1918	07/09/1918
Miscellaneous	R.E. Instructions No 24.	08/09/1918	08/09/1918
Miscellaneous	R.E. Instructions No 25.	09/09/1918	09/09/1918
Miscellaneous	R.E. Instructions No 26.	10/09/1918	10/09/1918
Miscellaneous	R.E. Instructions No. 27.	11/09/1918	11/09/1918
Operation(al) Order(s)	31st Divisional Engineers. Operation Order No. 35	11/09/1918	11/09/1918
Miscellaneous	R.E. Instructions No 28.	12/09/1918	12/09/1918
Miscellaneous	R.E. Instructions No 29.	13/09/1918	13/09/1918
Miscellaneous	R.E. Instructions No 30.	14/09/1918	14/09/1918
Miscellaneous	R.E. Instructions No 31.	15/09/1918	15/09/1918
Miscellaneous	R.E. Instructions No 32.	16/09/1918	16/09/1918
Miscellaneous	R.E. Instructions No 33.	17/09/1918	17/09/1918
Miscellaneous	R.E. Instructions No. 34	19/09/1918	19/09/1918
Miscellaneous	R.E. Instructions No 35.	19/09/1918	19/09/1918
Miscellaneous	R.E. Instructions No 36.	20/09/1918	20/09/1918
Operation(al) Order(s)	31st Divisional Engineers. Operation Order No 36.	20/09/1918	20/09/1918
Miscellaneous	31st Divisional Engineers. Amendment No 1 to Operation Order No 36.	21/09/1918	21/09/1918
Miscellaneous	R.E. Instructions No 37.	21/09/1918	21/09/1918
Miscellaneous	R.E. Instructions No 38.	22/09/1918	22/09/1918
Miscellaneous	R.E. Instructions No 39.	24/09/1918	24/09/1918
Miscellaneous	R.E. Instructions No 40.	25/09/1918	25/09/1918

Miscellaneous	R.E. Instructions No 41.	25/09/1918	25/09/1918
Miscellaneous	R.E. Instructions No 42.	26/09/1918	26/09/1918
Miscellaneous	R.E. Instructions No 43.	26/09/1918	26/09/1918
Miscellaneous	R.E. Instructions No 44.	27/09/1918	27/09/1918
Heading	War Diary of Headquarters, 31st Divisional Engineers. From 1/10/18 to 31/10/18. Volume XXXIV.		
War Diary	Caestre	01/10/1918	16/10/1918
War Diary	U.13.c.6.0	17/10/1918	18/10/1918
War Diary	Croix Blanche	19/10/1918	20/10/1918
War Diary	Lannoy	21/10/1918	26/10/1918
War Diary	Courtrai	27/10/1918	31/10/1918
Miscellaneous	R.E. Instructions No 45.	30/09/1918	30/09/1918
Miscellaneous	R.E. Instructions No 46.	01/10/1918	01/10/1918
Miscellaneous	R.E. Instructions No 47.	02/10/1918	02/10/1918
Miscellaneous	R.E. Instructions No 48.	03/10/1918	03/10/1918
Operation(al) Order(s)	31st Divisional Engineers. Operation Order No 37.	03/10/1918	03/10/1918
Miscellaneous	R.E. Instructions No 49.	04/10/1918	04/10/1918
Miscellaneous	R.E. Instructions No 50.	05/10/1918	05/10/1918
Miscellaneous	R.E. Instructions No 51.	06/10/1918	06/10/1918
Miscellaneous	R.E. Instructions No 52.	07/10/1918	07/10/1918
Miscellaneous	R.E. Instructions No 53.	08/10/1918	08/10/1918
Miscellaneous	R.E. Instructions No 54.	09/10/1918	09/10/1918
Miscellaneous	R.E. Instructions No 55.	10/10/1918	10/10/1918
War Diary	R.E. Instructions No 56.	11/10/1918	11/10/1918
Miscellaneous	R.E. Instructions No 57.	12/10/1918	12/10/1918
Miscellaneous	R.E. Instructions No 58.	13/10/1918	13/10/1918
Operation(al) Order(s)	31st Divisional Engineers. Operation Order No. 38.	13/10/1918	13/10/1918
Operation(al) Order(s)	31st Divisional Engineers. Operation Order No 39.	13/10/1918	13/10/1918
Miscellaneous	R.E. Instructions No 59.	16/10/1918	16/10/1918
Miscellaneous	R.E. Instructions No 60.	17/10/1918	17/10/1918
Miscellaneous	R.E. Instructions No 61.	18/10/1918	18/10/1918
Miscellaneous	R.E. Instructions No. 62.	19/10/1918	19/10/1918
Miscellaneous			
Miscellaneous	R.E. Instructions No. 63.	21/10/1918	21/10/1918
Miscellaneous	Distribution		
Miscellaneous	R.E. Instructions No. 64.	21/10/1918	21/10/1918
Miscellaneous	R.E. Instructions No. 65.	22/10/1918	22/10/1918
Operation(al) Order(s)	31st Divisional Engineers. Operation Order No. 41	24/10/1918	24/10/1918
Miscellaneous	Distribution:-		
Miscellaneous	R.E. Instructions No 66.	22/10/1918	22/10/1918
Miscellaneous	R.E. Instructions No. 67.	29/10/1918	29/10/1918
Miscellaneous	Subject.		
Heading	War Diary of Headquarters, 31st Divisional Engineers. From 1/11/18 to 30/11/18. Volume XXXV.		
War Diary	Courtrai	01/11/1918	02/11/1918
War Diary	Halluin	03/11/1918	07/11/1918
War Diary	Sweveghem	08/11/1918	09/11/1918
War Diary	Ruyen	10/11/1918	10/11/1918
War Diary	Renaix	11/11/1918	14/11/1918
War Diary	Lauwe	15/11/1918	24/11/1918
War Diary	St. Omer.	25/11/1918	29/11/1918
Operation(al) Order(s)	31st Divisional Engineers Operation Order No 45.	23/11/1918	23/11/1918
Miscellaneous			
Miscellaneous	R.E. Instructions No 71.	19/11/1918	19/11/1918
Miscellaneous	R.E. Instructions No 70.	11/11/1918	11/11/1918
Miscellaneous	R.E. Instructions No 69.	10/11/1918	10/11/1918

Miscellaneous	R.E. Instructions No. 68.	08/11/1918	08/11/1918
Operation(al) Order(s)	31st Divisional Engineers Operation Order No 44.	07/11/1918	07/11/1918
Miscellaneous	Distribution:-		
Operation(al) Order(s)	31st Divisional Engineers (Warning) Order No 43.	06/11/1918	06/11/1918
Operation(al) Order(s)	31st Divisional Engineers (Warning) Order No 42.	02/11/1918	02/11/1918
Heading	War Diary of Headquarters, 31st Divisional Engineers. From Dec. 1st to Dec. 31st, 1918. Volume XXXVI.		
War Diary	St. Omer	01/12/1918	31/12/1918
War Diary	R.E. Instructions No 74.	24/12/1918	24/12/1918
Miscellaneous	R.E. Instructions No 73.	13/12/1918	13/12/1918
Miscellaneous	R.E. Instructions No 72.	08/12/1918	08/12/1918
Heading	War Diary. of the Headquarters, 31st. Divisional Royal Engineers. for the month of January, 1919. Vol 35.		
War Diary	Stomer	01/01/1919	29/01/1919
War Diary	R.E. Instructions No 75.	05/01/1919	05/01/1919
Miscellaneous	R.E. Instructions No 76.	05/01/1918	05/01/1918
Heading	War Diary of Headquarters, 31st Divisional Engineers. February, 1919. Vol. 36.		
War Diary	St. Omer	03/02/1919	24/02/1919
Miscellaneous	R.E. Instructions No. 78.	13/02/1919	13/02/1919
War Diary	St. Omer	01/03/1919	23/03/1919

WO 95/2348/2

31ST DIVISION
DIVL ENGINEERS

C. R. E.

MAR 1916 – MAR 1919

BEF. XXI

Army Form C. 2118.

WAR DIARY
or
INTELLIGENCE SUMMARY.
(Erase heading not required.)

CRE
31st Div
Vol I

Confidential

War Diary
of
Headquarters 31st Divisional RE
from 1.3.16 to 31.3.16

Volume 3

Mar 19

Place	Date	Hour	Summary of Events and Information	Remarks and references to Appendices

Army Form C. 2118.

WAR DIARY
or
INTELLIGENCE SUMMARY.
(Erase heading not required.)

Instructions regarding War Diaries and Intelligence Summaries are contained in F.S. Regs, Part II. and the Staff Manual respectively. Title pages will be prepared in manuscript.

Place	Date	Hour	Summary of Events and Information	Remarks and references to Appendices
KANTARA	1.3.16	4 AM	Left KANTARA by train for PORT SAID. Adjt RE 52nd Divn reports for final orders, but does not actually take over stores.	
		11 PM	HQ horses (six) with 3 drivers leave KANTARA for ALEXANDRIA to embark on HMT "TINTORETTO"; also chargers of 223 Coy RE. Weather - Fine, warm. Wind - moderate.	TWM
ditto	2.3.16	6 AM	223 Coy RE left KANTARA by train for PORT SAID.	
		12 noon	HQ RE (3 offrs 1 WO 5 OR.) left KANTARA by train for PORT SAID, embarking on HMT "Dunluce Castle". Left PORT SAID 9 pm. Weather; Dull, warm. Wind SW, strong. Sand blowing.	TWM
at Sea	3.3.16 to 7.3.16		CRE on duty as O.C. Troops, adjt as Ships Adjt, RSM as Ships Sergt Major.	TWM
	8.3.16	—	Arrived MARSEILLES 11 AM. Received orders about 4 pm and commenced unloading ship. Entrained about 11 pm and left about midnight. 223 Coy travelling same train. Weather LD right. Very cold.	TWM

Army Form C. 2118.

WAR DIARY
or
INTELLIGENCE SUMMARY.
(Erase heading not required.)

Instructions regarding War Diaries and Intelligence Summaries are contained in F. S. Regs., Part II. and the Staff Manual respectively. Title pages will be prepared in manuscript.

Place	Date	Hour	Summary of Events and Information	Remarks and references to Appendices
—	9.3.16		All day in train, stopped MACON 4–5 pm. Weather AM bright PM gloomy cold.	TWM
—	10.3.16		In train, only stop 9 am to 10 am. PM. Passed round Paris, snow lying thickly. Arrived PONT REMY 10.30 PM and detrained. Loaded kits into lorry.	
			Very cold, roads frozen, considerable snow lying.	TWM
HALLENCOURT	11.3.16		Arrived HALLENCOURT 1.30 am. Spent night in empty house. Got billets 9 am. 210 Coy passed through about noon.	
		PM	Went to HOCQUINCOURT to see three Field Coys billetted there. 10.30 pm. Horses arrived, has one driver lost at ALEXANDRIA, fairly fit. Weather – Fine, very cold.	TWM
do	12.3.16	AM	Stores of H.Q. T.R.E. at last recovered from station. CRE to (AM) HOCQUINCOURT, (PM) to PONT REMY to arrange for timber. Adjt to HOCQUINCOURT (PM). Most of the day spent in sorting out stores and arranging correspondence. Weather – Fine, dry. Snow almost gone.	TWM

T.M. 1.

CRE's Move Order in
accordance with
31st Div'n Order No. 10.

31.3.16.

1. 211th Coy RE will withdraw from the trenches on the 3rd inst: and on the 4th inst. will proceed to BERTRANCOURT where they will proceed with the improvement of the accomodation for which detailed instructions will be issued later.

2. 210th Coy RE will send one section from BUS to COLINCAMPS on the 3rd inst. where it will come under the orders of OC 223 Coy RE. On the 4th prox. this section will move to COURCELLES and take up work in connection with the store there. The remainder of the Coy will remain at BUS.

3. 223rd Coy RE will send 2 sections on the 3rd prox. to new area — approximately COLINCAMPS — COURCELLES — and in conjunction with one section 210th Coy RE will work in trenches occupied by 94th Brigade. On the 4th, the other two sections will move to the same area

TM 1 (2).

Headquarters will move as most convenient to O.C.

4. The exact times of moves and details as to working parties will be settled direct with Bde HQS by the O.C's Field Companies

T. W.

Copies to   O C   210 Coy
     211 Coy for 92nd Bde ✓
     223 Coy for 93rd + 94th Bde
   Divn H Q ✓
   O. C. 31st Divn Train ✓
   O C Signals
   C R E 48th Divn ✓
   C R E 29th Divn ✓

Place	Date	Hour	Summary of Events and Information	Remarks and references to Appendices
			Remarks on Move. The HQRE has a difficult enough job to move all its stores when at full strength. On this occasion it moved in three portions. Three men are not enough to look after six horses with horse blankets and the new kits complete. The remainder are not able to properly look after the kits, saddlery and stores (especially medical stores) of the HQRE. The work could not have been done if assistance had not been obtainable from RE Units all along the line.	
HALLANCOURT	13.3.16		CRE and adjt to HOCQUINCOURT to inspect Sanitary arrangements of Field Coy billets. Many things were found requiring improvement.	
			Stoves issued TM to enable improvements to be carried out. Weather – Fine	TWN

Army Form C. 2118.

WAR DIARY
or
INTELLIGENCE SUMMARY.
(Erase heading not required.)

Instructions regarding War Diaries and Intelligence Summaries are contained in F. S. Regs., Part II. and the Staff Manual respectively. Title pages will be prepared in manuscript.

Place	Date	Hour	Summary of Events and Information	Remarks and references to Appendices
HALLANCOURT	14.3.16	AM	Orders received for Field Coys to be ready to move by 19th inst. Maps received showing portion of line we shall take over. Part of morning spent in considering arrangement of trenches, weak and strong points, possible distribution of Field Coys.	
			CRE to HOCQUINCOURT to confer with O.C.'s companies as to refitting and further tramway. Adjt. overhauling stores and kits and arranging for replacements.	T
			PM CRE and Adjt. to ABBEVILLE to purchase timber. Weather - Bright, rain 9pm to 10pm. Wind NW moderate	TWM
do	15.3.16		Conference on return at DHQ. CRE to HOCQUINCOURT. Weather - Fair, rather dull.	TWM
do	16.3.16		Work in offices practically all day. Orders to send 2 sections 210th Coy RE to VII Corps HQ at MARIEUX. Weather AM - Fine PM slight rain from 1pm until 10pm.	TWM

Army Form C. 2118.

WAR DIARY
or
INTELLIGENCE SUMMARY.
(Erase heading not required.)

Instructions regarding War Diaries and Intelligence Summaries are contained in F. S. Regs., Part II. and the Staff Manual respectively. Title pages will be prepared in manuscript.

Place	Date	Hour	Summary of Events and Information	Remarks and references to Appendices
HALLANCOURT	17.3.16		Only routine work all day. Weather - Fair, dull	TWM
do	18.3.16		CRE and adjt to MARIEUX to see CE VIII Corps Shewter (Brig. Gen. CARTWRIGHT) also to ACHEUX to see CRE 36th Divn (Lieut Col DENNIS DE VITRÉ). A fair amount of information obtained as to work of Divnl R.E., state of trenches, means of getting into touch with work, advanced parties from Field Coys for instructional purposes. Weather - Fair, drizzle in P.M. Wind S.E.	TWM
do	19.3.16		CRE and adjt to HOCQUINCOURT to talk over information recd with Coys. Weather Dull.	TWM
do	20.3.16		CRE goes on leave. Adjt to HOCQUINCOURT. Weather Fair, rather dull	TWM
do	21.3.16		Officers work most of the day. Weather - Fair, rain in evening. Orders issued for move ; 211 on 24th, 223 on 25th, 210 on 26th.	TWM
do	22.3.16		Advanced parties (1 off. + 4 NCO's) from 210 and 223 Coys sent up to front for instructional purposes. HQ RE ordered to move with 210 Coy. Weather - Dull cold, slight rain all day	TWM

Army Form C. 2118.

WAR DIARY
or
INTELLIGENCE SUMMARY.
(Erase heading not required.)

Instructions regarding War Diaries and Intelligence Summaries are contained in F. S. Regs, Part II. and the Staff Manual respectively. Title pages will be prepared in manuscript.

Place	Date	Hour	Summary of Events and Information	Remarks and references to Appendices
HALLANCOURT	23.3.16		advanced party of 211 Coy goes up for instruction a/CRE and adjt to ACHEUX to arrange taking over of line from 36th Divn: decided to try and send parties up in advance. Weather - Fine, Very cold	TWM
do.	24.3.16		all day arrangements about move. Heavy snow fall night of 23rd/24th mostly melting during day. 211th Coy leaves HOCQUINCOURT for their march to the trenches.	TWM
do	25.3.16		CRE Adjt, RSM and 1 man to ACHEUX to take over from 36th Divn RSM sent on to RE Store, MAILLY-MAILLET. Weather bright but cold 223rd Coy starts march	TWM
do	26.3.16		210th Coy and HQ RE (remainder of) start march vi: Wilhelting at LONGPRE adjt in office of CRE 36th Divn taking over papers. very heavy rain in AM : fine but cold PM	TWM
do	27.3.16		Bdjt round trenches in front of ENGELBELMER with officers of 122 Coy RE. Fair in AM : very wet in PM. 211th Coy arrives MAILLY-MAILLET	TWM

T2134. Wt. W708-776. 500000. 4/15. Sir J.C. & S.

Army Form C. 2118.

WAR DIARY
or
INTELLIGENCE SUMMARY.
(Erase heading not required.)

Instructions regarding War Diaries and Intelligence Summaries are contained in F. S. Regs., Part II. and the Staff Manual respectively. Title pages will be prepared in manuscript.

Place	Date	Hour	Summary of Events and Information	Remarks and references to Appendices
On the move	28/3/16		Adjt to ACHEUX WOOD and No 7 RE Store	
			211 Coy to ENGELBELMER. 223 Coy arrives MAILLY-MAILLET. HQRE billetted at BEAUVAL. Weather - Fine, cold	TWM
ditto	29/3/16		Adjt to Field Coys. HQRE arrives at BUS-les-ARTOIS; CRE returns from leave, adjt rejoins. Weather - Cold, snow 4-6p	TWM
B.y.S. ditto	30/3/16		Preliminary orders re move received. CRE and Adjt to COLINCAMPS and COURCELLES to select site for new store. Weather - Fine, very cold	TWM
ditto	31/3/16		CRE and Adjts to COUIN to interview CRE 48th Divn, re taking over 48th Divn area. Decided to move store to COURCELLES. Much office work in connection with move. Evening - Detailed orders re move received, and CRE's orders issued.	Copy attached TWM
			Weather - Fine. Wind NW. Put to Divn. that Cpl Auotchenny, Engineer Clerk is unfit for the duties of his rank, and should be sent back to England	TWM

T2134. Wt. W708-776. 500000. 4/15. Sir J. C. & S.

Army Form C. 2118.

WAR DIARY
or
INTELLIGENCE SUMMARY.
(Erase heading not required.)

Instructions regarding War Diaries and Intelligence Summaries are contained in F. S. Regs., Part II. and the Staff Manual respectively. Title pages will be prepared in manuscript.

Place	Date	Hour	Summary of Events and Information	Remarks and references to Appendices
			The remarks of February on the composition and equipment of H.Q.R.E. still hold good. The want of a decent clerk has been very much felt this	

T.W. Miller
Capt RE
Adjt 31st Divn R.E.

A.Hugh Stokes
1.4.16. Col. &c. RE

Confidential

War Diary
of
C.R.E. 31st Division.

from 1.4.16 to 30.4.16

Volume 4.

Army Form C. 2118.

WAR DIARY
or
INTELLIGENCE SUMMARY.
(Erase heading not required.)

Instructions regarding War Diaries and Intelligence Summaries are contained in F. S. Regs., Part II. and the Staff Manual respectively. Title pages will be prepared in manuscript.

Place	Date	Hour	Summary of Events and Information	Remarks and references to Appendices
BUS les ARTOIS	1.4.16	AM	CRE into trenches in front of MAILLY-MAILLET with O.C. 223rd Coy R.E. Adjt to R.E. stores, MAILLY	
		PM	CRE 29th Divn reports for information as to taking over line. One section 210 Coy RE to COURCELLES. Weather, fine, bright. Wind, faint.	TWM
ditto	2.4.16	AM	All day in office. CRE 48th Divn comes in. Two sections 223 Coy miles East COCHRAN to COURCELLES.	
		PM	CRE reconnoitring round including WARNIMONT WOOD. Adjt laid up with bad leg. Weather - fine, bright.	TWM
ditto	3.4.16		CRE in motor car to COURCELLES, COLINCAMPS, and AMIENS to buy tool stores. Major GOODWIN to conference Remainder 223 Coy to COURCELLES. Adjt still laid up. One section 210 Coy to COURCELLES. Weather - fine, bright.	TWM
ditto	4.4.16		All morning in office. Lieut-Col J.P. MACKESY comes to take over duties of CRE, goes to DHQ. Weather - Dull, cold. 2/1 Coy RE comes in at BERTRAND COURT.	TWM

T2134. Wt. W708—776. 500000. 4/15. Sir J. C. & S.

Army Form C. 2118.

WAR DIARY
or
INTELLIGENCE SUMMARY.
(Erase heading not required.)

Instructions regarding War Diaries and Intelligence Summaries are contained in F.S. Regs., Part II. and the Staff Manual respectively. Title pages will be prepared in manuscript.

Place	Date	Hour	Summary of Events and Information	Remarks and references to Appendices
BUS	6.4.16	—	CRE and Lt Col MACKESY to COURCELLES and COLINCAMPS: in PM to MARIEUX to see CE, and DOULLENS. Lt MALLINSON comes into CRE's Office to assist with stores work: adjt - he to COURCELLES stores	TWM
ditto	6.4.16		CRE into trenches with G.S.O.1, discussing arrangements for new distribution of troops which was later communicated to O.C's Companies. Decided that 223 Coy is to complete front of line, 211 Coy back front of line, 210 Coy to work behind the defense line. Weather - Dull, cold, slight katterly wind. Work 210 Coy Erecting offices for Divn Staff - Well-aubrey 211 Coy - Hutting 223 Coy - Clearing & retaining BORDEN AVENUE: improving Comm Trenches and protecting Batln HQ a against gas when O.C. 211 Coy work to be done CRE to COURCELLES	TWM TWM TWM
ditto	7.4.16		223 Coy - Improving front line and communication trenches	TWM

WAR DIARY
or
INTELLIGENCE SUMMARY.
(Erase heading not required.)

Army Form C. 2118.

Place	Date	Hour	Summary of Events and Information	Remarks and references to Appendices
BUS	9.4.16	—	C.E. VIII Corps comes in to discuss water supply, corps lines etc.	
			CRE to RE stores. System of dealing with RE stores fixed	
			210 Coy — Well sinking, hutting, stores	
			223 Coy — Tunnelling under SERRE road, clearing communication trenches, repairing firing trenches and strong points	
			Weather — Fine, cold	TWM
ditto	10.4.16	—	CRE to trenches with OC 223 Coy RE.	
			210 Coy RE — as above	
			211 Coy RE — construction of armoured Headquarters, dug-outs etc	
			223 Coy RE — improvement of communication trenches.	
			Weather — Fair, cool	TWM
ditto	11.4.16	—	CRE to DOULLENS for stores.	
			Coy Companies — as above	
			Weather — Rain nearly all day. Very heavy about 1 p.m.	TWM

Army Form C. 2118.

WAR DIARY
or
INTELLIGENCE SUMMARY.
(Erase heading not required.)

Instructions regarding War Diaries and Intelligence Summaries are contained in F. S. Regs., Part II. and the Staff Manual respectively. Title pages will be prepared in manuscript.

Place	Date	Hour	Summary of Events and Information	Remarks and references to Appendices
BUS	12.4.16		CRE to visit 211 Coy work. Adjt to stores at MALLINSON and 2 Lorries to AMIENS	
			Weather - very wet all day	TWM
do	13.4.16		Companies at work as before. Controller of Mines came to talk over mining work with Divn. Staff, but WATLING (stores officer to CE) made RE Stores.	
			Weather - Dussell, wet at times. Strong wind from South.	TWM
do	14.4.16	AM	CRE to trenches	
		PM	O.C. 223 Coy comes in to discuss water supply	
			Weather - Dry, Cold, sometime bright. Strong Sunset	TWM
do	15.4.16		CRE at Divn conference. later RE Conference in CREs Office	
			Weather - Fine, dry, cold.	TWM
do	16.4.16		CRE with CE to COLINCAMPS and to AUTHIE valley. Weather dull, cold	TWM

T2134. Wt. W708-776. 500000. 4/15. Sir J. C. & S.

Army Form C. 2118.

WAR DIARY
or
INTELLIGENCE SUMMARY.
(Erase heading not required.)

Instructions regarding War Diaries and Intelligence Summaries are contained in F.S. Regs., Part II. and the Staff Manual respectively. Title pages will be prepared in manuscript.

Place	Date	Hour	Summary of Events and Information	Remarks and references to Appendices
B.U.S.	17.4.16	—	CRE to AMIENS to purchase stores.	
			Weather — Dull, cold, showers at intervals; very wet in evening.	
			First R.E. casualties in the Division; wagon party of 211 Coy R.E. caught by shrapnel.	
			210 Coy — Erecting huts at D.H.Q., sinking wells, Corps Defence Line.	
			211 Coy — Constructing advd. D.H.Q., Dressing Stations, improving comn. trenches.	TWM
			223 Coy — Improving front line trenches, and forward comn. trenches.	TWM
do	18.4.16		Office work all day. Weather — very wet and stormy.	TWM
do	19.4.16		Conference at Corps Headquarters: CRE attends.	
			Weather — Wet, very cold.	
do	20.4.16		CRE to trenches to site new mines.	
			Weather very variable; frequent rain storms, occasionally very fine.	
			210 Coy — Completing huts at D.H.Q.; constructing dumps for R.A. and A.S.C.; work for gas experts; entanglements for T.M.O.; tree felling and shafting in B.U.S. WOOD.	
			211 Coy — Work on Divn. Battle Headquarters, Bde Battle Headquarters; Medical DVs, cleaning trenches at ELLIS and FORT HOYSTED; improving accommodation of BERTRADCOURT.	TWM

T2134. Wt. W708—776. 500000. 4/15. Sir J. C. & S.

Army Form C. 2118.

WAR DIARY
or
INTELLIGENCE SUMMARY.
(Erase heading not required.)

Instructions regarding War Diaries and Intelligence Summaries are contained in F. S. Regs., Part II. and the Staff Manual respectively. Title pages will be prepared in manuscript.

Place	Date	Hour	Summary of Events and Information	Remarks and references to Appendices
BUS	20.4.16	—	223 Coy - Ble and Battn Dug-outs: tunnelling under SERRE Road: cleaning and repairing JORDAN, LEGEND, NEW ZAMBUK, SACKVILLE St, FLAG AVEN, BORDEN AV, improving water supply COLINCAMPS.	TWM
ditto	21.4.16	—	Little outside work possible owing to very wet weather.	TWM
ditto	22.4.16	—	Again very wet. Chief Engineer came in. Conference of Field Coy Comdrs at DHQ.	TWM
ditto	23.4.16	—	CRE with GOC RA to site Ammn Dumps. Conference at DHQ. 38 lorries of timber received at Q-inn Stone. Orders received to construct 100 huts in WARNIMONT WOOD. Weather - Very fine, bright.	TWM
ditto	24.4.16	—	CRE to front line with OC 211 Coy RE to inspect all 211 Coys work. Weather - Fine bright. One man 223 Coy killed by grenade.	TWM
ditto	25.4.16	—	CRE round 223 Coys work. Adjt to SUCRERIE. Weather Fine bright.	TWM
ditto	26.4.16	—	CRE round 210 Coys work: also preparing RE. Scheme. Weather - Very fine, bright, warm. Wind East to South East.	TWM

Army Form C. 2118.

WAR DIARY
or
INTELLIGENCE SUMMARY.

(Erase heading, not required.)

Instructions regarding War Diaries and Intelligence Summaries are contained in F. S. Regs., Part II. and the Staff Manual respectively. Title pages will be prepared in manuscript.

Place	Date	Hour	Summary of Events and Information	Remarks and references to Appendices
BUS	27.4.16		CRE to DOULLENS. Weather - Very fine. Wind East	TWM
do	28.4.16		CRE to trenches, especially 'B' area. 2nd Lt GRIFFIN arrived from 4th Div. and is attached to 223 Coy for work in (future) 4th Div. area. Weather - Very fine, warm. Wind East	TWM
do	29.4.16		CRE to trenches with G.S.O.I. New scheme of Working Parties promulgated. Weather A.M. Very fine. Warm. Wind E to NE. P.M. Thunder shower. Work of Companies -	TWM
			210 Coy - Erecting huts in WARNIMONT WOOD; erecting RA Dump and ASC Shelters; sinking wells at BUS and WARNIMONT; constructing Div. Baths, and Huts for Div. Bombing Off; and dug-out for gas expert. Police patrol hut. General carpenters and painters work + ironwork.
211 Coy - Erection of Bath-house and huts for 4th Div. Divn Battle H.Qs. OPs; new ning stations; Div. - RA OPs; cleaning trenches, concrete slabs.
223 Coy - New trenches, HYDE PARK CORNER to LEGEND, and VALLADE CORNER, CAT, BEET, FREDDY; clearing narrow trenches; making concrete slabs	TWM

T.W. Mullett
Captain R.E.
31st DIVISIONAL ENGINEERS.

J. Ormerod Lt Cn
2/5/16
31st Division. R.E.

31 DIV RE
Vol 3

Confidential

War Diary
of
Headquarters 31st Division
Engineers

from 1.5.16 to 31.5.16

Volume 5.

Army Form C. 2118.

WAR DIARY
or
INTELLIGENCE SUMMARY.
(Erase heading not required.)

Instructions regarding War Diaries and Intelligence Summaries are contained in F. S. Regs., Part II. and the Staff Manual respectively. Title pages will be prepared in manuscript.

Place	Date	Hour	Summary of Events and Information	Remarks and references to Appendices
BUS.	1.5.16		Conference of C.R.E. with Field Coy Commanders and with O.C. Brigade Permanent Working Parties	
ditto	2.5.16		COURCELLES Park shelled 5 p.m. Several casualties among RE and working parties	TWM
ditto	3.5.16		C.E. VIII Corps comes to see C.R.E.	TWM
ditto	4.5.16		Ordered to finish huts for 3 battns in WARNIMONT by 7th inst. Lieut G.B. WHITAKER, 211 Coy, badly injured by explosion	TWM
ditto	5.5.16			
	6.5.16		Relief night. 93rd IB moves from BERTRANDCOURT to BUS. Three Battns 94th IB from trenches to bivouac in WARNIMONT Wood. R.E. Conference	
	2.5.16		Huts for three Battns completed in WARNIMONT Wood	
	7.5.16		C.R.E. to trenches with G.S.O.I.	
	8.5.16		Work in hand. 210 Coy R.E. - Huts in WARNIMONT Wood; Pife line AUTHIE - BUS: Roadmaking; tree-felling, and homeward. R.E. Workshops 211 Coy R.E. - Erecting huts BERTRANDCOURT, constructing & clearing stations	TWM

WAR DIARY or INTELLIGENCE SUMMARY.

Army Form C. 2118.

Place	Date	Hour	Summary of Events and Information	Remarks and references to Appendices
BUS	Saturday		and Dug-outs at COLINCAMPS and EUSTON. Qum and R.A. O.P's improving C.T's at EXCEMA, JEREMIAH, SACKVILLE ST, TAUPIN, PYLON : Laying down Beaumont Track : work on PALESTINE, ELLES SQUARE, FORT HOYSTED. Concrete work at SUCRERIE.	
"			223 Coy R.E. — Cleary and improving NEWCUT, EXCEMA, JORDAN, CORSE T.R. ROB ROY, CAMPION, MONK, ROLLAND, BABYLON. Constructing Brigade and Battn Headquarters ; R.A. O.P's and telephone DU's : improving water supply gear at LA SIGNY and erecting new supply points	TWM
"	8.5.16			
"	9.5.16			
"	10.5.16		CRE to WARNIMONT WOOD in P.M. with O.C. 4th Survey Sect. to ELLES SQ.	TWM
"	10.5.16		Arrival of 2 Lt. STEVENS R.G. for 211 Coy R.E., 2nd Lt. KEATING R.F.A. for 223 Coy R.E.	TWM
"	12.5.16		Pumping plant at SUCRERIE struck by shell, rising main cut and water supply to trenches cut off.	TWM
"	13.5.16		Orders received to complete forward pipe line by 31.5.16. O.C. 223 Coy reports LA SIGNY — SUCRERIE plant still out of action. O.C. 223 Coy reports LA SIGNY FARM Water Supply ready for use.	TWM

Army Form C. 2118.

WAR DIARY
or
INTELLIGENCE SUMMARY.
(Erase heading not required.)

Instructions regarding War Diaries and Intelligence Summaries are contained in F. S. Regs., Part II. and the Staff Manual respectively. Title pages will be prepared in manuscript.

Place	Date	Hour	Summary of Events and Information	Remarks and references to Appendices
BUS	14.5.16		SUCRERIE W.S. gear reformed by 3.30 am. New system of holding trenches proposed, viz, 94 Inf Bde with HQ permanently at COURCELLES to have one Battn permanently in trenches	TWM
"	16.5.16	—	Decided to move one section 210 Coy to COURCELLES to work with 94th Inf Bde.	TWM
"	17.5.16	—	Orders given to make front line continuous all through. Practically all parties taken from this week.	TWM
"	18.5.16	—	Lieut COXCL..... to replace Lieut SWALES.	TWM
"	21.5.16	—	General offensive work stopped to prepare defensive lines. LA SIGNY Farm to become strong point.	TWM
"	22.5.16	—	Bombardment of support line; many casualties among RE Working Parties. Major GOODWIN severely injured by shell fire; two NCO's of 223 Coy RE wounded	TWM
"	23.5.16	—	COUR. BUS. Water Supply Scheme: task completed, pumping started, but stopped owing to break in pipe line	TWM
"	24.5.16		Water supply still delayed owing to faults in pipe line, water gets through about 6 pm	TWM

WAR DIARY
or
INTELLIGENCE SUMMARY.

(Erase heading not required.)

Army Form C. 2118.

Place	Date	Hour	Summary of Events and Information	Remarks and references to Appendices
BUS	26.5.16		Capt SLATER, R.E. arrives for special reconnaissance work in divisional area	TWM
"	28.5.16		Capt R.E. Dewing, R.E. arrives to command 223 Coy R.E. 2/Lieut W INGHAM, R.E.(T.C.) joins 210 Coy R.E. to replace 2/Lieut HARGREAVES transferred to office of C.E. 4th Army	TWM
"	29.5.16		One section 223 Coy R.E. replaces one section 210 Coy R.E. at R.E. stores COURCELLES, the latter returning to BUS. One section 210 Coy R.E. (Lieut MARSHALL) to COURCELLES for work on front line	TWM

WAR DIARY
or
INTELLIGENCE SUMMARY.
(Erase heading not required.)

Army Form C. 2118.

Place	Date	Hour	Summary of Events and Information	Remarks and references to Appendices
			Stations of Companies during month. 210 Coy R.E. Headquarters - BUS, three and afterwards two sections at BUS, one afterwards two section COURCELLES. 211 Coy R.E. BERTRAN- COURT, 223 Coy R.E. COLINCAMPS mounted section BER- TRANCOURT. Principal work during month; opening up front line and rendering it continuous, construction of continuous support line, constructing new communication trenches, cleaning, deepening and traversing many existing trenches, construction of medical dug-outs, five at EUSTON, five at COLINCAMPS, five at shelter for motor lorry at COURCELLES, and construction of 6 grenade stores at COLINCAMPS and during Posthilt for Army Survey Section and numerous OP's for Divn. Brigade and R.A. Two R.A. Ammunition Dumps erected. Huts for 4 battns and 1 Field ambulance	

WAR DIARY
or
INTELLIGENCE SUMMARY.
(Erase heading not required.)

Army Form C. 2118.

Place	Date	Hour	Summary of Events and Information	Remarks and references to Appendices
			constructed in WARNIMONT wood. COUIN - BUS water supply in working order. BUS wells drawn down to water level, but pumps not connected to to LA SIGNY farm supply restored and put in working condition. SUCRERIE water supply conduit protected from shells by 400' tramway laid. About 2500 trees cut for artillery emplacements, dug outs and pickets. Repairs to roads Remarks on work of H.Q., Div. and R.E. by a Clerk & a Draughtsman. The staff has had to be extended considerably recently to deal with the amount of correspondence received. The authorized establishment of Engineers Clerks is quite inadequate.	

T W Mulley
Capt. R.E.
ADJUTANT,
31st DIVISIONAL ENGINEERS

J Brunton
Lt Col
C.R.E.
31st DIVISION.

R.E. 31 D.3
Vol 4
June

Confidential

WAR DIARY

of

31ˢᵗ DIVISIONAL ENGINEERS

From 1-6-16 to 30-6-16

Volume VI

Army Form C. 2118.

WAR DIARY
or
INTELLIGENCE SUMMARY.
(Erase heading not required.)

Instructions regarding War Diaries and Intelligence Summaries are contained in F. S. Regs., Part II. and the Staff Manual respectively. Title pages will be prepared in manuscript.

Place	Date	Hour	Summary of Events and Information	Remarks and references to Appendices
BUS	4.6.16	1am	Raid on German trenches. Fairly successful use of Bangalore torpedo.	TWM
	5.6.16		Relief night. 94th B withdrawn to GEZAINCOURT for training	TWM
	6.6.16			TWM
	7.6.16		4th Division takes over charge of all work in this area	TWM
	9.6.16		Capt DEWING slightly wounded by shell fire, remaining at duty.	TWM
	11.6.16		2/Lieut KEATING wounded.	TWM
	12.6.16		Capt DEWING leaves 31st Divn to command 126th Field Coy RE. No working parties owing to whole of one Brigade being away for training	TWM
	13.6.16		Orders to accelerate work. No working parties. Capt COLLIN assumes to command 223 Coy RE	TWM
	14.6.16		Dump at OBSERVATION Wood filled at night. Work pushed on at O.P. WAGRAM Avenue, Construction of bridges, construction of return Dumps and Russian Sap	TWM

Army Form C. 2118.

WAR DIARY
or
INTELLIGENCE SUMMARY.

(Erase heading not required.)

Instructions regarding War Diaries and Intelligence Summaries are contained in F. S. Regs., Part II. and the Staff Manual respectively. Title pages will be prepared in manuscript.

Place	Date	Hour	Summary of Events and Information	Remarks and references to Appendices
	15.6.16		Dump at SACKVILLE STREET filled. Shortage of water in front line.	TWM
	16.6.16		Dump at CHICHESTER CAMP filled. 2 Lieut H.W. COULTAS joins for duty with 223 Coy R.E. Shortage of picks and shovels in store observed.	TWM
	17.6.16		Work on EUSTON reserve Dump. RE Conference. One of the advanced galleries blown in by enemy mine. Decided to move Keystone home to BUS Wells.	TWM
	18.6.16		EUSTON Dump completed.	TWM
	20.6.16		Water again off in front Trenches.	TWM
	21.6.16		Water still off; one well reported dry, other pump broken down.	TWM
	22.6.16		Water again restored at SUCRERIE but no water reaching 31st Divn area.	TWM
	23.6.16		Boreholes stuck. Keystone home starts work on BUS Well.	TWB

Army Form C. 2118.

WAR DIARY
or
INTELLIGENCE SUMMARY.
(Erase heading not required.)

Instructions regarding War Diaries and Intelligence Summaries are contained in F. S. Regs., Part II. and the Staff Manual respectively. Title pages will be prepared in manuscript.

Place	Date	Hour	Summary of Events and Information	Remarks and references to Appendices
	24.6.16		Bombardment continues	CRE'O Operation Order No. 1
	25.6.16		Bombardment continues. Enemy retaliate on COLINCAMPS and COURCELLES	TWM
	26.6.16		Enemy bombard COURCELLES and BUS	TWM
	27.6.16			
	28.6.16		Assault postponed on account of wet weather. Ordered to make up large number of BANGALORE torpedoes from wire cutting.	TWM
	29.6.16		More trouble with water supply. Top tank at SUCRERIE connected to pipe line to Start. Guns away, but now result. Army partly to pipe line in 4th Div. area being hit by shell and partly to unforeseen fault.	TWM
	30.6.16		LA SIGNY engine damaged by shell. Decided to leave holes in HEBUTERNE pipe line to supply trenches. 210 Coy R.E. to trenches for work in trenches during assault.	TWM

WAR DIARY
or
INTELLIGENCE SUMMARY.
(Erase heading not required.)

Army Form C. 2118.

Work done during month

Construction of new support lines; these new trenches,
24 Bombardment slits off front line trench. New communication trench.

Many trenches cleaned, revetted, improved, deepened and
where necessary traversed; including front and support to
LA SIGNY Farm connected into strong point.

Dugouts 10 Medical, 5 for Bde Battle Head
quarters, 1 for Battn Headquarters, 6 for Coys Signals,
1 for R.E., 1 for motor lorry (Electoral comm.)
all completed. Two experimental but not completed to
Deep Mined dug-outs. 36 entrances started to
form 18 deep dug-outs. Depth needed gives at least 15
feet earth cover. Chambers started at that depth
should have been connected up to form 18 D.Vs
each with two entrances, if labour had permitted.

Army Form C. 2118.

WAR DIARY
or
INTELLIGENCE SUMMARY.
(Erase heading not required.)

Instructions regarding War Diaries and Intelligence Summaries are contained in F.S. Regs., Part II. and the Staff Manual respectively. Title pages will be prepared in manuscript.

Place	Date	Hour	Summary of Events and Information	Remarks and references to Appendices
			OP's 3 of mannual OP's, 1 Army Survey Post numerous Brigade and RA OP's completed. miscellaneous 12 dumps for food, water and SAA completed. 8 REQ dumps completed. Special experiments for shelters constructed in front line. Roads in forward area. Forward and Return road marked out and bridged to front line. Cross country tracks marked out and bridged. Extra heavy constructed at EUSTON; several spare bridges deposited in forward dumps. Four portable bridges constructed for RA Tramways. Acomville Track laid in trench between EUSTON and COLINCAMPS. Wooden tramway overhauled. 16 railway trucks constructed. Water Supply Wells and pumping plant at SUCRERIE put into protected by steel and concrete double roof	

WAR DIARY
or
INTELLIGENCE SUMMARY.
(Erase heading not required.)

Army Form C. 2118.

Place	Date	Hour	Summary of Events and Information	Remarks and references to Appendices
			New engine erected at LA SIGNY and installation there put in working order. 2 wells at BUS sunk to depth of 130 feet giving good supply; pumps tried, tanks erected and staged. Approximate capacity COVIN – BUS supply in working order: new reservoir, capacity 12000 gals constructed: new 4" pipe lead from reservoir to watering place: watering pond much enlarged and separate place being established for 4th Div. Huts. Two huts completed for 2nd school, 1 for officers of Bde. Trees. About 250 cut down for dug-outs and gun shelter. Branches used as revetting posts, entanglement pickets. Roads steady repair to roads. Both watering ponds metalled. Stone for roads quarried at WARNIMONT. Muschouse. Russian sap constructed to form flash trench & bomb stores constructed. Stores. Gun huts supplied with R.E. stores on [crossed out] as state in Parkes would permit. Work somewhat hampered owing to motor lorries being withdrawn. Occasional shortage of timber, girders, pickets + sheets	

Army Form C. 2118.

WAR DIARY
or
INTELLIGENCE SUMMARY.
(Erase heading not required.)

Instructions regarding War Diaries and Intelligence Summaries are contained in F. S. Regs., Part II. and the Staff Manual respectively. Title pages will be prepared in manuscript.

Place	Date	Hour	Summary of Events and Information	Remarks and references to Appendices
			Remarks on composition etc of Headquarters Div R.E. Have been without an Engineer clerk for two months now. T W Molloy Capt RE ADJUTANT. 31st DIVISIONAL ENGINEERS 1/7/16 [signature] C.R.E. 31st DIVISION.	

T2134. Wt. W708—776. 500000. 4/15. Sir J. C. & S.

Operation Orders No 1   Copy No 5
by Lieut. St Mackay   SECRET
Commanding 31 Divisional Engineers
                                    BUS.
                                    25.6.16

1. Field Companies and 2' day will be
distributed as follows
  210 F.Co.R.E (less 1 section) SAPPER TRENCH
                      1 section Foreman in charge of
                      water supply at BUS.
  211 F.Co.R.E.   COURCELLES.
  223   "   "   COURCAMPS.
  Mounted Sections } at BUS. under Officer 211 Co.
  of 210, 211, 223 }

2. During the operations 210 F.Co.R.E. will be
responsible for keeping the bridges in repair &
for bridging the front trenches and the German
trenches so form a roadway to north of the
Road Junction K.35.a.1.9.
It is of the greatest importance that the bridges for
forward traffic should be fit for the passage of
guns into NO MANS LAND not later than the
attainment of the 2nd Bound, a 2 Batteries advance
                                  there at 1.30.
210 Coy. will also be responsible for repairing
breaks in the 2" water main & taps and for
destroying guns or blowing up buildings in
SERRE, and other RE within forward area

midday during 2 day.
OC 210 will keep in touch with Battle HQrs
94 Inf Bde for purposes of receiving and
sending messages.

3. 211 & 223 Field Cos RE will remain in
Reserve ready to act on receipt of orders from
CRE
Probable employment, at dusk
(a) Wiring Front Line or Supporting Points
   or
(b) Helping in Completion of Supporting Points
or Front Line
   or
(c) Constructing a Support Line
   or
(d) 211 Co. RE preparing road into & through SERRE for motor traffic

4. 211 Coy will maintain tramway in
working order from CEIWCAMPS to BLACKFRIARS
Bridge, and 210 Co the tramways in front
of BLACKFRIARS Bridge.

5. The 10% dismounted Branch of 211 & 223 Cos
under an Officer of 223 Co will remain at the
RE Park COURCELLES until ordered to rejoin
their Companies by CRE

6. O.C. 211, 223 Coys to keep in touch with telephone stations at COURCELLES & COURCELMPS respectively for the purpose of receiving & despatching messages.

7. When work in hand has been completed men should reassemble at places specified in para 1 and get washed &c ready for other work.

8. Reports to be sent to C.R.E.'s office BUS. Negative reports to be sent periodically.

.... C.R.E.
31st DIVISION.

Copy No 1 to OC 210 Coy
    2   „ 211
    3   „ 223
    4   HQrs 31 Div for information
    5   War Diary
    6   Office

CONFIDENTIAL.

WAR DIARY

OF

HEADQUARTERS,
31ST DIVISIONAL ENGINEERS.

FROM 1-7-16 TO 31-7-16

VOLUME VII

Army Form C. 2118.

WAR DIARY
or
INTELLIGENCE SUMMARY.
(Erase heading not required.)

Instructions regarding War Diaries and Intelligence Summaries are contained in F. S. Regs., Part II. and the Staff Manual respectively. Title pages will be prepared in manuscript.

Place	Date	Hour	Summary of Events and Information	Remarks and references to Appendices
BUS-lès-ARTOIS	17/6/15	5.23 am	210 F. Coy RE reaches SAPPER TRENCH and reports assault launched.	two
		7.30		
		12.35	Message received from 210 Coy RE (sent off about 11.45) that G.O.C. 94 Inf Bde did not want bridges over front trenches erected during daylight, and asking for assistance from another Field Company from maintenance. Message above intermessage received asking for two one inch twist drills for boring holes in 4 inch main from HEBUTERNE, or any 9 mills obtained about 8 pm — two from VARENNES — and sent up to SAPPER TRENCH. Casualties to 12 noon 1st inst: Wounded 211Coy one OR, 223 Coy RE 2 OR	7 am
"	27/6	—	CRE goes up to SAPPER trench and decides to withdraw 210 Coy — two sections to COURCELLES, one section to BUS.	two
			Casualties to 12 noon 2nd inst. nil	

WAR DIARY
or
INTELLIGENCE SUMMARY.
(Erase heading not required.)

Army Form C. 2118.

Place	Date	Hour	Summary of Events and Information	Remarks and references to Appendices
	3/7/16		Quiet Day. Arrangements made for 211 Coy RE to assist 210 Coy RE in forward 94th Bde area. Work on repairing trenches.	TW M
	4	10.30 pm	Warned to be prepared for possible gas or infantry attack. Casualties to 12 noon - nil	TW M
	4/7/16	noon	31st Divn. Order No 33 received notifying move to Corps Reserve and later to G.H.Q reserve at BERNAVILLE.	TW M
	5/7/15		223 Coy RE relieved by Field Coy from 48th Divn. moves under orders to G.O.C 92 Inf Bde to BEAUVAL. 211 and 223 Coys move into BUS for the night. 210 Coy RE move to BEAUVAL	TW M
	6/7/15	9.15 am	HQ RE (strength 3 offrs 1 WO 140 R 3 vehicles) marched via LOUVENCOURT, SARTON, TERRAMESNIL to BENVAL where it goes into billets for the night: arriving 5 pm. 211 Coy RE marches to BEAUVAL under orders of O.C.12Kors under orders 93rd Inf Bde. 223 Coy RE to GEZAINCOURT under orders of 94 th Inf Bde.	TW M

WAR DIARY
or
INTELLIGENCE SUMMARY.
(Erase heading not required.)

Army Form C. 2118.

Place	Date	Hour	Summary of Events and Information	Remarks and references to Appendices
	7/7/16	6.45am	HQRE leaves BEAUVAL and marches under orders of 12 KOYL to RIBEAUCOURT via CANDAS and BERNAVILLE. Receive orders at once to be prepared to move 12 noon.	
			210 Coy RE moves to BERNAVILLE. 211 Coy RE to CANDAS again.	TWM
	8/7/16		Quiet day.	
		9pm	Orders to march to FREVENT. HQRE move independently. Route — BERNAVILLE, FROHEN-LE-GRAND, VILLERS L'HOPITAL, BONNIERES. Arriving 4am to find 223 Coy RE already entraining.	TWM
	9/7/16		Left FREVENT 6.30am, travelling via ST POL, MARLES, LILLERS, detraining at STEENBECQUE at 10am. March to St VENANT arriving 1pm.	
			210 Coy RE to ROBECQ, 211 Coy RE to BUSNES, 223 Coy RE to QUENTIN	TWM
	10/7/16		CRE and adjutant to HINGES to see CE XI Corps.	TWM
	11/7/16		CRE and outfit to LA GORGUE to arrange for practice bridging by Field Coys.	TWM

Army Form C. 2118.

WAR DIARY
or
INTELLIGENCE SUMMARY.
(Erase heading not required.)

Instructions regarding War Diaries and Intelligence Summaries are contained in F. S. Regs., Part II. and the Staff Manual respectively. Title pages will be prepared in manuscript.

Place	Date	Hour	Summary of Events and Information	Remarks and references to Appendices
ST VENANT	14/7/16	1am	Orders received to be prepared to move to take over front of line. Officers packed up	
	15/7/16	11.30pm	move postponed until 15th	TWM
		1pm	March from ST VENANT to LESTREM via CALONNE. O/and RE Dump at FOSSE taken over. 210 Coy RE moves to RUE du PONCH, 211 Coy RE to new L'EPINETTE, 223 Coy RE to LES 8 MAISONS	TWM
		10pm	Orders received so to work of Field Companies. 210 Coy RE to work in Right Brigade Sector, 211 Coy RE in Left Brigade Sector, 223 Coy RE to work behind the trenches	WM
	16/7/16		CRE 61st Division comes to hand over	TWM
	17/7/16		Ordered to make M members of Bangalore torpedoes for raid.	TWM
	19/7/16		Owing to weather conditions attack of 61st Divn postponed, attack launched.	TWM

T2134. Wt. W708—776. 500000. 4/15. Sir J. C. & S.

Army Form C. 2118.

WAR DIARY
or
INTELLIGENCE SUMMARY.
(Erase heading not required.)

Instructions regarding War Diaries and Intelligence Summaries are contained in F. S. Regs., Part II. and the Staff Manual respectively. Title pages will be prepared in manuscript.

Place	Date	Hour	Summary of Events and Information	Remarks and references to Appendices
	19/7/16		As 61st Divn. had to maintain their objective, 92 Inf Bde only carried out raids and does not attempt to capture enemy's German trenches. In consequence RE were not sent forward	TWA
	23/7/16		31st Divn. commences to change part of his corps' moving to its right.	TWA
	24/7/16		211 Coy RE in consequence moves to billets at LACOUTURE. Move of Divisional line completed.	TWA
			Position of Coys on 31/7/16 — 210 Coy RE - between LACOUTURE and Les 8 MAISONS : 211 Coy RE — LACOUTURE : 223 Coy RE Les 8 MAISONS. Work 210 Coy RE and 211 Coy RE working in trenches, clearing and improving communicating dug-outs. 223 Coy RE. Work behind trenches on defensive posts, on sanitary, water supply and instructional works. TW Mole Captain	

[signature] Captain CRE 31 Divn

ORIGINAL

CONFIDENTIAL

Vol 6

War Diary

of

Headquarters: 31st Divisional Engineers

from 1-8-16 to 31-8-16

(VOLUME VIII)

Army Form C. 2118.

WAR DIARY
or
INTELLIGENCE SUMMARY.
(Erase heading not required.)

Instructions regarding War Diaries and Intelligence Summaries are contained in F. S. Regs., Part II. and the Staff Manual respectively. Title pages will be prepared in manuscript.

Place	Date	Hour	Summary of Events and Information	Remarks and references to Appendices
LESTREM	7.8.16	—	Orders recd as to 30th Divn being replaced by 30th Divnxn 93rd Bde to take over part of line held by 39th Divnxn	TWM
	9.8.16	—	CRE to see CRE 30th and CRE 30th Divn arranged that one Field Coy 30th Divn should take over from 30th Divn and be responsible for work in that area. Enemy ordered to send 1 section 223 Field Coy RE to work in trenches taken over by 93rd Bde	
			Casualties to 12 noon 9th 210 Coy RE wounded 2	TWM
	15/8		CRE gone on leave	TWM
	16/8		Section 223 Coy RE rejoins company	TWM
	19/8		Casualties to 12 noon 19th 211 Coy RE killed 1	TWM
	20/8		Q wanted to arrange for erection of 'tree O.P.' in ORCHARD POST	TWM
	21/8		Preliminary instructions for offensive actions received. Ordered to construct new tramway line from CADBURY C.T. to FACTORY CORNER	TWM

Army Form C. 2118.

WAR DIARY
or
INTELLIGENCE SUMMARY.
(Erase heading not required.)

Instructions regarding War Diaries and Intelligence Summaries are contained in F. S. Regs., Part II. and the Staff Manual respectively. Title pages will be prepared in manuscript.

Place	Date	Hour	Summary of Events and Information	Remarks and references to Appendices
	23/8		CRE asyon from leave	TWM
	25/8		Conference of Field Company Commanders	TWM
	26/8		Tree O P carried to position ingh CHALFONT from ou by club	WM
			Cranlit to 12 noon 29th 211 Cy RE required accidentally 1 O.R.	WM
	29/8		Remarks on months work	
			copy of CRE's report on months work attached	

_____ O.R.E.
31st Division.

T.W. Morley
Capt. R.E.
ADJUTANT,
31st DIVISIONAL ENGINEERS

T2134. Wt. W708—776. 500000. 4/15. Sr: J.C. & S.

(Copy.)

Hd Qrs 31st Div.

I beg to report work carried out during the month by R.E. & Pioneer Battn. is as follows:-

Signed J. P. Mackesy. Lt. Col
C R E 31st Division.

24/8/16

TRENCHES

TRENCH	FROM	TO	PROGRESS
O.B.L.	CADBURY	North	250ˣ Remade
new "B" Line	CADBURY	PIPE	300ˣ Remade
	PIPE	South	120ˣ Remade
"B" Line	BOND ST.	South	100ˣ Remade
"	PIONEER	LANSDOWNE	7 Bays completed
"	PIONEER	CRESCENT	Cleaned up
"	CRESCENT	50ˣ	Cleaned up
NEW SWITCH near HUSH HALL	BALUCHI	SIGN POST LANE	164ˣ dug 120ˣ revetted & hurdled. 160ˣ wired complete
GUARDS	LANSDOWNE	COPSE	350ˣ reclaimed
COVERED WAY 6.7			450ˣ cleaned out, drained & Trench Bds. replaced.
BALUCHI & NEW CUT.			750ˣ do.
LANSDOWNE			350ˣ do
CADBURY	Both sides of BOURNVILLE		Parapet built up
FRONT LINE	QUINQUE RUE (new)	North	5 Bays strengthened & long Traverses built
ditto	BALUCHI	South	Breaches repaired
ditto	OXFORD STREET	LANSDOWNE	ditto
SUPPORT LINE	SHETLAND	North	Opened up
RICHMOND	PIONEER	SHETLAND	Two steps provided
COVER TRENCH	ARGYLE	North	

R.A: O.P's.

FACTORY KEEP. } Completed.
PUMP HOUSE
CORNER Ho. BARRICADE Ho. MAXIMS. } In hand
MOOR HEN, BOOT FACTORY.
Camouflage Tree (ORCHARD POST). foundation in hand
LADDER. O.P.   1 Completed. 1 in hand

R.A Gun Pits

'B' line. Excavation & framing for one is complete.

Dug-Outs

'B' line.   XI Corps frame pattern.   4 Completed
   "   another pattern. 5 men   1 Completed.
front line. Baby Elephants. } { 1 Experimental & 6
              6 men each   }   Ordinary completed
front line. timber pattern   { 30 repaired & reconstructed
              (various)   { between SIGN POST LANE
                               { & CHURCH ROAD.

CHURCH Redoubt. Divisional pattern   2 Constructed.
                (3 men each).

PONT LOGY   Batt. H.Qrs   Commenced
ST VAAST.   1. S.A.A & 1 Bomb Store Completed
EUSTON   do   do   do.
ST VAAST.   Concrete bursting layer added to existing
            Adv. Dressing Station dugout
GREEN BARN Bursting layer & double roof   ditto
RUE DE BOIS. ? Cellar converted for O. I. to O. to
             store bombs

Junction KING'S Rd } Dugouts for Dressing Station in hand
KING GEORGES Road }

KEEPS

Repairs to FACTORY & TUBE STATION

DRAINAGE

Reopening drains blocked by shellholes, cutting grass & removing weeds, & cleaning out thick black mud continued. Particular attention has been paid to the following, working up against the flow.
GRAND COURANT, COURANT HARQUIN, SUEZ CANAL, BUTTERWORTH'S DRAIN, BERCEAUX DRAIN.
Notice boards are being gradually erected where required.

INSTRUCTIONAL CLASSES

Have been held as under:-

    94th Bde — 4 days
    93rd Bde — 4 "
                2 "
    Divl. School — 3 days & 1 Night.

The subjects taught comprise:-
Sandbag work, revetments, U frames, Inval Braces, Pumps, Mining, Dug outs, laying-out trenches, Bangalore torpedoes.

MISCELLANEOUS

18 Horse troughs constructed & issued. Model trenches. Three floors of barns concreted for Field Ambulance. Huts for Divl. School on hand. Mortuary completed. R.A Ammunition Dump being altered. Moving various huts to new sites. A.S.C dumps providing bridges & revetting sides of ditches. 4 Bread ovens & more constructed. Numerous sign boards made & fixed.

                        Signed J.F. Smitley Lt Col
                                C.R.E
                              31st Divsn.

Confidential

Vol 9.
VOL 4

War Diary.

Headquarters 31st Divisional Engineers

September 1916.

Army Form C. 2118.

WAR DIARY
or
INTELLIGENCE SUMMARY.
(Erase heading not required.)

September

Instructions regarding War Diaries and Intelligence Summaries are contained in F. S. Regs., Part II. and the Staff Manual respectively. Title pages will be prepared in manuscript.

Place	Date	Hour	Summary of Events and Information	Remarks and references to Appendices
LESTREM	Sept 1	–	Preparing for offensive operations. Forward dumps to be completed by 6th inst.	
	5	–	Casualties to 12 noon. 211 Coy RE wounded OR 1.	TWM
	8	–	All forward dumps completed.	TWM
			Casualties to 12 noon. 210 Coy RE wounded OR 1.	TWM
	13	–	4 Permanent Base men employed at RE Park sent to their Base Depots.	
	14	–	Warned to either move, survey to alteration of lines to be held.	TWM
	17	–	Divnl Headquarters move to LE TOURET. 223 Coy RE moves from HVIT MAISONS to LE TOURET, 211 Coy RE remains at LACOUTURE, 210 Coy RE moves from near HVIT MAISONS to GORRE. RE Park moved from FOSSE to LE TOURET.	TWM
	22	–	Casualties to 12 noon. 223 Coy RE killed OR 1.	
	29	–	Warned to be ready to move.	TWM
	29	–	Adjutant (Capt Millington) proceed to ??? Capt RE Act. Adjutant	

G.K.???? Capt RE
31st DIVISIONAL ENGINEERS
O.R.E.

Army Form C. 2118.

WAR DIARY
or
INTELLIGENCE SUMMARY.
(Erase heading not required.)

Place	Date	Hour	Summary of Events and Information	Remarks and references to Appendices
			Short report on months work. First half of month. – 2 Field Coys in trenches, 2/1 on night, 210 on left. 223 doing back work. B. line, cleared and extended. Parados constructed where required, dugouts built. Repairs to C.T.'s, dugouts constructed in front line. Two forward gun emplacements constructed. 5 O.P.'s built. Two large D.O.'s built for Battⁿ H.Q.S. 3 (including 2 Elephant D.O's) erected for Dressing Stations. Tramways extended and repaired. Drains cleared. Second half of month. – All Field Coys in trenches, 210 on right. 223 in centre, 211 on left. B. Line cleared and improved. Islands connected up and improved.	

Army Form C. 2118.

WAR DIARY
or
INTELLIGENCE SUMMARY.
(Erase heading not required.)

Instructions regarding War Diaries and Intelligence Summaries are contained in F. S. Regs., Part II. and the Staff Manual respectively. Title pages will be prepared in manuscript.

Place	Date	Hour	Summary of Events and Information	Remarks and references to Appendices
			Village line. General Repairs O P's — work done on 5 Repairs to tramways. General Drainage work	

"ORIGINAL"

CONFIDENTIAL

WAR DIARY

of

HEADQUARTERS, 31st DIVISIONAL ENGINEERS.

from 1/10/16 to 31/10/16.

VOLUME X

WAR DIARY or INTELLIGENCE SUMMARY.

Army Form C. 2118.

October

Place	Date	Hour	Summary of Events and Information	Remarks and references to Appendices
LOCON	Oct 1		Warned to be prepared to move on the 5th	
	3		Lt R.V.M. Buchanan R.E. reported to 223rd Coy R.E. for duty	
	4		No 53721 Dr Simpson G.H. transferred from H.Q. R.E. to 223 Coy R.E	
	"		No 95532 " " " " 223 Coy R.E. & H.Q. R.E.	
	6		Lt R.C. Stevens R.E. (T.C) evacuated from 1/2 London C.C.S	
			MERVILLE to base (and to England)	
	8		Entrained at MERVILLE 9-30 P.M.	
MARIEUX	9	7.15 AM	Arrived at CANDAS 7.15 AM proceeded to MARIEUX	
AUTHIE	17		Moved to AUTHIE. Casualties up to 12 noon 223 Coy R.E. 1 O.R. Killed	
	19		Lt C.J. Pound R.E. (S.R) reported to 111th Coy for duty	
	20		Lt C.L. Cox R.E. (T.C) admitted to hospital	
	25		Lt Pope R.E. (TC) reported to 223 Coy R.E. for duty.	
	26		Casualties up to 12 noon 210th Coy R.E. 1 O.R Killed 4 O.R Wounded	
	27		Casualties up to 12 noon 210th Coy R.E. 1 " 1 "	
			" " " " " " 1 O.R Shell shock	

Confidential

Volume XI
Vol 9

War Diary

Headquarters R.E.   31st Division

November 1916

Army Form C. 2118.

WAR DIARY
or
INTELLIGENCE SUMMARY.
(Erase heading not required.)

HQ Offr 31st Div R.E.

Place	Date	Hour	Summary of Events and Information	Remarks and references to Appendices
AUTHIE	1/11/16		Weather continued bad for R.E. work	
	2/11/16		2/Lt Bennell R.E.(T.C) joined for duty 223 Cy R.E.	
	5/11/16		2/Lt R.C. Stevens R.E.(T.C) rejoined 211 Cy R.E. for duty	
	13/11/16		We commenced attack at 5.45 am. aimed Geulan Pt. I. had later to fall back to our own lines. Casualties 211 Cy R.E. no officer killed. 2 N.C.O.'s wounded & Sappers wounded. Casualties up to 12 noon 211 Cy. 1 O.R. Killed 4 O.R. Wounded while in 223 Cy R.E. 1 O.R. Wounded.	
			2/Lt R.C. Stevens R.E.(T.C) admitted to hospital	
	19/11/16		Lieut. J.M. Farrell R.E.(T.C) joined 211 Cy R.E. for duty	
	23/11/16		2/Lt R. Norman R.E.(T.C) for duty Headquarters moved from AUTHIE to COUIN	
COUIN	30/11/16		Casualties up to 12 noon 210th Cy R.E. 1 O.R. killed, 223rd Cy R.E. 1 O.R. wounded	

C.K.Walker Capt. R.E.
pr H. OC
C.R.E. 31st Div.

ORIGINAL.

C O N F I D E N T I A L.

WAR DIARY
of
HEADQUARTERS, 31st DIVISIONAL ENGINEERS.

FROM   1st December.1916   to 31st December.1916.

VOLUME ~~XII~~

****

Army Form C. 2118.

WAR DIARY
or
INTELLIGENCE SUMMARY.
(Erase heading not required.)

HQ Ops 31st Div R.E.

Place	Date	Hour	Summary of Events and Information	Remarks and references to Appendices
COUIN	1/12/16		C.R.E. went to England on leave. Capt Collin took over & acts as C.R.E. in his absence. Companies at work on YELLOW LINE, repairing billets etc., also M.G. dug outs. Casualties – 210 Co, 1 O.R. killed, 1 O.R. wittles	
	11/12/16		C.R.E. returned from leave. Wiring of RED LINE started	
	24/12/16		Adjutant went to England on leave	
	22/12/16		Major E. Hopper left 210th Co RE & took command of 24th advanced Park R.E.	
	24/12/16		Capt A.B. Clough from 56th Fd Co R.E. arrived & take command of 210th Fd Co R.E.	
			Capt J.S. Collin left 223rd Co R.E. & takes command of 5th Fd Squadron R.E. Capt Oldham took command of 223 Co RE. Casualties 12 noon 210th Co R.E. 1 O.R. wounded at billets	
	28/12/16		II U.K. Ingham (T) R.E. joined 223 Co R.E.	
	29/12/16			

L.K. Walker Capt R.E.
for C.R.E. 31st Div R.E.

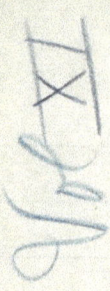

ORIGINAL.

CONFIDENTIAL.

WAR DIARY

of

HEADQUARTERS, 31st DIVISIONAL ENGINEERS.

From 1/1/17 to 31/1/17.

Volume XIII

Army Form C. 2118.

WAR DIARY
INTELLIGENCE SUMMARY.
(Erase heading not required.)

Hd Qrs
31st Div. RE

Instructions regarding War Diaries and Intelligence Summaries are contained in F. S. Regs., Part II. and the Staff Manual respectively. Title pages will be prepared in manuscript.

Place	Date	Hour	Summary of Events and Information	Remarks and references to Appendices
GOUIN	1.1.17		Lieut. H. Rankin R.E. (T.C.) joined 223 Fd Coy R.E. (N Sub)	
	5.1.17		Nos 1 & 3 secs. 211th Coy R.E. left COIGNEUX (in lorries) for BERNAVILLE & FIENVILLERS respectively. Taking over from 2 sections 94th Fd Coy R.E.	
	"		Nos 1 & 3 secs 210 Fd Coy R.E. left COIGNEUX for GEZAINCOURT	
	9.1.17		Remainder of 211th Coy left COIGNEUX & proceeded to BERNAVILLE. Remainder of 210th Coy left COIGNEUX & proceeded & occupied Hd Qrs 31st Div RE moved from COUIN & proceeded to BERNAVILLE.	
	11.1.17		223 Coy R.E. remain behind at COIGNEUX	
	25.1.17		210th Fd Coy R.E. proceeded by motor lorry to BEAUSSART & took over from 1st & 5/6th Fd Coy R.E. (Work yellow line in front of BEAUMONT HAMEL) under C.E. V" Corps Men work by companies in rest during month. Huntin, repairs billets, erecting NISSEN HUTS, baths etc. work at our School & Laundry.	

J. H. Walter Capt RE
for C.R.E 31st Div

T2134. Wt. W708—776. 500000. 4/15. Sir J. C. & S.

Vol 12

Original

Confidential
War Diary
of
31st Divisional Engineers
from 1-2-17 to 28-2-17.
Vol. XIIII

Army Form C. 2118.

WAR DIARY
or
INTELLIGENCE SUMMARY.
(Erase heading not required.)

Hd Qrs 31st Div RE

Instructions regarding War Diaries and Intelligence Summaries are contained in F. S. Regs., Part II. and the Staff Manual respectively. Title pages will be prepared in manuscript.

Place	Date	Hour	Summary of Events and Information	Remarks and references to Appendices
BERNAVILLE	1/2/17		Hd Qrs, RE + 211th Coy HdQrs with one section at BERNAVILLE. 1 Sect Dil Coy at VAUCHELLES. 1 Sec BERTEAUCOURT. 1 Sec BAYNEU. 210th Coy working on Yellow Line in front of BEAUMONT HAMEL. 223rd Coy still at COIGNEUX	
	5/2/17		211th Coy moved to SAILLY DELL in lorries. 210th Coy moved from back. 223rd Coy to BERNAVILLE. 210th Coy moved from BEAUSSART to BERNAVILLE in lorries. 223rd Coy left in aeroplanes at VAUCHELLES for intk at Our School + alone to ...	
	8/2/17		Also he moved to Our Laundry Capt Washington attacked & works RE in instruction CAME with my leave. MAJ ANDERSON TOOK over from him. 223rd Coy Hd Qrs moved to BONNEVILLE. Li RANKIN H. RE left
	9/2/17		223 Coy & from No 1 aeft Coy RMRE	
			II A. BARKER H.E. R.E. returned to 223 Coy RE for duty. Lt R.M. PADDINSON joined in Coy RE for duty 210th Coy RE + 223 Coy RE concentrated at BERNAVILLE & BONNEVILLE respectively	
	16/2/17		210 Coy RE Marched to BEAUVAL	
	19/2/17		Hd Qrs Div Hd Qrs RE 211th Coy RE moved to BEAUVAL	
	20/2/17		...	

T2134. Wt. W.708-776. 500000. 4/15. Sir J.C. & S.

Army Form C. 2118.

WAR DIARY
or
INTELLIGENCE SUMMARY.
(Erase heading not required.)

Instructions regarding War Diaries and Intelligence Summaries are contained in F. S. Regs., Part II. and the Staff Manual respectively. Title pages will be prepared in manuscript.

Place	Date	Hour	Summary of Events and Information	Remarks and references to Appendices
	26.2.17		Lt. J.M. Favell R.E. transferred to 5th 7th Survey Coy R.E.	
	20.2.17		No 4 Coy R.E. marched to Coigneux	
COIGNEUX	21.2.17		Hd Qrs Div moved to AUTHIE. Hd Qrs R.E. moved to COIGNEUX	
	24.2.17		C.R.E. returned from leave	
	25.2.17		Maj Anderson R.E. reported this Coy	
	26.2.17		Capt Hitchman line transferred to A & Q for instruction & Hd Qrs R.E. for machine Capt of 11 had Hayot was attached to Hd Qrs R.E. for instruction	
			SERRE evacuated by enemy. 93rd Bde attempted to take	
			GOMMECOURT. Lt ATKINSON & Lt PADDISON admitted to hospital sick (trench). Lt MARSHALL still away on a Course. C.R.E. inspected trenches + pool point area	
	27.2.17			
	28.2.17		GOMMECOURT taken by 93rd Inf/Bde	

R.T. Walker Capt R.E.
for CRE 8th Div
28/2/17

SECRET.   COPY No......11......

31st DIVISIONAL ENGINEERS ORDER No.3.
****

26/2/17.

Reference Map
HEBUTERNE 1/10,000

                           12th K.O.Y.L.I.
1. R.E. and detachment are detailed for work as follows :-

   (a) 210th Field Coy.R.E.----- To repair HEBUTERNE - SERRE Road
                                 from K.16.a.2.6. to THE POINT, so as
                                 to take 1st Pack Animals and then
                                 later Vehicles.

   (b) 223rd Field Coy.R.E.----- To repair HEBUTERNE - 16 POPLARS
                                 Road from K.16.a.2.6. to 16 POPLARS, so
                                 as to take 1st Pack Animals, and then
                                 later Vehicles.

2. The Tramways Officer (2nd.Lieut. Barker 223rd Field Coy.R.E.)
   assisted by 1 Section 223rd Field Coy.R.E. & 12th K.O.Y.L.I. to
   put tram line from K.20.c.central along JEAN BART in good order,
   and on completion to put the HEBUTERNE -SERRE Road tram line in
   good order. Trucks to be collected at Tram Bases.

3. Field Coys.R.E. to reconnoitre and examine the Tank Traps and
   dug-outs in captured territory with a view to discovering and
   disconnecting mines or traps as under :-

   223 ~~210~~th Field Coy.R.E.----- SUNKEN Road (inclusive) to North.

   210 ~~223~~rd Field Coy.R.E.----- SUNKEN Road (exclusive) to South.

   To report result to Troops and Brigade in the above areas.

4. Detachment 12th K.O.Y.L.I. will repair SAILLY - HEBUTERNE Road, and
   Road through HEBUTERNE to K.16.a.2.6.   Also provide party of
   30 for R.E.Park at COIGNEUX.

5. 211th Field Coy.R.E. will remain in reserve at BAYENCOURT.

6. Please acknowledge receipt.

H.Q.R.E.   Lt.Colonel.R.E.
26/2/17.   C.R.E. 31st Division.

Copies to :-

No.1.----- 210th Field Coy.R.E.
No.2.----- 211th Field Coy.R.E.
No.3.----- 223rd Field Coy.R.E.
No.4.----- Detachment 12th K.O.Y.L.I.
No.5.----- R.E.Park COIGNEUX.
No.6.----- 31st Divisional Arty.
No.7.----- 92nd Inf.Bde.
No.8.----- 93rd Inf.Bde.
No.9.----- 31st Divisional Headquarters,"G"
No.10----- 31st Divisional Headquarters,"Q"
No.11----- War Diary
No.12----- File.

ORIGINAL.

CONFIDENTIAL.

WAR DIARY

of

HEADQUARTERS, 31st DIVISIONAL ENGINEERS.

From 1/3/17 to 31/3/17.

VOLUME XV

* * * * * * * * * * * *

Army Form C. 2118.

WAR DIARY
INTELLIGENCE SUMMARY.
(Erase heading not required.)

Instructions regarding War Diaries and Intelligence Summaries are contained in F.S. Regs., Part II. and the Staff Manual respectively. Title pages will be prepared in manuscript.

Hd. Qrs. 31st Div. R.E.

Place	Date	Hour	Summary of Events and Information	Remarks and references to Appendices
COIGNEUX	1.3.17		C.R.E. investigated roads + dugouts in area evacuated by the enemy. Enemy still retiring along 11.5 Mallison admitted to hospital	
COUIN	4.3.17		Left COIGNEUX - moved to COUIN. Taking over billets from 19th Div R.E.	
	5.3.17		2/Lt Tordingesm joined No 1st Co, R.E. for duty 11/Lt RES 2nd Lt RE. joined	
	6.3.17		C.R.E. inspected forward roads. Still in bad condition. improving slightly. Slight frost.	
	7.3.17		Slight frost continued	
	8.3.17		Hard frost. Had previously received for day June or hold to date approx L.1.a.33. L.2.C.23. L.9.a.2.9. L.9.a.93. L.15.6 behind L.22.a.2.2 Attempts to take BUCQUOY not altogether successful.	
	9.3.17		Frost, very heavy	
	10.3.17		Thaw. Precautions taken in 2/1st Co, RE in party again in I2 Sec. C.R.E. about to QR came to Couin to take over work on roads	
	11.3.17			
	12.3.16		Gave to Thompson line Hospital 1/1 R.E. rendered evening by Fr to Plain unable to get man I have helpers asked for	

J Mather Capt RE
Ag 1 C R E 31st Divn

Army Form C. 2118.

WAR DIARY
INTELLIGENCE SUMMARY.
(Erase heading not required.)

Hd Qrs
31st Divn R.E.

Instructions regarding War Diaries and Intelligence Summaries are contained in F.S. Regs., Part II. and the Staff Manual respectively. Title pages will be prepared in manuscript.

Place	Date	Hour	Summary of Events and Information	Remarks and references to Appendices
COUIN	14.3.17		Orders received from Divn to be prepared to move into 1st army area, to concentrate at BOUQUEMAISON. Div to move	
	15.3.17		Hd received from Div to effect that move East is probable.	
			Div to be ready to move at 2 hrs notice	
	16.3.17		Orders confirmed to move north	
	18.3.17		Received orders to move to BOUQUEMAISON Div 11th inst	
	20.3.17		Hd Qrs moved to BOUQUEMAISON	
	21.3.17		" " " RAMECOURT	
	22.3.17		" " " PERNES	
	23.3.17		Remained one day at PERNES	
	24.3.17		Hd Qrs moved to NORRENT FONTES	
	25.3.17		" " " ST VENANT	
	26.3.17		1/1 Pt Crowther joined 211th Fd Coy RE for duty	
	27.3.17		All Fd Cos killed he has also	
			All companies engaged in training	
	29.3.17		All companies + Hd Qrs inoculated	

J R Mathew Capt RE
Adj for C.R.E. 31st Divn R.E.

Vol 14

ORIGINAL

CONFIDENTIAL

WAR DIARY
OF
HEADQUARTERS. 31st DIV. R.E
APRIL 1ST to APRIL 30TH 1917
VOL. XVI

Army Form C. 2118.

WAR DIARY
or
INTELLIGENCE SUMMARY.
(Erase heading not required.)

1st Qrs
31st Div R.E.

Instructions regarding War Diaries and Intelligence Summaries are contained in F.S. Regs., Part II. and the Staff Manual respectively. Title pages will be prepared in manuscript.

Place	Date	Hour	Summary of Events and Information	Remarks and references to Appendices
ST VENANT	2.4.17		Orders received for 2" Coy to be in readiness to move for work in 1st Canadian Corps area. 223rd Fd Coy traveled	
	3.4.17		Heavy fall of snow. 223rd Coy moved to BETHUNE	
	4.4.17		223rd Coy RE moved to GUOY SERVINS to work in 1st Canadian Corps area	
	6.4.17		Warned to move into COUNEHEM area on 7th inst. Order about later to 8th inst	
	8.4.17		Moved into GONNEHEM and 2" Coy & 1st Qrs RE marched to 211th Coy at GONNEHEM. 1st Qrs RE at LANNOY (Billeting)	
LANNOY	10.4.17		Warned to be prepared to move by 11 am 11th inst	
	11.4.17		1st Qrs RE & 2" Coys moved from LANNOY - GONNEHEM respectively to 211th Coy to 210 2" Coy from & BRUAY to 211.	
			& MAISNIL les RUITZ	
BRUAY	12.4.17		210th Coy warned to move	
	13.4.17		210th — moved to BARLIN. 211th Coy RE march to RUESTREVILLE	
OURTON	14.4.17		1st Qrs RE moved from BRUAY to OURTON	

Army Form C. 2118.

WAR DIARY
or
INTELLIGENCE SUMMARY.
(Erase heading not required.)

Instructions regarding War Diaries and Intelligence Summaries are contained in F. S. Regs., Part II. and the Staff Manual respectively. Title pages will be prepared in manuscript.

Place	Date	Hour	Summary of Events and Information	Remarks and references to Appendices
OURTON	15.4.17		223 Coy R.E. Hanet to move to ECOIVRES	
	16.4.17		Moved to ECOIVRES	
	17.4.17		20th + 21st Coy moved to X huhments at ECOIVRES	
	18.4.17		Third field Coys within anders C.E. XIII Corps	
	22.4.17		C.R.E. visited ECOIVRES area to invesligate accommodation. Cavalry up to 1 new. Capt F. Horsepool + Lt R H Padmore wounded, shell fire	
	23.4.17		Capt Horsepool + Lt Padmore another to Hospital	
	24.4.17			
	29.4.17		Moved from OURTON to VILERS- CHATEL - billet here / lik night	
	30.4.17		Moved from VILERS CHATEL to C.4.a.6.) near ROCLINCOURT	

J M Walker Capt R.E.
for C.R.E. 31st Div

ORIGINAL.

Vol 15

CONFIDENTIAL.

WAR DIARY

of

HEADQUARTERS, 31st DIVISIONAL ENGINEERS.

From 1st May 1917 to 30th May 1017.

Volume XVII.
****

WAR DIARY
INTELLIGENCE SUMMARY.
(Erase heading not required.)

Army Form C. 2118.

Hd Qrs 31st Divn RE

Place	Date	Hour	Summary of Events and Information	Remarks and references to Appendices
ROCLINCOURT G.4.a.6.3	1.5.17		Move from G.4.a.6.3 & G.S.a.S.8 ROCLINCOURT. 210th Coy at G.S.a.S.S. 211th Coy at C.10.a.2.2. 223rd Coy at G.4.b.s.c.	
	2.5.17		Heard that attack would be made on OPPY on May 3rd. Camp fired on by German Aeroplane at night. One officer wounded.	
	3.5.17		Attacked at 3.45 am. Very strong counter attack by enemy. Attack on OPPY failed. Casualties up to 12 noon 211th Coy RE. O.R. 10 wounded. All Coy? 223rd Coy RE. O.R 1 wounded. All Coy? Casualties up to noon 211th Coy RE. 1 Off killed. 4 O.R wounded. (A/Capt. Crosthe killed)	
	4.5.17		Casualties to 12 noon 223rd Pn Coy RE wounded 2 O.R All Coy? 211th Fn Coy RE wounded 2 O.R all Coy?	
	5.5.17		Casualties to 12 noon. Wounded A/Major M.A.Crosthmas M.C. RE 2 O.R. All Coy 3m	

Army Form C. 2118.

WAR DIARY
or
INTELLIGENCE SUMMARY.
(Erase heading not required.)

1st Pro 31st Div
R E

Instructions regarding War Diaries and Intelligence Summaries are contained in F. S. Regs., Part II. and the Staff Manual respectively. Title pages will be prepared in manuscript.

Place	Date	Hour	Summary of Events and Information	Remarks and references to Appendices
ROCLINCOURT Q.u.a 6.3	6.5.17		2nd Lieut Mansfield J.E. (T.C.) & 2nd Lieut Burfield F.R. (T.C.) joined 211th Coy RE for duty.	
	7.5.17		Casualties to 12 noon 210th Coy RE. OR 1 all fill artillery	
	10.5.17		Casualties to 12 noon 210th Coy RE. OR 7 Ros. 1 Artillery wounded	
	11.5.17		2nd Lieut A. Blair (R.E.) reported to 211th Coy RE for duty.	
	14.5.17		Casualties to 12 noon 210th Coy RE OR 2 wft 1 artillery wounded	
	16.5.17		Casualties to 12 noon 210th Coy RE OR 2 Killed & Howitzer artillery 4	
	17.5.17		Casualties to 12 noon 210th Coy RE. OR 1 wounded for OR 1.	
			Work continued on Red and Green Lines	
			2nd Lieut H.F.A. Keating joined 211th Coy RE for duty & was transferred to 210th Coy R.E.	
	30.5.17		Northern sector of RED LINE handed over to 5th Division	

M. Cahill
ADJUTANT,
31st DIVISIONAL ENGINEERS
Or CRE

ORIGINAL

CONFIDENTIAL.

WAR DIARY

of

Headquarters, 31st Divisional Engineers.

From 1/11/17 to 30/11/17.

VOLUME XXIII

WAR DIARY

INTELLIGENCE SUMMARY. 31st Div RE

Army Form C. 2118.

H.Qrs

(Erase heading not required.)

Place	Date	Hour	Summary of Events and Information	Remarks and references to Appendices
ROCLINCOURT	1.11.17		Changed to B.6 morn No 1st Fd Cy	
	9.11.17		No 4 + 223 Fd Cys in line. No 2d Cy on back work. Raid Mt. FRESNOY in which 16 captured. No 2 Fd Cy took part each taking matl. charges for destruction of dugouts & dyouts. No manoeuvre + one SAA dump were destroyed. Casualties 1 Offr & 6 wounded. No injury.	
	14.11.17		11 Rnks inc 1 Offr on 4 days leave to Paris	
	16.11.17		Maj Cochrane 223 Fd Cy left on 14 days leave to England	
	17.11.17		Casualties + Recon No 2d Cy OR 2 found. Wounded	
			self	
	18.11.17		Lt Biglman returned 223d Fd Cy from Paris leave	
			Capt Powell 11th Fd Cy left to attend bridging course at AIRE	
	21.11.17		No 11th Fd Cy handed over ACHEVILLE section to CANADIANS	
	22.11.17		Casualties + 12.0 morn No 2d Cy. 1 OR accidentally wounded, Gunshot	
	25.11.17		"	1 OR wounded Shell	
	26.11.17		"	1 OR killed T.M.	
	30.11.17		2-11 Fd Cy	1 OR wounded M.G. 1 OR wounded M.G.	

R K Nesham Capt RE
A/ng 31st Div RE
For CRE

ORIGINAL.

CONFIDENTIAL.

WAR DIARY
of
Headquarters, 31st Divisional Engineers.

From 1/12/17   to 31/12/17.

VOLUME XXIV

Army Form C. 2118.

WAR DIARY
or
INTELLIGENCE SUMMARY. HQ Corps Engrs R.E.
(Erase heading not required.)

Instructions regarding War Diaries and Intelligence Summaries are contained in F. S. Regs., Part II. and the Staff Manual respectively. Title pages will be prepared in manuscript.

Place	Date	Hour	Summary of Events and Information	Remarks and references to Appendices
Boulincourt	1/3/17		Capt. Powell 211 Fld Coy returned from Heavy Bridging Course A.I.F.	
	2/3/17		Major Cochran 223 Fld Coy Returns from leave to England	
	3/3/17		Lieut Ford proceeds on leave to Tank Corps for 96th Division conjunction with 2nd Lieut Lawton on 211 Fld Coy & Mr Grosbety transfer. 211 Field Coy moved to Masnieres. 223 Fld Coy moved to HQ.RCE — 210 Fld Coy	
	4/3/17		moved to Masnieres.	
	5/3/17		Capt H.S. Arthurton Escott 210 Fld Coy proceeds to HQ Corps RE Art. Capt Pickmore RE 223 Field Coy left RE Course at BISNOSCOPES Brigade relieved by 56th Division. 3rd Brit. HQ remained at Equincourt	
			Lieut Foye showing rebuilding Tilloy R.E.	
	11/3/17		Lieut Ingham RE 223 Fld Coy on leave to England. Lt Cpl Wood R.E. 211 Field Coy	
			Lt F. Birkinshaw RE 210 Fld Coy and Lt Loughton RE 210 Lawton returns from England on transfer to Tank Corps. Lt Cyril Buchanan M.C.R.E. left for Camouflage Course Honsieux.	
	13/3/17		H.Q. R.E.M.Q. 211 Field Coy. left for duty with C.R.E. Hayes.	
	14/3/17		Lt R.G. Corp R.E. and 2/Lt J.E.D. Makepeace reported for duty to 210 Fld Coy H.Q. HQ 113th Fd. Coy reports for duty to 211 Fld Coy	
	15/3/17		Lt. Cyril Buchanan M.C. RE. 223 Fld Coy returned from Camouflage Course Honsieux	
	18/3/17		Capt Hodgson RE 211 Lawton on leave to England	
	29/3/17		Capt Bright RE 210 Fld Coy on leave to England	

Army Form C. 2118.

WAR DIARY
or
INTELLIGENCE SUMMARY. 3rd Div. R.E.
(Erase heading not required.)

Instructions regarding War Diaries and Intelligence Summaries are contained in F. S. Regs., Part II. and the Staff Manual respectively. Title pages will be prepared in manuscript.

Place	Date	Hour	Summary of Events and Information	Remarks and references to Appendices
Roisincourt	26/9/17		Field Coys. moved to ECOUST to look over work of 56th Div. 223 Field Coy. went to Bois in ORIEUX SECTOR. 211 Fd. Coy. went to 7 Bois in ACHEVILLE SECTOR.	
	23/9/17		3rd Div. took over command of HILLEUX + ACHEVILLE sectors from 56th Div.	
	24/9/17		2/o Labr. Coy. commence Capt. Ming. Scheme.	
	9/9/17		Work in own command's Langrais moving to front and rear of Yours.	
	29/9/17		Major MENZEL R.E. 211 Field Coy. left for R.E. School of Instruction BLENDECQUES	
	27/9/17		67 HIGHAM R.E. 223 Field Coy. returns from Leave to ENGLAND.	
	29/9/17		Capt. POUND R.E. 211 Field Coy. left for 1st Army School of Instruction MAROEUIL. Capt. WALKER R.E. 203 H.Q.R.E. on leave to England. Capt. MOORE R.E. 223 Fd Coy. returns from R.E. School BLENDECQUES and took over Temporary Command of 211 Field Coy.	
	3/9/17		Enemy had front Mist Campiès unit in line.	

M. Ingham
Lt. R.E.
Adjutant 3rd Div R.E.
C.R.E. 3rd Div

G. ADJUTANT,
3rd DIVISIONAL ENGINEERS.

War Diary.

SECRET.

31st Divisional Engineers. Copy No. 11

OPERATION ORDER No. 19.

5/12/17

Reference 31 Div. Orders No 247 and 248, and Administrative Instructions.

1. Field Coys.R.E. of 56th Division are sending advanced parties consisting of about 2 Officers and 10 O.R. to take over work and forward billets,etc., from Field Coys.R.E. of 31st Division on 6th inst.
To arrive about 9 a.m.

2. Field Coys.R.E.,31st Division will move on 7th inst to billets in Brigade areas as under :-
    211 Field Coy.R.E. to MAROEUIL.
    223 Field Coy.R.E. to ACQ.
    210 Field Coy.R.E. to ST. CATHERINE.
and hand over present hutments to Field Coys. of 56th Division.
To start from ECURIE as under:-
    223 Field Coy.R.E. 9-45 a.m.
    211 Field Coy.R.E. 10-15 a.m.
    210 Field Coy.R.E. 10-30 a.m.

3. Billets to be taken over and subsequent moves made under Brigade arrangements.

4. Handing over of front line work and completion of moves to be reported immediately to C.R.E., 31st Division.

[signature]
Lt.Col.R.E.
C.R.E., 31st Division.

Issued at   p.m.

210 Fd.Coy.R.E.	Copy No 1.
211 Fd.Coy.R.E.	No 2.
223 Fd.Coy.R.E.	No 3.
C.R.E. 56th Div.	No 4.)
31 Div.'G'.	No 5)
31 Div.'Q'.	No 6.)
31 Div. Signal Coy.	No 7.) For information.
92 Inf. Bde.	No 8.)
93 Inf. Bde.	No 9.)
94 Inf. Bde.	No 10.)
War Diary.	(No 11.
	(No 12.
Office Copy.	No 13.

SECRET.

**31st Divisional Engineers
Operation Order No.20.**

Copy No. 6

6/12/17.

1. Command of Brigade Sectors will change at 10.50 a.m. on 8th inst.

    Command of Divisional Front will pass to G.O.C. 56th Division at 11 a.m. on 8th inst.

2. Headquarters 31st Division will close at ROCLINCOURT at 11 a.m. on 8th inst., and open at VILLERS CHATEL at same hour.

    C.R.E's Office 31st Division will reopen at MINGOVAL at 6 p.m. on 8th inst.

3. Code names to be handed over to all relieving units.

4. It is possible that the Division will move about 10th inst. to another back area for training.

    O.C.Field Coys. to be prepared to start one week's training.

Lieut-Colonel.R.E.
C.R.E. 31st Division.

Copy No.1   O.C. 210th Field Coy.R.E.
      No.2   O.C. 211th Field Coy.R.E.
      No.3   O.C. 223rd Field Coy.R.E.
      No.4   C.R.E. 56th Division.
      No.5) War Diary.
      No.6)
      No.7   Office Copy.

SECRET. *War Diary*

Copy No 11

31st Divisional Engineers.

OPERATION ORDER No 21

16/12/17.

1. Field Coys. 31st Division will send advanced parties on 18th inst. to take over previous advanced billets, work, and hutments from 56th Division Field Coys.R.E.
223rd Field Coy.R.E. will however, take over dugout B.11.a.2.6. instead of B.10.a.6.1.

2. On 19th, Field Coys.R.E. will move and take over former hutments near ECURIE from 56th Div. Coys.

3. Field Companies R.E. will carry out R.E. work in Brigade areas as under :-
   RIGHT Brigade Area - 211th Field Coy.R.E.
   CENTRE   do   do - 210th Field Coy.R.E.
   LEFT   do   do - 223rd Field Coy.R.E.
   with 2 Sections living forward.

4. Completion of moves to be reported immediately to C.R.E. 31st Division.

J.R.Maclay
Lt.Col.R.E.
C.R.E., 31st Division.

Issued at 1 p.m.

Copy No. 1. 210 Field Coy.R.E.
       2. 211 Field Coy.R.E.
       3. 223 Field Coy.R.E.
       4. C.R.E. 56th Div.   )
       5. 31 Div."G".   )
       6. 31 Div."Q".   )
       7. 92 Inf. Bde.   ) For information.
       8. 93 Inf. Bde.   )
       9. 94 Inf. Bde.   )
      10. 12th K.O.Y.L.I.   )
      11) War Diary.
      12)
      13. Office Copy.

ORIGINAL

C O N F I D E N T I A L.

WAR DIARY

of

Headquarters, 31st Divisional Engineers.

From 1/1/18 to 31/1/18.

VOLUME XXV

Army Form C. 2118.

WAR DIARY
or
INTELLIGENCE SUMMARY.
(Erase heading not required.)

Hqrs 31st Div
RE

Place	Date	Hour	Summary of Events and Information	Remarks and references to Appendices
ROCLINCOURT	1.1.18		1st Jt Coy working under 13th Corps on Corps heavy scheme with 2nd Coy working in left sector	
	4.1.18		Major Cochran 223rd Ft Coy & Major Clough 210th Ft Coy warned M.C. on New Year Honours List. Capt Halfen RE returned to duty from leave in England. 2/Lt Ingham RE who was acting as adjutant. On frost snap on the whole trenches little damaged by frost + rain	
	14.1.18		RE Stores difficult. Transport (light railway) had trucks particularly scarce. CRE, CC Mackay, DSO RE, left for England on 3 days leave. Major Clough MC OC taking over from him until return of Major Marindale	
	31.1.18			

R Wrighton
Capt RE
Adjutant for CRE
31st Div

T2134. Wt. W708—776. 500000. 4/15. Sir J.C. & S.

Army Form C. 2118.

WAR DIARY
-or-
INTELLIGENCE SUMMARY.   Hd Qrs 31 Div R.E

(Erase heading not required.)

Instructions regarding War Diaries and Intelligence Summaries are contained in F.S. Regs., Part II. and the Staff Manual respectively. Title pages will be prepared in manuscript.

Place	Date	Hour	Summary of Events and Information	Remarks and references to Appendices
A.27.a.17. ROCLINCOURT	1.10.17		Weather conditions continue favourable to work. 223rd Coy employed forward in mft area. 210 Dr Coy employed forward in rift area. 211 Dr Coy on back work	
	4.10.17		Capt. J.H. More 223rd Dr Coy returned from leave to England	
	9.10.17		2/Lt Inston 211th Dr Coy returned from leave CRE 13th Corps took over area	
	11.10.17		2/Lt Pagel reported to 223rd Dr Coy for duty. Casualties 2/Lt morn 223rd Dr Coy 3. OR wounded, all by	
	16.10.17		Casualties 2/Lt moon 223rd Dr Coy. 1 O.R. Killed all by SR wounded, all by	
	16.10.17		2/Lt Collins 223rd 223rd Dr Coy left H.Q. for course at Rodgers school AIRE	
	21.10.17		2/Lt Blair proceeded on leave to England	
	27.10.17		Sgt Chapman 223rd Dr Coy R.E. awarded Military Medal	
	29.10.17		Casualties 2/Lt moon 210 Dr Coy 1 OR wounded all by	
	30.10.17		2/Lt Collins returned from Rodgers School at AIRE	

A Knowles Capt R.E
Adj 31 Div R.E
2/ C.R.E.

ORIGINAL.

CONFIDENTIAL.

WAR DIARY

of

Headquarters., 31st Div. Engineers.

October 1st.1917 to October 31st.1917.

VOLUME XXII

WAR DIARY
INTELLIGENCE SUMMARY

1st Div 31st Div R.E.

Army Form C. 2118.

Place	Date	Hour	Summary of Events and Information	Remarks and references to Appendices
ECLINGCOURT	6.9.17		31st Div handed over to 3rd Canadian Div Casualties to 12 noon 211th Fd Coy RE 8 OR 8 evacuated on duty (caused by mustard gas)	
	7.9.17		31st Div took over from 8th Division Casualties to 12 noon 210th Fd Coy 2 OR wounded (gassed) 1 OR killed	
	11.9.17		Casualties to 12 noon 211th Fd Coy wounded on OR 223 Coy wounded. Ten OR 210th Fd Coy one OR aeroplane bomb	
	30.9.17		Casualties to 12 noon 211th Fd Coy 2 OR accidentally injured. Weather conditions fresh throughout month.	

J. K. Mather Capt RE
Adj. 1st CRE
31st Div

30.9.17

ORIGINAL.

CONFIDENTIAL.

WAR DIARY
of
Headquarters, 31st Divisional Engineers.
from 1/9/17 to 30/9/17.

VOLUME XXI.

Army Form C. 2118.

WAR DIARY
INTELLIGENCE SUMMARY
(Erase heading not required.)

HQ 31st Div
R.E.

Instructions regarding War Diaries and Intelligence Summaries are contained in F. S. Regs., Part II. and the Staff Manual respectively. Title pages will be prepared in manuscript.

Place	Date	Hour	Summary of Events and Information	Remarks and references to Appendices
St George	14.8.17		New Camps for 31st Div HQ in course of construction at F.12.a.3.i. 2/3rd Div Coy carrying out work	
	16.8.17		Chevaux on balloon again shelled by 6" HV gun. Several dugouts considerably upset, personnel	
	20.8.17		One on left attacked - whole of LENS evacuated	
	22.8.17		Divisional Hhnent into new camp at F.12.a.3.c.	
	23.8.17		HQ R.E. moved its new headquarters at F.12.a.3.c.	
	24.8.17		Heard that Div will have to move into 5th Div area again. Army & Canadians taking over this area again.	
	25.8.17		Weather continually bad. Move arranged for 7th Sept.	
			In HQRS	

Rhuthus Capt RE
ADJUTANT,
31st DIVISIONAL ENGINEERS
for C.R.E.

Army Form C. 2118.

WAR DIARY
INTELLIGENCE SUMMARY.
(Erase heading not required.)

of 1st On 31" Div
R.E

Instructions regarding War Diaries and Intelligence Summaries are contained in F. S. Regs., Part II. and the Staff Manual respectively. Title pages will be prepared in manuscript.

Place	Date	Hour	Summary of Events and Information	Remarks and references to Appendices
FORT GEORGE	1.8.17		Weather hot, much rain & wind. Front quiet, uneventful. An unusual stillness. No 1 Cy R.E. working on right sect N. No 11 Cy in left sect. 2/3 Cy R.E. in reserve & open in back area work. Heather column uneventful.	
	4.5.?			
	9.5.?		Observation balloons in evidence shelled by enemy 4.V guns.	
			Shrapnel & direct to drive in forwards line.	
	10.5.?		Observation balloons again shelled by enemy.	
	11.5.?		Observation balloons again shelled, called by our heavy cal. to follow forward our B enemy line in spite of an	
			enemy aircraft again attempting to keep down observation balloon.	
	12.5.?		Fire broken out of AA gun fire. enemy planes afterwards brought down. Observers on recuts.	
	13.8.17		Heather continuing wet.	

T2134. Wt. W708—776. 500000. 4/15. Sir J. C. & S.

ORIGINAL

CONFIDENTIAL.

WAR DIARY
of
Headquarters, 31st Divisional Engineers.

From August 1st. 1917 to August 31st. 1917.

Volume XX

WAR DIARY
or
INTELLIGENCE SUMMARY.
(Erase heading not required.)

Army Form C. 2118.

HQ Ono
31st Dn RE

Place	Date	Hour	Summary of Events and Information	Remarks and references to Appendices
ACQ	4.7.17		HQ Ono RE moved to Ivry & Billets in ACQ	
	6.7.17		C.R.E. proceeded on leave to England. Maj R.A.S. Manuel acting as C.R.E. in his absence.	
	10.7.17		Received warning order from Divn. I probably relieve 1st Canadian Div in line on 13th inst	
	14.7.17		Canadian Div relieved in line during 13th, 13th & 14th inst. 31st Dn HQ moved to FORT GEORGE F.6.c.Cen Shel S1c C.NE	
	16.7.17		HQ Ono Dn RE moved to F6.c.2.4 Shel S1c NE	
	17.7.17		C.R.E. Returned from leave.	
	23.7.17		Maj R.A.S. Manuel rejoined his unit.	
	25.7.17		Casualties to date 31st Dn Coy Wounded 1 OR Artillery	
	26.7.17		" " " " " 1 OR	
			" " " " " 1 OR	

JK Arthur Capt RE
Dr C.R.E 31st Dn

CONFIDENTIAL.

WAR DIARY

for

Headquarters., 31st Divisional Engineers.

July 1st.1917.   to   July 31st.1917.

VOLUME XIX

* * * * * * * * * * *

Army Form C. 2118.

WAR DIARY

Hd Qrs
31st Divn R.E.

INTELLIGENCE SUMMARY.

(Erase heading not required.)

Instructions regarding War Diaries and Intelligence Summaries are contained in F. S. Regs., Part II. and the Staff Manual respectively. Title pages will be prepared in manuscript.

Place	Date	Hour	Summary of Events and Information	Remarks and references to Appendices
ROCLINCOURT	29.6.17		Casualties to 1 NCO 223rd Tn Coy. 1 OR wounded artillery. Our attack on CADORNA TRENCH at 7.10 pm all objectives gained. No casualties to R.E.	
	30.6.17		Up to date no counter attack made by enemy	

A.K. Miller
Capt R.E.
2i/c C.R.E. 31st Divn
30.6.17

Army Form C. 2118.

WAR DIARY
of H. Qrs
INTELLIGENCE SUMMARY. 31st Div. R.E.
(Erase heading not required.)

Instructions regarding War Diaries and Intelligence Summaries are contained in F. S. Regs., Part II. and the Staff Manual respectively. Title pages will be prepared in manuscript.

Place	Date	Hour	Summary of Events and Information	Remarks and references to Appendices
ROCLINCOURT	1.6.17		11 D. Inclination. No 4 Dn Coy R.E. admitted to hospital sick	
G.S.6.3.9.	5.6.17		Capt F. Hertford R.E. attached to 11th Dn Coy R.E. for duty Casualties. 2 min O.R. 1 inj.	
	8.6.17		223rd Coy R.E. moved from ECOIVRES to North of ST CATHERINE	
	G.9.d.17		took over work from 247 Coy R.E.	
	10.6.17		11th Dn Coy R.E. took over work from 248 Coy R.E. No 4 Dn Coy R.E. took over from 249 Dn Coy R.E.	
	11.6.17		Hd. Qrs 31st Dn. Moved from HILLERS CHATEL to ROCLINCOURT G.S.6.3.9. 31st Div. took over line from 63rd Div.	
	13.6.17		Conference arranged on G.T.O. Subject Trenches. New Paths. H.Q. & c.	
			Annual Horse Show took place 1 O.R. wounded	
	15.6.17		Casualties. 1 Dn. No. 211 Dn Coy R.E. 1 O.R. wounded Artillery. 223 Coy R.E. 1 O.R. wounded	
	22.6.17		Casualties. 1 Dn. N.C. Jn	

ORIGINAL.

Vol 16

CONFIDENTIAL.

WAR DIARY

of

31st DIVISIONAL ENGINEERS.

From June 1st.1917.   to June 30th.1917.

Volume XVIII.

* * * * * * * * * * * * *

ORIGINAL

CONFIDENTIAL.

War Diary
of
Headquarters, 31st Divisional Engineers.

From 1/2/18 to 28/2/18.
VOLUME XXVI.

Army Form C. 2118.

WAR DIARY
or
INTELLIGENCE SUMMARY.

HQ 31st Div RE

(Erase heading not required.)

Instructions regarding War Diaries and Intelligence Summaries are contained in F. S. Regs., Part II. and the Staff Manual respectively. Title pages will be prepared in manuscript.

Place	Date	Hour	Summary of Events and Information	Remarks and references to Appendices
ROCLINCOURT	4.2.15		Maj Manuel 211th Fd Coy took over duties as acting CRE from Maj Clough 210th Fd Coy	
	6.2.15		Cavalries & 15 men 223rd Fd Coy RE L.O.R. artillery command	
	12.2.15		" " 211th " " " "	
	17.2.15		" " 223rd " " " "	
	22.2.15		Maj Clough M.C. O.C. 210th Fd Coy left for England to take over duties as instructor at senior officers school ALDERSHOT	
			Companies returning as follows 210th Fd Coy RE took over house [illegible] Corps on morning October, 211th Fd Coy RE working on left Bde sector, 223 Fd Coy RE working on right Bde sector	
	27.2.15		Many other moved that HqRE 31 Div would move on 1st March & relieved by Hq RE 62 Div	
			[signature] Capt RE Adjutant 31st Div CRE	

T2134. Wt. W708—776. 500000. 4/15. Sir J. C. & S.

31st Divisional Engineers

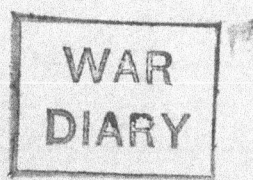

C. R. E.

31st DIVISION.

MARCH 1918

ORIGINAL.

CONFIDENTIAL.

WAR DIARY
of
Headquarters, 31st Divisional Engineers.

From 1/3/18 to 31/3/18.

VOLUME XXVII

Army Form C. 2118.

HQ RE 31 Div
RE

WAR DIARY
or
INTELLIGENCE SUMMARY.
(Erase heading not required.)

Instructions regarding War Diaries and Intelligence Summaries are contained in F.S. Regs, Part II. and the Staff Manual respectively. Title pages will be prepared in manuscript.

Place	Date	Hour	Summary of Events and Information	Remarks and references to Appendices
MAROEUIL	1.3.18		HQ RE moved by lorries from ROCLINCOURT to MAROEUIL. Maj HOMER of 9th Fd Coy 4th Div expected to relieve 11CR Mackay DSO as CRE 31 Div. message from 13 Corps that expected 11 Col Mackay returned.	F 9 & 9.4
	4.3.18		11 Col Mackay arrived back from leave in England & handed over to Maj HOMER M.C. RE.	
	6.2.18		Maj HOMER M.C. RE. arrived & took over duties from 11 Col Mackay as CRE 31 Div.	
	12.2.18		11 Col Mackay left for England to take command of reserve battalion R.E. BEAUMORIS.	
	21.3.18		German offensive commenced. MAROEUIL shelled by HV guns. Received orders to move to BASSEUX.	
	22.3.18		Fd Coys to HQ RE entrained 6.0 a.m. for BASSEUX. 210th Fd Coy received orders to proceed to line during evening.	
	23.3.18		Div HQ & HQ RE moved to AYETTE. All companies into huts near COURCELLES LE COMTE	

Army Form C. 2118.

HQ 31 Dn
RE

WAR DIARY
or
INTELLIGENCE SUMMARY.
(Erase heading not required.)

Instructions regarding War Diaries and Intelligence Summaries are contained in F.S. Regs., Part II. and the Staff Manual respectively. Title pages will be prepared in manuscript.

Place	Date	Hour	Summary of Events and Information	Remarks and references to Appendices
AYETTE	24.3.18		Fd Coy to previous retreat to new line near COURCELLES & ABLAINZEVELLE	
	25.3.18		Div HQ – HQ RE withdrew to HUMBERCAMP. Canals & 12 Nov 223 FdCy 1 OR Killed 15 Wounded	
	26.3.18		Received message from VI Corps that enemy had broken through near HÉBUTERNE, & was approaching SOUASTRE in armoured cars. HQ RE moved to Plack Hole & fallen	CRE Lt Col Homer Wounded
			there across canal. Div HQ moved to NARLUS & HUMBERCAMP in evening to spot & enemy breaking through Field Coys all billeted in MONCHY-SUR-BOIS front to Fulae & ADINFER	
			Fd Coy commenced work on PURPLE LINE in front of ADINFER WOOD. Canals & 12 men 1 OR Killed 4 OR Wounded. No Fd Coy	
	27.3.18		Coy withdrew to WosQ ADINFER HOOD Canals & 12 Nov 223 FdCy 1 OR Killed, 211 FdCy	
	28.3.18		3 OR Wounded. No FdCoy 1 OR Killed 2 OR Wounded	
	29.3.18		Fd Coys advanced by 31 Dn Fd Cy	

AMallery Capt Lt for Col R.E.
C.R.E. 21ST DIVISION.

31st Divisional Engineers

C. R. E.

31st DIVISION

APRIL 1918.

ORIGINAL.

CONFIDENTIAL.

WAR DIARY
of
Headquarters, 31st Divisional Engineers.

From 1/4/18 to 30/4/18.

VOLUME XXVIII

WAR DIARY
INTELLIGENCE SUMMARY
(Erase heading not required.)

Army Form C. 2118.

HQ RE
31 Div

Place	Date	Hour	Summary of Events and Information	Remarks and references to Appendices
	1.4.18		31 Div HQ moved from HUMBERCAMP to LUCHEUX.	
	2.4.18		Division moved from LUCHEUX to VILLERS CHATEL area. Div HQ & Hq RE at VILLERS-CHATEL. HQ RE at CAMBLIGNEUL. Field Coys moved as follows. 210 Coy CAUCOURT. 211 Coy MARQUAY. 223 Coy CAUCOURT.	
	4.4.18		Coys to salvage material required in fresh fields in area & carry out necessary work. 3.4.18 Capt Glave buried & taken up temporarily at Division in M.O.	
	9.4.18		Lt Col Riley DSO reported & taken over duties as CRE. relieved Major Mitchell MC. 211 Coy who moved to Hq Coy. Received orders to be prepared to advance at once in lorries. 211 Coy embussed opposite Kleber. 212 Coy 223 Coy at 3 pm with 93rd (Bde.) & 1st OCA NOEUX. 211 Coy 4 pm with 4 Gds Bde. with 2nd Bde. No DA Coy. 11 from with 4 Glo Bde.	
			Div HQ + CRE moved to VIEUX BERQUIN 11th inst. & moved back on 4 to LAMOTTE.	
	12.4.18		Div HQ. CRE moved from LAMOTTE to Cd HAZARD. Field Coys in line Lestrem & Rue round	

WAR DIARY or INTELLIGENCE SUMMARY

HQ 31st Div RE

Army Form C. 2118.

Place	Date	Hour	Summary of Events and Information	Remarks and references to Appendices
	12.4.18		Casualties. No 211 Coy 1 OR killed, No 212 Coy 1 OR killed 8 OR wounded. No 211 & 223 Field Coys withdrawn from line & 0R wounded. 0 HONDEGHEM. No 212 Coy still in line owing to situation.	
	13.4.18		No 212 Coy withdrawn from line to LE BREARDE. Div HQ & HQRE moved from Gd HAZARD to HONDEGHEM. Div under two hours notice to move.	
	14.4.18		Capt G.K.Mathur RE admitted to hospital. Conference re working on rear defences. Casualties No 212 Coy 1 OR killed 3 wounded.	
	15.4.18		No 212 Coy moved from LE BREARDE to HONDEGHEM.	
	16.4.18		Div HQ & HQRE moved from HONDEGHEM to WALLON-CAPPEL. No 211 & 223 Field Coys to AU SOUVERAIN. No 212 Coy to HAZEBROUCK.	
	18.4.18		Field Coys employed Wiring, preparing trenches, repairing roads & preparing bridges for demolition. Casualties No 212 Coy 1 killed & 13 wounded (OR)	
	21.4.18		Casualties 223 Fd Coy 1 OR wounded.	
	22.4.18		Casualties No 212 Coy 3 OR wounded (Gas)	

WAR DIARY
— or —
INTELLIGENCE SUMMARY.

(Erase heading not required.)

Army Form C. 2118.

HQ. 31 Div. RE

Instructions regarding War Diaries and Intelligence Summaries are contained in F. S. Regs., Part II. and the Staff Manual respectively. Title pages will be prepared in manuscript.

Place	Date	Hour	Summary of Events and Information	Remarks and references to Appendices.
	23.4.18		Companies employed in wiring, pulling, excavating trenches, preparing hutments for demolition. Casualties 211 2A Coy 1 OR wounded	
	26.4.18		Casualties 213 2A Coy 1 OR killed 2 OR wounded	
	27.4.18		Casualties 211 2A Coy 1 OR wounded	
	28.4.18		2A Coy returned in line by 29th Div.	
	29.4.18		Div HQ & HQRE moved from WALLON-CAPPEL to HONDEGHEM. 2A Coy to Meaux no - V.13.6.5.9. 211 - V.I.C.6.0. 212 - V.S.d.2.4. Sheet 27. 432 2A Coy. & 14 ATCy attached to CRE 31 Div. 2A Coys employed on 2nd Zone defences, improving trench etc.	
	30.4.18		Capt. Mallock RE Ajt. returned to duty from hospital	

Mallock Capt RE
Ajt. LT. COL: R.E.,
C.R.E. 31ST DIVISION.

ORIGINAL.

CONFIDENTIAL.

WAR DIARY

of

Headquarters, 31st Divisional Engineers.

From 1/5/18 to 31/5/18.

VOLUME XXIX.
-oOo-

WAR DIARY or INTELLIGENCE SUMMARY

Army Form C. 2118.

HQ 31 Div RE

Place	Date	Hour	Summary of Events and Information	Remarks and references to Appendices
HONDEGHEM	1.5.18		Capt Ingham acting adjutant returned to his unit.	
	2.5.18		H/C Kenton left to join 11 Col Homer RE DSO at Liverpool Merchants Hospital.	
	6.5.18		CRE presented MM (military) to Cpl Bowich 2nd Dr Cy RE	
	8.5.18		Received orders that 31 Div would relieve left Bde 1st Australian Div in line. 31 Div to have on Bdes in line, one in support & one in reserve. 223rd Dr Cy & 64 inf. Bns with 92nd Bde. 11 Barker 223rd Dr Cy. Mounted shell fire. Casualties to CRE arranged with French RE on left not when line should join.	
	10.5.18		92nd Bde relieves in front line by 92nd Bde but Lieutenant Keogh wounded came to	
	12.5.18		Work continued same as before. 16/5/18 1 OR killed by 919 Army Troops Coy Horrorghem	
	15.6 18.5.18		10 R. wounded ditto	
	20.5.18		Adjutant posted 9th Div RE came to take over. 223 Field Coy relieved on front line work by 64/2 Field Coy. 223 Field Coy move to Le REPROE.	
	22.5.18			

Army Form C. 2118.

WAR DIARY
or
INTELLIGENCE SUMMARY.
(Erase heading not required.)

Instructions regarding War Diaries and Intelligence Summaries are contained in F. S. Regs., Part II. and the Staff Manual respectively. Title pages will be prepared in manuscript.

Place	Date	Hour	Summary of Events and Information	Remarks and references to Appendices
HONDEGHEM	23/5/16		223 Field Coy. moved from LE CRESNE DE- to rest at RACQUINHEM.	
	24/5/16		211 Field Coy. relieved by 63rd Field Coy. and moved from MT LEVIN to LE BRESROE and Rwy. by 'bus to HEURINGHEM.	
			210 Field Coy. relieved by 90th Field Coy. and moved from HONDEGHEM TO BLARINGHEM.	
MARDEEQUES	25/5/16		C.R.E. handed over to C.R.E. 9th Divn. and moved to MARDEEQUES.	
	26/5/16		Coys. settling down & cleaning up. 211 Hbty. rail and one section to LUMBRES, remainder to rest. 92nd S.P.Bn.	
	27/5/16		Coys. arms & clothing programme, working 6 am to 12 noon daily.	
	28-31/5/16		Continuous training.	
	31/5/16		211 Field Coy. proceed by bus to QUELMES to practise Ceremonial parade with 92nd Bde.	
			223 Field Coy. practise Ceremonial parade with 93rd Bde. at HEURINGHEM.	
			Capt. Q.K. Nolan R.E. on leave to U.K. Capt. Ingham 210 Coy a/Adjutant	

M. Ingham
Capt L
ADJUTANT,
31st DIVISIONAL ENGINEERS

for LtCol R.E. CRE 31st Divn.

SECRET.

War Diary

Copy No. 14

31st Divisional Engineers.

OPERATION ORDER No 30.   9/5/18.

1. The 31st Division takes over Left Brigade front in the line of 1st Australian Div on night 9th/10th May

2. 31st Divisional Boundary is (Sheet 27 S.E. 1/20,000)

   N. BOUNDARY.
   X.11.a.5.0. to cross roads at X.4.c.4.3. thence round FONTAINE HOUCK to cross roads at X.3.d.3.8. thence to R.31.central thence Q.36.b.3.0. to Q.35.b.4.0. and thence due West to cross roads in Q.31.b.

   S. BOUNDARY.
   X.20.central, along METEREN Becque inclusive through X.13.central., W.12.d.,c.,and a. through W.11.b. and a., W.10.b. and a. and thence in a straight line through W.9.,8., and 7. to junction of roads at V.12.d.9.7.

   The French are on the North and Australian Division on the South.

3. (a) The 93rd Bde. will be Bde. in Front Line responsible for defences of front and support line.
   223rd Field Coy. will work in conjunction with the Bde, taking over on night 9th/10th from No 1 Australian Field Coy. camped at X.1.b.3.9.

   (b) The 92nd Bde. will be supporting Bde and responsible for defences of reserve line of front system (2) FLETRE Strong Point (3) the ROUKLOSHILLE Switch.
   211th Field Coy. and 2 Coys. Pioneer Batt. will supervise and assist.
   211 Fd. Coy. will take over from No 2 Australian Fd. Coy. (camped at W.6.b.7.4.) and O.C. K.O.Y.L.I. will detail 2 Coys. to take over from A Coy.,1st Australian Pioneers (camp at X.1.c.5.8.) and B Coy. 1st Australian Pioneers (camp at Q.35.d.7.4.) respectively.
   211 Fd. Coy. will camp at W.1.d.5.9. and the 2 Coys. K.O.Y.L.I. will camp at X.1.c.5.8. and Q.35.d.7.4.

   (c) The work on "B" and "C" Lines (2nd Zone) will be directly under C.R.E. and will be carried out by 210th Field Coy.R.E. and 1 Coy. K.O.Y.L.I., Infantry Parties being found by the Reserve Brigade as required.
   O.C. 210th Field Coy. will notify Div.R.E.,H.Q. by 4 p.m. 9/5/18 of numbers, time, and rendezvous of working party required for 10th inst.
   C Coy. 1st Australian Pioneers are working on "B" Line and O.C. K.O.Y.L.I. will arrange a Coy. to take over from them. This Coy. will be accommodated in COMMANDERIE FARM at Q.33.c.2.4..
   210 Fd. Coy. will remain at present location, U.12.b.5.9. moving up daily to work.

4. Reconnaissance and liaison by and between the units concerned will be carried out during daylight of 9th inst (except 223 Fd. Coy.) Moves to locations West of CAESTRE may be completed during daylight. E. of CAESTRE moves must be made during hours of darkness.

5. Transport Lines will remain as at present.

6. All work E. of "B" Line, 2nd Zone will be carried out at night.

7. Os.C. Coys. will make a special point of ascertaining and reporting on siting and nature of defences adjoining the boundaries of their respective areas.

(2)

8. Daily Progress Reports will be rendered to this office as usual. Tracings to accompany same will be issued later.

9. Location of Divisional R.E. Dump will be notified later.

10. Reliefs to be completed by 8 a.m. 10th inst and completion to be reported to H.Q., R.E.

11. ACKNOWLEDGE.

F. Giles.
Lt.Col.R.E.
C.R.E. 31st Division.

Issued at 1-30 a.m.

Copies to:- 31st Div.'G'. 1
31st Div.'Q'. 2
C.E. XV Corps. 3
4th Gds. Bde. 4
92 Inf. Bde. 5
93 Inf. Bde. 6
210 Fd. Coy. 7
211 Fd. Coy. 8
223 Fd. Coy. 9
12th K.O.Y.L.I. 10
C.R.E. 1st Aust. Div. 11
1st Aust. Pioneer Battn. 12
Office Copy 13
War Diary 14
" " 15

ORIGINAL.

CONFIDENTIAL.

WAR DIARY

of

Headquarters, 31st Divisional Engineers.

From June 1st 1918 to June 30th, 1918.

VOLUME XXX

Army Form C. 2118.

H.Q. 31 Div. R.E

WAR DIARY
or
INTELLIGENCE SUMMARY.
(Erase heading not required.)

Place	Date	Hour	Summary of Events and Information	Remarks and references to Appendices
NARDRECQUES	1/6/18		Field Companies continue training in Field Area. 211 Field Coy inspected by G.O.C. Bn. along with 92nd Brigade.	
	3/6/18		223 Field Coy inspected by G.O.C. Division along with 93rd Bde. Army Command parade & Operations.	
	4/6/18 & 6/6/18		Training continued as before.	
	10/6/18		Divisional R.E. Sports on Polo Ground. RACQUINGHEM.	
	12/6/18		Vanport of 210 Field Coy, inspected by C.R.E.	
	13/6/18		Vanport of 211 Field Coy inspected by C.R.E.	
	14/6/18		31 Div. Warning order to be ready to move forward in case of enemy attack.	
EBLINGHEM	15/6/18		Advanced H.Q. R.E established at CHATEAU V19C77. 90 Field Coy moved from BLARINGHEM to STAPLE. 211 Field Coy moved from HEURINGHEM. To RYCK HOUT CAPPEL. 223 Field Coy moved from RACQUINGHEM to HONDEGHEM in readiness to move to new HAZEBROUCK defences in case of attack. Rear H.Q. R.E remain at NARDRECQUES	
	16/6/18		Remain in above positions under communication orders.	
NARDRECQUES	17/6/18		Advanced H.Q. R.E. move back to NARDRECQUES. 210 Field Coy move from STAPLE to RACQUINGHEM. 211 Field Coy move back from RYCK HOUT CAPPEL TO RACQUINGHEM.	

Army Form C. 2118.

WAR DIARY
or
INTELLIGENCE SUMMARY.
(Erase heading not required.)

Instructions regarding War Diaries and Intelligence Summaries are contained in F. S. Regs., Part II. and the Staff Manual respectively. Title pages will be prepared in manuscript.

Place	Date	Hour	Summary of Events and Information	Remarks and references to Appendices
WARDRECQUES	17/6/15		223 Field Coy. moved from HONDEGHEM to FECK. MONT CASSEL and 93 "Bde" to work under C.E. XV Corps on HAZEBROUCK defences.	
	18/6/15		210 and 211 Field Coys continue training but under 1 hours notice to move.	
	19.6.15		D.11 Cav. advanced to effect that 31st Div. would relieve 29th Div in line 20/6/15 inst.	
	20.6.15		223" Fd Coy relieved 455" Fd Coy	
	21.6.15		210 Fd Coy relieved	
			" 211 Fd Coy relieved, leaving 2 sections of Capt. G.K. Maker Act.	
			210 Fd Coy D.g.c.b.s.4. 211 Fd Coy D.g.c.6.3. 223 Fd Coy D.c.c.g.1 returned from leave	
	22.6.15		223" Fd Coy handed over to 211" Fd Coy.	to duty.
	23.6.15		210" Fd Coy moved to D.S.C.g.1. 223" Fd Coy to D.g.b.s.4. Companies employed on head trenches, excavating for & erecting R.E. Shelters	
	24.6.15		Advanced Bde H.Q. New Div H.Q. defensive works etc	
	25.6.15		Fd Cartridge to K.O.G.41. Wrecker force on above efforts	
			Fd Coys preparing for "Under Cover" operations 93 Bde allotted Lead 2	
	26.6.15		do -	ANKLE FARM. E.17.6.0
	27.6.15		31 Div. attacked 6.0 am. all objectives gained. R.E. successfully	
			used showy jumps, constructed mule tracks Cavalry	210" Fd Coy
				211" Fd Coy

Army Form C. 2118.

WAR DIARY
— or —
INTELLIGENCE SUMMARY.
(Erase heading not required.)

Place	Date	Hour	Summary of Events and Information	Remarks and references to Appendices
	25.6.15		110th Fd Coy. Lt Keating and 1 OR killed, 3 OR wounded. 211th Fd Coy. 2 OR wounded. Lt W. Ingham 110th Fd Coy returned to his unit. Adjutant returned to duty. Casualties 210th Fd Coy 2 OR wounded slightly, remained at duty	
	29.6.15			
	30.6.15			

Abraham Capt RE
ADJUTANT.
31st DIVISIONAL ENGINEERS
for CRE

War Diary

R.E. INSTRUCTIONS No 1.

SECRET

Copy No ...9...

Should no further news regarding an impending attack be received before 6 a.m. tomorrow morning, the Companies will remain in their present locations.

The men should be given half an hours Physical Training before breakfast and one hours Close Order Drill after breakfast.

All animals must be exercised for one hour in the morning.

[signature]
Lt.Col.R.E.
C.R.E. 31st Division.

June 16th 1918.

```
Copy No. 1 H.Q. 31st Division. "G"
         2 210th Field Coy.R.E.
         3 211th Field Coy.R.E.
         4 223rd Field Coy.R.E.
         5 C.R.E.
         6 Adjutant
         7 H.Q. Secret File
         8)
         9) War Diary.
```

War Diary SECRET. Copy No. 6

R.E. Instruction No. 2.

1. 31st Divisional Engineers Operation Order No.31 is cancelled.

2. Coys will move in accordance with 31st Div. Order No.326 (Copy attached)

3. 210th and 211th Field Coys will report arrival and forward Training Programme for remainder of week to H.Q. 31st Div. Engineers at WARDRECQUES.

4. 253rd Field Coy. R.E. will report location of new camp on arrival there to WARDRECQUES.

                                                                    Lt. Col. R.E.

17/6/18.   C.R.E. 31st Division.

         Copy No. 1   C.R.E.
                 2   Adjutant
                 3   210th Field Coy. R.E.
                 4   211th Field Coy. R.E.
                 5   253rd Field Coy. R.E.
                 6) War Diary.
                 7)
                 8   H.Q. 31st Div. Engineers File.
                 9   H.Q. 31st Div. "G".

War Diary.

SECRET.   Copy No 7

R.E. INSTRUCTIONS No 3.

Orders in case of attack.

Until further notice, following are orders for R.E. Field Companies in case of attack.

1. All R.E. in Company billets will stand to in billets ready to move on receipt of orders.

2. All R.E. (other than R.E. i/c Demolitions) out on the works, will rendezvous at points selected by Os.C. Field Companies, and be marched back <u>in formed bodies</u> to Company billets, report, and carry on as in (1).

3. Os.C. Coys. to report to C.R.E. by both orderly and wire, the numbers available and their location.

4. R.E. i/c Demolitions will stand to and be on the alert for orderlies bearing orders for them.

F. Giles.

Lt.Col.R.E.

C.R.E. 31st Division.

20/6/18.

Copies to:- No 1. 31 Div.'G'. (Ref. S.G.83/515 of 20/6/18.)
        2. C.R.E.
        3. Adjt.
        4. 210 Fd. Coy.R.E.
        5. 211 do   do
        6. 223 do   do
        7.) War Diary.
        8.)
        9. File.
       10. 92 Inf. Bde.
       11. 93 Inf. Bde.
       12. 94 Inf. Bde.

CORRIGENDA.
==*=*=*=*

War Diary

Reference R.E. Instructions No 4 dated 23/6/18.

Delete last line of Table "A" - Road Mine, D.19.d.2.0.

J.Giles.
Lt.Col.R.E.
C.R.E. 31st Division.

23/6/18.

Copies to all recipients of above Instructions.

SECRET.   WAR DIARY   Copy No. 11

R.E. INSTRUCTIONS No 4.

-2-

RIGHT BDE. AREA.   FRONT LINE. 1. (a). During the dusk of 23/6/18, O.C. 211 Field Company will arrange to tape out the inter-connecting portion of the present Front Line from LUG FARM (exclusive) E.23.c.3.8. to Southern Divisional Boundary to join on with 5th Division at about K.4.a.5.0.

(b) O.C. 'B' Coy, 12th K.O.Y.L.I. and the O's.C. Right and Left Battalions in line will arrange to send an Officer with the taping party, who will act as guide to the Working Party later on.

Officers will report to a representative of 211 Field Coy. as follows:-

1 Officer Left Battn.   ) at Brickfield Stack at
1 Officer and Orderly,K.O.Y.L.I.) E.20.b.7.0. at 8 p.m.

1 Officer Right Battn. at Sawmills, E.19.d.1.0. at 7-30 p.m.

2.(a). The digging of these connecting portions is divided up as follows :-

(i) 12th K.O.Y.L.I. 'B' Coy. will dig nightly until completion the portion from VOLLEY FARM exclusive to road running West and East through E.28.c. (exclusive).

(ii) G.O.C. 92 Bde. is arranging for Right Battn. in line to find 50 diggers nightly to dig the portion road West and East through E.28.c. inclusive to junction with 5th Division at about K.4.a.5.0. and Left Battn. in line to find 50 diggers nightly to dig the portion LUG FARM exclusive to VOLLEY FARM inclusive.

(iii) O.C. 211 Field Coy. after due reconnaissance will decide on section of trench to be dug and issue dimensioned sketches to O.C.,K.O.Y.L.I. and O.C. Right and Left Battn. representatives before work commences.

(iv) Working Parties will provide their own tools and should not commence work before 11 p.m.

SUPPORT LINE. (a) A continuous breastwork line requires to be completed throughout. Present Posts need parapet and parados raising. Shelters for garrison to be provided as necessary outside and behind parados.
O.C. 211 Field Coy. will carry out general supervision

(b) O.C. 211 Field Coy. will find 2 Sections of his Company for the R.E. work, and G.O.C. 92 Bde. is providing 300 Working Party daily from Reserve Battn. for work on Support Line from E.21.central to junction with 5th Division at about K.3.b.7.0.
Work in the wood is by day; outside wood by night.

RESERVE LINE.(a) 1 platoon,'C' Coy.,K.O.Y.L.I. will continue wiring Reserve Line in the wood.

(b) 1 section,211 Field Coy.R.E. will erect Battn. H.Q. shelters, to be 4.2 proof, at about E.25.d.9.4.

-2-

        GENERAL. (a) O.C. 'C' Coy., K.O.Y.L.I. will find 3 platoons to work on hurdle making at Forestry Dump at E.25.d.9.5. under O.C. 211 Field Coy. instructions.

        (b) O.C. 211 Field Coy. will take over and be responsible for Right, Forward, and Rear groups of mines and places prepared for demolition (vide Table 'A' attached)

        (c) O.C. 211 Field Coy. will be responsible for upkeep of dry weather cross-country tracks in Right Brigade sector.

        (d) O.C. 211 Field Coy. will make gas-proof curtains to 4 M.G. positions in LA MOTTE (details from 210 Field Coy.)

        (e) O.C. 211 Field Coy. will complete shelters being erected in LA MOTTE Switch.

        (f) O.C. 211 Field Coy. will complete Forward Bde. Hd. Qrs. at FETTLE FARM on same lines as commenced i.e. concrete protection.

LEFT BDE. AREA.   SUPPORT LINE. (a) O.C. 'D' Coy., K.O.Y.L.I. will work by night on improvement of Support Line trenches between occupied Posts from E.10.a.4.6. to Southern Bde. Boundary at E.21.central.

        Particular attention will be paid to making parapets and parados bullet proof and building firesteps where necessary.

        (b) G.O.C. 93 Bde. is instructing garrison of this Support Line that they will carry out improvement of their own Posts themselves.

        (c) O.C. 210 Field Coy. will generally assist with technical advice and inspection but is not responsible for the work or rate of progress.

SEC BOIS and SWARTENBROUCK DEFENCES.

        G.O.C. 93 Bde. is arranging that improvements of these Defences shall be carried out by the garrison under supervision of O.C. 210 Field Company, who will be responsible that the scheme already decided on is strictly followed.

        GENERAL. (a) O.C. 210 Field Coy. will construct protection for Bde. Hd. Qrs. at GRAND MARQUETTE FARM in accordance with the plan already decided on.

        (b) O.C. 210 Field Coy. will take over the responsibility for the Left forward and rear groups of mines and places prepared for demolition. (vide Table 'A' attached.)

        (c) O.C. 210 Field Company will be responsible for dry weather cross-country tracks in Left Bde. sector.

        (d) O.C. 210 Field Company will be responsible for upkeep and repair of Railway Line from AU SOUVERAIN to LA MOTTE Station.

        He will also prepare 25 lengths of rail on Railway Line for demolition near LA MOTTE Station.

-3-

REAR AREA. 223 Field Coy. will :-

    (a) Erect D.H.Q. at U.30.c.0.8.

    (b) Complete a Gas Hut for D.G.O. at D.13.a.7.5.

    (c) Be responsible for upkeep of roads
        (i) TIR ANGLAIS to LA MOTTE.
        (ii) PAPOTE - SCALLOP FARM - SPOOK COTTAGE.

                                                    F. Giles.

23/8/18.   Lt.Col.R.E.
                                                 C.R.E. 31st Division.

Copies to:- No 1. 31 Div.'G'.
               2. C.R.E.
               3. Adjt.
               4. 210 Fd. Coy.
               5. 211 do
               6. 223 do
               7. 92 Inf. Bde.
               8. 93 Inf. Bde.
               9. 12th K.O.Y.L.I.
             10. File.
             11) War Diary. ✓
             12)

T A B L E "A".

Group.	Object for Demolition.	Location.
Right Forward.	Bridge.	1. D.30.c.9.8.
	"	2. D.30.a.6.3.
	"	3. D.30.b.9.8.
	"	4. E.19.d.1.1.
	Road Mine.	5. D.30.d.1.8.
	Railway Bridge.	6. D.24.d.5.1.
	Road Bridge.	7. K.1.c.7.2.
Left Forward.	A. Road Mine.	1. E.9.a.4.4.
	"	2. E.8.a.9.8.
	"	3. E.8.c.6.6.
	B. Road Bridge.	1. E.13.c.3.4.
	"	2. D.18.b.9.3.
	"	3. D.12.d.5.0.
Right Rear.	Road Bridge.	1. D.24.a.7.1.
	"	2. D.24.a.0.2.
	"	3. D.18.c.6.2.
	"	4. D.16.d.2.2.
	Road Mine.	5. D.16.d.2.2.
	"	6. D.21.a.4.2.
	"	7. D.24.a.1.1.
	Road Bridge.	8. D.23.d.0.7.
Left Rear.	Road Bridge.	1. D.17.b.9.2.
	"	2. D.17.b.4.6.
	"	3. D.11.d.2.0.
	"	4. D.17.a.1.2.
	"	5. D.11.a.4.3.
	"	6. D.6.c.9.1.
	Road Mine.	7. D.11.b.8.1.
	"	8. D.16.b.9.6.
	Railway Bridge.	9. V.29.c.4.4.
	Road Mine.	D.19.d.2.0.

War Diary

<u>R.E. INSTRUCTIONS No 5.</u>   Copy No **13**

SECRET

<u>FORESTRY DUMP.</u>

The Forestry Dump at E.26.c.2.4. is under control of the Right Field Company in the line.
The sapper i/c will issue only on signature of

    (a) R.E. Officer for use of an R.E. Unit.

    (b) O.C. Right Field Coy. for use of other Units.

At present, 211th Field Coy. is Right Field Coy.

                                                             Lt.Col.R.E.

23/6/18.   C.R.E. 31st Division.

Copies to:-   No 1. 31st Div.'G'.   No 8. 223 Fd. Coy.
                    2. 31st Div.'Q'.   9. 12th K.O.Y.L.I.
                    3. 92 Inf. Bde.   10. C.R.E.
                    4. 93 Inf. Bde.   11. Adjt.
                    5. 94 Inf. Bde.   12) War Diary.
                    6. 210 Fd. Coy.   13)
                    7. 211   do   14. File.

War Diary

SECRET.

R.E. INSTRUCTIONS No 8.

Copy No 11

R.E. Instructions No 4 are modified as follows:-

Under instructions from H.Q. 31st Division,

12th K.O.Y.L.I. 1. (a) "B" and "D" Coys. will move into the fortified localities of SWARTENBROUCK and PETIT SEC BOIS respectively and form garrison there, taking over from present Infantry garrison after dark on evening of 24/6/18 at a time to be arranged with 93rd Bde.

Necessary reconnaissance of the defence works will be carried out during daylight.

(b) These Coys., under O.C. K.O.Y.L.I. will be responsible thereafter for the improvement of those defences and that the work is completed in accordance with the scheme already decided on.

2. (a) "C" Coy. will similarly take over from Infantry garrison the LA MOTTE Defences on the morning of 24/6/18. On arrival, Lewis Guns and crews will be left in their battle positions, and remainder of Coy. will proceed to work as in (b)

(b) ½ Coy. will work on hurdle making at Forestry Dump at E.26.c.2.4.
½ Coy. will take over maintenance and extension of tramway track in forward Forest area.

3. O.C. K.O.Y.L.I. will obtain his tactical orders direct from Left Brigade for PETIT SEC BOIS and SWARTENBROUCK, and from Right Brigade for LA MOTTE Defences. He will get into touch with Brigades to obtain same at once.

F. Giles.

Lt.Col.R.E.

23/6/18.

C.R.E. 31st Division.

Copies to:- No 1. 31st Div.'G'.
2. 92 Inf. Bde.
3. 93 Inf. Bde.
4. 94 Inf. Bde.
5. 210 Fd. Coy.
6. 211 do
7. 223 do
8. 12th K.O.Y.L.I.
9. C.R.E.
10. Adjt.
11)
12) War Diary.
13. File.

SECRET.

WAR DIARY

SECRET.

Copy No 11

R.E. INSTRUCTIONS No 7.

OPERATION. 1. On morning of 28th inst, at an hour to be notified later, the 5th and 31st Divisions, under XI Corps, will attack and capture the enemy line from SWINGBRIDGE at K.15.d.5.8. - LE CORNET PERDU (K.5.b.) - K.6.c. - LA BECQUE - (E.23.central.)
The operation will be referred to as "BORDERLAND".

BOUNDARY. 2. The boundary for the attack, between 5th and 31st Divisions, runs from K.3.central through K.6.central.

FORMATION. 3. The attack of 31st Division will be carried out by 92 Inf. Bde. on right, and 93 Inf. Bde. on left.
Inter-Brigade Boundary runs from E.28.a.8.8. - E.29.a.0.7. - E.29.b.0.6.

R.E. 4. 211 Field Coy.(less 1 section) and 2 sections 210 Field Coy. under O.C. 211 Field Coy. are detailed for work with 92 Bde.

5. 3 sections will work as soon as the situation is sufficiently clear on consolidating strong points E., F., G. and H. (see Map 'A') of which the sites will be fixed by Infantry. The Section Commander will take his instructions from the Battalion Commander to whom he is attached as to when to move forward to site, and will be given name of Commander, and number and unit of platoon forming garrison of respective Strong Points.

6. 2 sections will be employed on :-

(a) Making Mule Tracks.

No 1 from Dump at K.4.a.6.2. to K.5.b.0.7.
No 2 " " " E.28.a.2.2. to E.29.a.5.2.

(b) Exploiting water supply in captured area.

O.C. 211 Field Coy. will make arrangements for drawing water from any well that appears to contain drinkable water, and reporting location of supply to 92 Bde. so that water may be tested by a Medical Officer.
O.C. 211 Field Coy. will also arrange for bottles to send samples to A.D.S. at D.18.a.4.2. for testing.

7. 150 Infantry from 94 Inf. Bde. will be detailed by 92 Bde. for work as carrying parties to the various R.E. parties. O.C. 211th Field Coy. will get in touch with O.C. Battalion and arrange distribution at his own discretion. He will make sure that his Section Officers get into touch with the Officers commanding carrying parties, and thoroughly rehearse their respective roles, and also reconnoitre as far as practicable, the ground over which they are going to act.

PIONEERS. 8. O.C. 12th K.O.Y.L.I. will detail 2 Coys. to work with 92 Bde. and 1 Coy. with 93 Bde. Work will consist in wiring front line posts with festooned double apron fence, (a trip wire 30 yards in front of same if time permits) and will commence at 11 p.m. on site.

92 Bde. AREA. 9. (a) In 92 Bde. Area.

1 Coy. will work on 'A' Post.)
3 platoons "   " 'B' Post.) see attached map.
1 platoon "   " 'C' Post.)

-2-

Wiring parties of 1 N.C.O. and 9 men each will be detailed as under :-

    'A' Post. - 4 parties.
    'B' Post. - 4 parties.
    'C' Post. - 2 parties.

Remainder of Coys. will carry, doing two trips.

(b) Carrying parties for K.O.Y.L.I. from the Battalion of 94 Bde. under 92 Bde. are as follows :-

150 men will make one journey in morning going out with 4th wave under arrangements to be made by 92 Bde. (For detail see Bde. Orders.) Forward R.E. Dumps to which they will carry are K.5.b.55.70. - E.29.d.30.95. - E.29.a.85.50. These men will again carry to same places at night, under arrangements to be made by O.C. 12th K.O.Y.L.I. Rendezvous in 'B' ride at E.27.a.0.4. at 9 p.m. and there await instructions from 12th K.O.Y.L.I.

92 Bde. will also arrange for 60 mules to take up loads at night to Mule Track termini.

(c) O.C. 12th K.O.Y.L.I. will arrange for an Officer or responsible N.C.O. to be at each dump of R.E. Stores to superintend loading of carrying parties, both morning and evening, and that the location of dumps, tracks, and the ground over which action will take place is carefully reconnoitred.

(d) He will ensure that liaison with Officer i/c Infantry carrying parties is instituted at once.

(e) The detail of loads to go up is worked on a basis of

    36 long screw pickets - 6 men.)
    128 medium "   " - 16 men.) per 100 yards wire.
    38 coils barbed wire. - 38 men.)

    1 man load equals - 1 coil barbed wire,
                   or 6 long screw pickets,
                   or 8 medium screw pickets.

(f) In morning 150 Infantry take equivalent of 250 yards of entanglement.

In evening Infantry carry a similar amount, and 50 mules under Bde. arrangements take

    Long Screw Pickets - 180)
    Medium do   do   - 560) equals 400 yards
    Barbed Wire, coils. - 120) entanglement.

to mule track termini.

Pioneers will take up with them sufficient for a further 200 yards entanglement.

(g) In morning, Infantry draw stores from dump at E.20.b.9.1. In evening, mules draw from E.20.b.9.1. and 12th K.O.Y.L.I. with Infantry draw from dumps at K.4.a.6.2. and E.28.a.3.2.

93 Bde. AREA

10. a) In 93rd Bde area

1 Coy. K.O.Y.L.I. will work on LA BECQUE FARM Post, (see attached map) Work will be as in 8.
4 wiring parties of 1 N.C.O. and 9 men each will be detailed.
Remainder of Coy. will carry, doing two trips.

-3-

  (b) A company from Battalion of 94 Bde. under orders of 93 Bde. will be detailed as carrying party. O.C. 12th K.O.Y.L.I. will get into touch with this Coy. and make all detailed arrangements

  (c) The dump of R.E. Stores is at E.21.b.2.3.
    O.C. K.O.Y.L.I. will arrange a responsible N.C.O. to superintend loading.

MEDICAL ARRANGEMENTS.   11. DISPOSITIONS.

Relay Posts.	Left Sector.	E.8.c.8.2. (present R.A.P.)
Advanced Dressing Stations.	No. 1.	D.18.a.4.2.
	No. 2. (emergency)	D.9.d.0.8. (TEXAS FARM)
M.D.S.	C.5.a.6.9.	

                F. Giles.
                  Lt.Col.R.E.

26/6/18   C.R.E. 31st Division.

Copies to:- No 1. 31st Div. 'G'.
      2. 92 Bde.
      3. 93 Bde.
      4. 94 Bde X
      5. 210 Fd. Coy. X
      6. 211 do
      7. 223 do X
      8. 12 K.O.Y.L.I.
      9. C.R.E. X
      10. Adjt. X
      11.)
      12.) War Diary. ✓ X
      13. File. X

X map not attached.

War Diary

CORRIGENDA.

R.E. INSTRUCTIONS No 8.

Para 2 (b)

For 1 Section Reserve Battn.H.Q. at E.28.d.9.4.

Read 1 Section Reserve Battn.H.Q. at E.25.d.9.4.

HEADQUARTERS,
31st
DIVL. ENGINEERS.

No.
Date. 30/6/18.

Lt.Col.R.E.

C.R.E. 31st Division.

Copies to all recipients of above Instructions.

War Diary

S E C R E T.　　　　　　　　　　　　　　　　　　　　　　　Copy No 13

R.E. INSTRUCTIONS No 8.

The following is Programme of Work until further orders :-

210 Field Coy.R.E.
- (a) 1 Section on 5.9 proof dugout at B.H.Q. at GD. MARQUETTE.
- (b) ½ Coy. on COBLEY COTTAGE - VOLLEY FARM Switch.
- (c) 1 Section i/c Demolitions.

211 Field Coy.R.E.
- (a) 1 Section FETTLE FARM Bde. H.Q. working in double shifts.
- (b) 1 Section on Battn. H.Q. at E.20.central.
  1 Section on Demolitions.
  1 Section Reserve Battn.H.Q. at E.28.d.9.4.
- (c) Superintending hurdle making as carried out by ½ Coy. K.I.Y.L.I. at Forestry Dump.(E.25.d.9.4.)
- (d) Marking out tracks in wood in conjunction with K.O.Y.L.I.

223 Field Coy.R.E.

D.H.Q. at U.30.c.0.6.

K.O.Y.L.I.
- (a) Coy. garrisoning Pt. SEC BOIS Strong Point employed by night on improving trench line from Sanitas Corner (E.15.a.7.9.) to COBLEY COTTAGE (E.21.b.2.3.) The garrison of trenches will work on the portions they are occupying. The K.O.Y.L.I. will work on the intervening lengths.
- (b) Coy. garrisoning SWARTENBROUCK will work by night improving trench line into a solid breastwork from VOLLEY FARM (E.28.a.7.7.) to road at E.28.c.7.4. Arrangements to be made for shelters for accommodation behind the parados.
- (c) Coy. garrisoning LA MOTTE Defences will work by day as under :-
  - (i) ½ Coy. under 211 Fd. Coy. making hurdles at Forestry Dump, E.25.d.9.4.
  - (ii) ½ Coy. maintaining tram track, and rides and shooting tracks in AVAL WOOD, East of "C" ride inclusive.
    The Officer i/c this ½ Coy. will get in touch with O.C. 211 Fd. Coy. who will give him all information re tracks and notice boards for same.

F. Giles.
Lt.Col.R.E.
C.R.E. 31st Division.

P.T.O.

SECRET.   Copy No.

R.E. INSTRUCTIONS No. 2.

Copies to:- No 1. C.E. XV Corps.
           2. 31 Div. 'G'.
           3. 92 Inf. Bde.
           4. 93 "   "
           5. 94 "   "
           6. 210 Fd. Coy.
           7. 211 "   "
           8. 223 "   "
           9. 12 K.O.Y.L.I.
          10. C.R.E.
          11. Adjt.
          12.) War Diary.
          13.)
          14. File.

The following is PROGRAMME of work for night 30th June/1st July:-

210 Field   (a) 1 Section on S.P. Road Demolitions at B.H.Q. at
Coy. R.E.   GD. HARCOURTS.
             (b) ½ Coy. on GOBLIN CORNER & VALLEY FARM Cutting.
             (c) 1 Section l/o Ferrettas.

211 Field   (a) 1 Section SUTTLE FARM Strong Point, working in
Coy. R.E.   double shifts.
             (b) 1 Section on Dets. Road at R.E.30.central.
             1 Section on Demolitions.
             1 Section Reserve Batln.H.Q. at R.28.d.9.6.
             (c) Superintending Bundle making as carried out by ½
                 Coy. K.O.Y.L.I. at Forestry Dump.(R.28.d.8.4.)
             (d) Marking out tracks in wood in conjunction with
                 K.O.Y.L.I.

223 Field   D.H.E. at U.E.20.d.C.M.
Coy. R.E.

K.O.Y.L.I.   (a) Coy. garrisoning Pt. 70 BOIS Strong Point, employed
                 by night on improving trench line from Sanites Corner
                 (R.12.a.7.5.) to COBURY COTTAGE (R.21.b.2.5.). The
                 garrison of trenches will work on the portions they
                 are occupying. The K.O.Y.L.I. will work on the
                 intervening lengths.
             (b) Coy. garrisoning SPAFFINBOROUGH will work by night
                 improving trench line into a solid breastwork from
                 VOLLEY FARM (R.28.a.7.7.) to road at R.29.c.7.4.
                 Arrangements to be made for shelters for accommodation
                 behind the parados.
             (c) Coy. garrisoning 14 NORTH Defences will work by day
                 as under :-
             (i) ½ Coy. under 211 Fd. Coy. making bundles at
                 Forestry Dump, R.28.d.8.4.
            (ii) ½ Coy. maintaining tram track, and rides and
                 shooting tracks in AVAL WOOD, East of "D"
                 ride inclusive.
                 The Officer i/o this ½ Coy. will get in touch
                 with O.C. 211 Fd. Coy. who will give him all
                 information re trams and bolts boards for same.

                                                    Lt.Col.R.E.
                                                C.R.E. 31st Division.

P.T.O.

War Diary

C.R.E's CIRCULAR No 2.

STABLE MANAGEMENT etc.

S.S.648. Every R.E. Officer is to be in possession of S.S.648, "Notes on Horse Management in the Field" This circular in no way affects the principles therein laid down, but is intended to draw attention to certain salient points.

GROOMING TOOLS and CLEANING GEAR. (a) Every mounted man must be in possession of the following articles of cleaning gear :-

    1 Body Brush.
    1 Dandy Brush.
    1 Hoof Pick. (On clasp knife.)
    1 Currycomb. (To be manufactured locally.)
    2 Sponges. (1 for eyes, nostrils and dock.)
            (1 for saddlery.)
    1 Wisp.
    2 Stable rubbers.
    1 piece Sandpaper.
    1 tin Saddle Soap.

Where any of the above are not a Government issue, the O.C. Company will take steps to provide.
Every mounted man will show the above articles at each kit inspection. Fair wear and tear will be replaced by the Company. Losses by neglect will be made good by the man.

(b) In addition to the above, every Coy. must be provided with either a power clipping machine or else one pair hand clippers per section.

GROOMING. (a) Particular attention must be paid to the following points :-
    1. Sponging out eyes, nostrils and dock.
    2. Cleaning head, tail, legs, and under chest.
    3. Picking out hoofs at every stable time.

(b) Mane and tail combs are not allowed.

(c) Hand rubbing is to be instituted forthwith to complete the removal of long coats of animals which have not already shed them.
By the end of June every animal should have lost completely the winter coat.

(d) Grooming must be carried out smartly and energetically. A good driver can clean the dirtiest animal in an hour.
Lazy grooming is useless to the animal and a waste of time on the part of the driver.

SHOEING. Mules feet generally are too long.
On no account must the rasp be permitted on the outside wall of the foot of an animal, except under the clinches before turning down.
The frog must not be touched with the knife except to remove loose pieces.
Farriers' tools are to be inspected by an Officer once a week. He will see that the rasp is sharp and in good condition. A blunt rasp leads to too much knife work on the foot. If becoming blunt, a new rasp should be indented for at once.

                                                                                    TEETH.

(2)

TEETH. The back teeth of every animal must be examined by an Officer at least once a month and he will supervise personally whilst they are being filed by the Farrier Sergt. where necessary.

FEEDING. (a) Feeds must invariably be given in nose bag or hay net - never on the ground.

(b) Four feeds a day will be given in future. The scale laid down in Appendix B to S.S.646 will be followed.

(c) At this time of the year every opportunity must be taken to graze animals.

(d) When working in the front line, Officers must be on the look-out for fields of green forage which are in such a position that obviously no crop can be taken off them by the owners, owing to enemy action. Bags full of this forage can be sent back by empty transport returning after the R.E. material has been delivered on site. This must be done only under the orders and personal supervision of an officer.

(e) A double handful of chaff must be thoroughly mixed in every feed of oats given. A similar amount of green forage should be mixed with the hay food whenever obtainable.

WATERING. (a) A horse cannot have too much water, always allowing it is given at the right time.

(b) Invariably water before feeding, and allow each animal plenty of time to drink. Because an animal raises its head from the water it does not necessarily mean that it has slaked its thirst.

(c) When on the move, allow animals as much as they will take no matter how hot and sweaty they may be, unless very severe or fast work is expected immediately afterwards.

EXERCISE. Animals must be exercised for at least one hour per day when not otherwise at work. This will always be done under an Officer's supervision. Brisk walk and slow trot only paces allowed.

STABLE GUARD. 1. One man must always be on duty in the lines between stable hours and at night. He must be provided with a board of written orders, detailing his duties as under :-

(a) Keep every horse tied up proper length.
(b) Shorten nose bags of any horses that are tossing them up.
(c) Remove nose bags as soon as horses have finished feeding, turn them inside out, and collect them.
(d) Note and report to Mounted Sergt. the horses off their feed.
(e) Keep hay and hay nets in proper position so as to prevent them being trampled on, and allow horse to eat with comfort.
(f) Remove all droppings, and keep the lines clean.
(g) Prevent horses becoming frightened, by speaking to them, and call for assistance at least sign of stampede.

2. The Stable Guard must be visited after 11 p.m. at night at least twice a week by an officer.

CLIPPING.

CLIPPING. All manes will be kept close hogged.
Mules tails will be clipped, leaving a "bell" at the extremity.
Horses tails will be pulled carefully by hand by a knowledgeable man. The clippers must never touch a horse's tail.

GENERAL. 1. The tendency for the supervision of the horse lines and transport to be left in the hands of the 2nd in Command and the Mounted Sergt., and for the mounted portion of the Coy. to look on themselves as a section apart from the rest of the Coy. must be severely discouraged.

2. Each section officer is responsible for knowing as much about the mounted portion of his section as he does about his sappers.
When front line work prevents his giving as much time to stables as he should, he is helped out by the O.C. or 2nd in Command, but he must be at all times prepared to answer any question that may arise in connection with his drivers, animals, and vehicles.

Lt.Col.R.E.
C.R.E. 31st Division.

June 15th, 1918.

Distribution :-
```
        1 Copy   to Div.H.Q.
        7 Copies to 210 Fd. Coy. R.E.
        7   "    to 211  "   "    "
        7   "    to 223  "   "    "
        1 Copy   to C.R.E.
        1   "    to Adjt.
        1   "    to H.Q. File.
        2 Copies to War Diary.
        3   "    Spare.
```

SECRET.   Copy No. 5

War Diary

Operation Order No.1.
51st Divisional Engineers.

1. If the tactical situation permits Field Coys of the 51st Div. will return tomorrow to the former Camps and Billets which they left on 15/8/18. No Coy is to move until orders are issued tomorrow morning.

2. On receipt of definite orders to move, Coys will march off forth with by the same routes by which they came, in their own time and report arrival to Divisional Headquarters at WARDRECQUES as before, forwarding at the same time the proposed Training Programme for the remaining week of the ensuing week, which should be framed in accordance with my R.E. 119/ dated omitting route marches.

3. The transport of the 223rd Field Coy.R.E. will be inspected at 11 a.m. on the 18th inst.

4. Definite orders for the move as in para 2 will cancel R.E. Instructions No.1.

                                                    J. Giles
                                                    Lt.Col.R.E.
16/8/18.   C.R.E. 51st Division.

            Copy. No.1 Headquarters 51st Division "g"
                    2 C.R.E.
                    3 Adjutant.
                    4 H.Q. 51st Divn.Engineers. File
                    5)
                    6) War Diary
                    7 210th Field Coy.R.E.
                    8 211th Field Coy.R.E.
                    9 223rd Field Coy.R.E.
                   10 92nd Inf.Bde.
                   11 93rd Inf.Bde.
                   12 94th Inf.Bde.
                   13 C.E. 15th Corps.

War Diary. SECRET

Map Ref: 1/40,000   31st Divisional Engineers.   Copy No 12
Sheets 27 & 36A
                     OPERATION ORDER No 32.

1. 31st Division (less Artillery) will take over Right Divisional
   Sector of XVth Corps front from 29th Division on 20th/21st and
   22nd June.

2. The attached Table "A" gives relief of Companies and Pioneers.

3. All R.E. Stores, tools, machinery, dumps, maps, sketches, plans,
   gumboots, photos, works reports, demolition schemes, etc., will
   be taken over and receipts given.

4. 100 rounds S.A.A. per man extra to Mob. Tables will be taken over
   by Field Companies, and amount so taken over reported at once to
   this office.

5. H.Q., R.E. will close at WARDRECQUES at 10 a.m. and open at
   WALLON CAPPEL (U.23.d.4.9.) at the same hour, on the 22nd
   inst.

6. Completion of relief to be wired to H.Q., R.E. by Code Word
   "BEGIN at........"

7. ACKNOWLEDGE.

                                              F. Giles.
                                              Lt.Col.R.E.
20/6/18.   C.R.E. 31st Division.

Issued at 8-45 p.m.

Copies to:- No 1. C.E. XV Corps.
                2. 31 Div.'G'.
                3. 31 Div.'Q'.
                4. C.R.E. 29 Div.
                5. 210 Fd. Coy. R.E.
                6. 211 do   do
                7. 223 do   do
                8. 12th K.O.Y.L.I.
                9. C.R.E.
               10. Adjt.
               11. File.
               12)
               13) War Diary.

TABLE "A".

Item No.	Date.	31st Divsn. relieve 29th Divsn.	29th Divsn. Unit	Advance Parties. Numbers.	Rendezvous.	Time.	New Locations. Billets.	Transport Lines.	29th Div.Unit will be clear by.
1.	20/6/18.	223 Fd. Coy.	455 Fd. Coy.	4 Off., 2 N.C.O'n., 5 Sappers, Demolition party, 1 Storeman.	D.9.b.5.4.	9 a.m.	D.5.c.9.1.	D.1.d.8.8.	2 p.m.
2.	21/6/18.	211 Fd. Coy.	510 Fd. Coy.	3 Off., 2 Storemen., 1 N.C.O. & 14 men Demolition Party.	D.9.c.6.3	9 a.m.	D.9.c.6.3	V.25.d.0.7.	3 p.m.
3.	21/6/18.	210 Fd. Coy.	497 Fd. Coy.	4 Off., 21 Other Ranks Demolition Party.	D.9.b.5.4.	12 mid-day.	D.9.b.5.4.	D.7.b.1.9.	2 p.m.
4.	21/6/18.	12 K.O.Y.L.I.	1/2 Monmouth.	4 Off.	V.23.d.5.2.	10 a.m.	V.23.d.5.2.	V.23.d.5.2.	2 p.m.
5.	22/6/18.	H.Q.,R.E.	H.Q.,R.E.	R.S.M. 2 Sappers. (Dump) 1 Clerk.	D.2.d.5.6. U.22.d.6.9.	12 noon. 21/6/18. 9 a.m. 22/6/18.	D.2.d.5.6. U.22.d.6.9.	U.22.d.4.9.	10 a.m.

ORIGINAL.

CONFIDENTIAL.

WAR DIARY

of

Headquarters, 31st Div. Engineers.

from 1/7/18 to 31/7/18.

VOLUME XXXI

WAR DIARY
INTELLIGENCE SUMMARY

HQ. 31 Dn RE

Army Form C. 2118

Place	Date	Hour	Summary of Events and Information	Remarks and references to Appendices
WALLON-CAPPEL	1.7.18		Fd Coys employed as follows. 211th working on right Bde sector. 210th Left Bde sector. 223rd Fd Coy on back work including Dn HQ at V.30.C.0.7.	
	2.7.18		Capt Williams attached to HQRE for instruction	
	3.7.18		HQRE moved from WALLON-CAPPEL village to V.30.C.0.7. Location of Fd Coys as follows. 210 D.5.C.9.1. 211 D.9.C.6.3. 223 D.9.C.5.4.	
	6.7.18		Capt Hospel appointed to command 447th Fd Coy 5/O Division. Lt Buchanan appointed to proceed in command 211th Fd Coy.	
	7.7.18		2/Lt Balch T.C. joined No 210 Fd Coy for duty. 2/Lt Rogers joined 223rd Fd Coy for duty.	
	14.7.18		Casualties at 12 noon 210 Fd Coy 2 slightly wounded remain at duty. Capt Williams left HQRE & to attached to Dn Artillery	
	13.7.18		Casualties at 12 noon 211th Fd Coy 1 OR wounded.	
	29.7.18		Casualties at 12 noon 210 Fd Coy 1 OR wounded	
	31.7.18		Companies employed on following work. Main line of resistance (Z Line). Concrete shelters, repairing roads, etc. demolitions etc.	

R Knutton Capt RE Aj
Dn CRE 31 Dn

WAR DIARY

Report on part taken by 31st Div.R.E. and Pioneers in Operations of June 28th, 1918, East of NIEPPE Forest.

Map 'A'.
BEAULIEU FARM
1/10,000. 11/6/18.

HEADQUARTERS,
31st
DIVL. ENGINEERS.
No. RE168/15
Date.

R.E. (1) Following personnel were engaged:-

211 Field Coy.(less 1 Section) and 2 Sections 210 Field Coy., all under Command of Major MANSEL.M.C.,R.E.

150 Infantry were attached as carrying party to be distributed at discretion of O.C. 211 Field Coy. amongst his sections.

TASKS. (2) Tasks set were :-

(a) To construct two tracks for Pack Transport as shown (1 section on each.)

(b) To wire in Strong Points, 1 section on 'D', 1 section on 'E', 1 section on 'F' & 'G'.

(c) To search for sources of water supply and exploit any that might be found.

R.E. INSTRUCTIONS. (3) The orders given were that the R.E. Officer i/c each Section was to remain with the Battalion Commander with whom he was affiliated for the day until that Officer informed him that the situation was sufficiently clear to admit of the working parties going forward.
The O.C. Coy. was to remain at Bde. H.Q. until the working parties were committed to their tasks.

NARRATIVE. (4) Zero hour was 6 a.m. and all objectives were reported reached by 9 a.m. At 8-30 a.m. the situation was sufficiently clear for the R.E. to start out. By 2 p.m. the two tracks were both completed, and a double apron fence erected

at 'D' - 400 yards.
'E' - 300 yards.
'F' - 400 yards.
'G' - 200 yards.

The successful completion of the task was largely helped by the good work done by the Infantry Carrying Parties. The 'carry' was 1500 yards and some parties did six, and the average was four, journeys.
Only one shallow surface well was found, and the pump was put in working order, and a sample of the water sent to the Field Ambulance for testing.

PIONEERS. (5) Following were engaged :-

3 Coys. 12th K.O.Y.L.I. with 150 Infantry as carrying party.

TASKS. (6) To wire Front Line Posts,
1 Coy. at 'A' Post.
1 Coy. at 'B' & 'C' Posts.
1 Coy. at LA BECQUE FARM Post.

PIONEER INSTRUCTIONS. (7) The Pioneers were to reach site of work at 11 p.m., ascertain from the Infantry Officer i/c where the wire was wanted, erect same, and clear by 3 a.m. after the O.C. Post had expressed himself as satisfied with the work.

NARRATIVE. (8) The 150 Infantry carrying party, under Brigade arrangements, went forward with the 4th wave of the assault in the morning, and made dumps at 'J', 'K' and 'L', and then returned to their assembly positions. In the evening they were to report to and carry up one load each for the respective Coys. of K.O.Y.L.I., and then return to their Battn. H.Q.

The Pioneers, each Coy. being previously arranged as wiring parties and carrying parties reached site of work at 11 p.m.

One party of Infantry failed to materialise, and the confusion at the rendezvous in the dark between the parties of Infantry carrying for Pioneers, and the ration, water, ammunition and other carrying parties was so great as to cause considerable delay to the Pioneers in getting to the work.

Arrangements had been made for 60 mules to take up wire and pickets to the dumps forward at the termini of the tracks for Pack Animals, and by this means, an ample supply was ensured.

The Pioneers did their own carrying from these termini to the site of work to supplement the material in the dumps at 'J', 'K' and 'L'.

In spite of several 'S.O.S.' sent up during the night, the following lengths of double apron fence were erected successfully.

'A' Post. - 400 yards.
'B' Post. - 230 yards.
LA BECQUE FARM 'C' Post. - 200 yards.

At 'D' Post work was impossible, since the enemy had evidently discovered the working party and brought heavy machine gun fire to bear whenever they showed themselves over the parapet of the post.

Next night however, a party of 20 men went up and completed the work.

CONCLUSIONS. The operations brought no fresh points to light so far as the R.E. are concerned, but only emphasize the soundness of the principles
(a) that the R.E. must not go forward until the situation in the front line is quite clear,
(b) the closest liaison between R.E. and carrying parties attached to them. (Each R.E. Section Officer had personally on the day before the battle taken the Infantry Officer i/c carrying party attached to him and pointed out position of dumps of R.E. material, and together they made a visual reconnaissance of the ground over which the advance was to take place).
(c) The responsibility for siting of Posts after objective has been reached must remain with Infantry, who should at once begin to dig in. On arrival of R.E. the O.C. Post then points out where he wants the wire erected, and is given such assistance as possible by R.E. in consolidating.

POINTS OF INTEREST. 1. Bangalore Torpedos (6 feet, 1¼" piping filled ammonal) were carried to cut any thick hedges met with. No such obstacle was met with, but at a preliminary rehearsal, these small charges worked admirably, and the Infantry could lie within 15 or 20 feet during the explosion with impunity.

2. Infantry carried one shovel per man and all shovel edges were sharpened on a grindstone so that they could be used as a cutting tool where required.

-2-

not attached 3. For bridges for Mule Tracks a special bridge was made by 211 Field Coy. - details in Appendix 'B' - which proved very successful.

4. The Infantry Bridge (E-in-C. Plate No. D.P/618) proved most effectual.

5. A Pack Mule load worked out at

       30 long light screw pickets.
   or 40 medium light screw pickets.
   or 4 coils (50 yards) barbed wire.

per mule.

J. Giles.

Lt.Col.R.E.
C.R.E. 31st.Division.

3/7/18.

Copies to:- 31st Div.'G'.
           C.E. XV Corps.
           210 Fd. Coy.
           211 Fd. Coy.
           223 Fd. Coy.
           12th K.O.Y.L.I.
           C.R.E.
           War Diary (2) ✓
           File.

ADDENDUM No.3.

R.E. INSTRUCTIONS No. 9.

The following should now/be added.

RIGHT Brigade Area - after PAPOTE Group add :-

MORBECQUE.	1. Road Mine near MORBECQUE D.19.d.2.0.	1 N.C.O.& 2 sappers 556 A.T. Coy. living at D.19.d.2.0.	C.R.E. on instructions from Divn.

LEFT Brigade Area - Include in Left Forward. B Group.

    4. Road Bridge at E.13.a.4.6.

F Giles.

Lieut-Colonel.R.E.

31/7/18.

C.R.E. 31st Division.

Copies to all recipients of above Instructions.

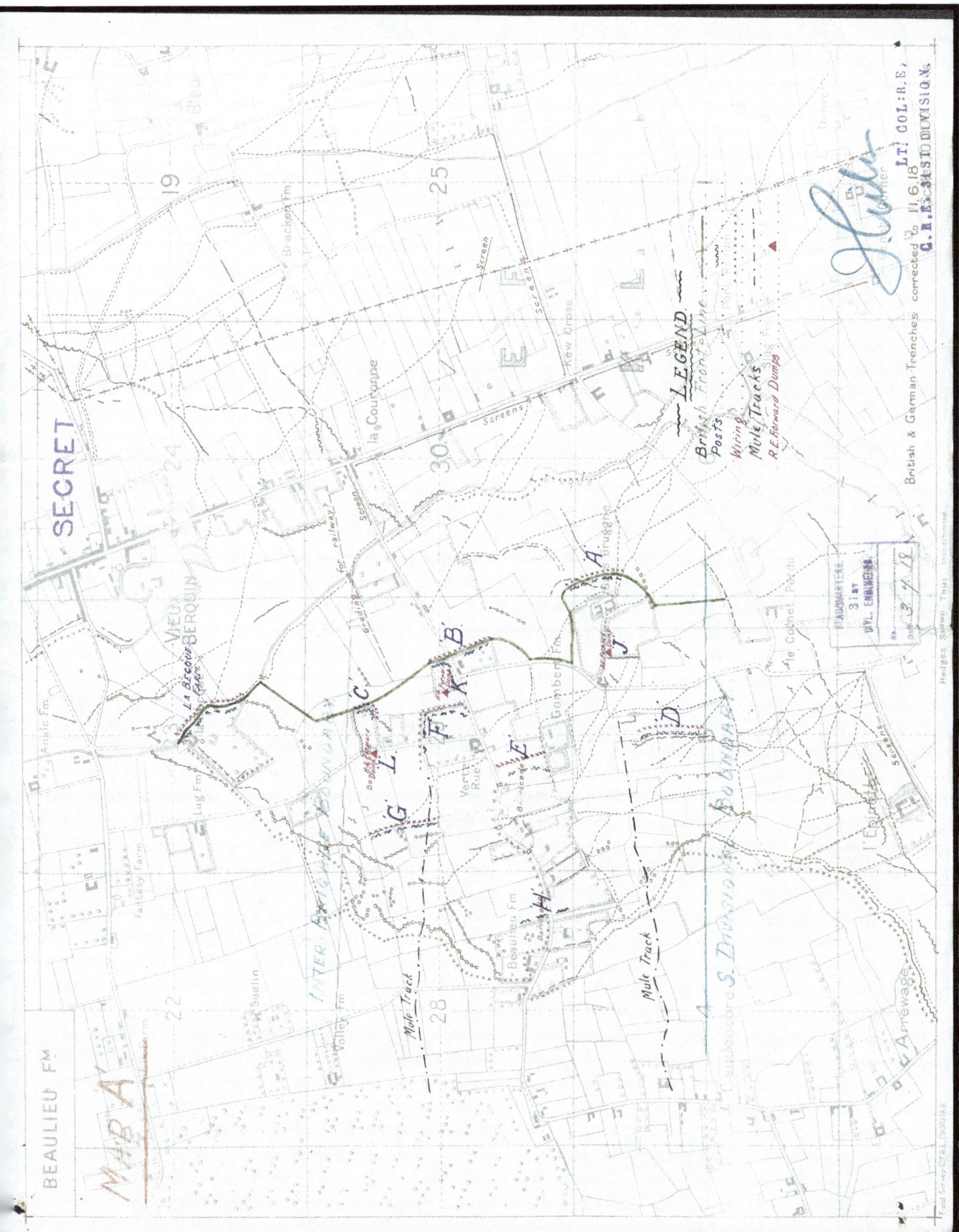

SECRET — War Diary

R.E. Instructions No 9.

The following should now be added to the map attached.

Road Mines blown at K.5.d.4.5., E.29.c.8.6. and E.29.d.4.8.

[signature]
Lt.Col.R.E.
C.R.E. 31st Division.

8/7/18.

Copies to all recipients of above Instructions and Map.

WAR DIARY

SECRET.

R.E. INSTRUCTIONS No 9.

Copy No 31

Demolitions in Divisional Area.

GENERAL INSTRUCTIONS.

DETAIL OF DEMOLITION PARTIES.
1. Parties as shewn in attached table will be detailed by Right and Left Coys to live at places stated. No changes are permitted without reference to C.R.E.

DUTIES OF OFFICER i/c DEMOLITIONS.
2. The Officer i/c Demolitions will be responsible that

   (a) One sapper per charge and the N.C.O. i/c is always either in the billet or on his charge.

   (b) A runner with bicycle is always at the billet and that he knows the position of all the mines, and thus be able to go round and warn any men who may be out on their charges when the alarm is given.

   (c) All charges are in proper order and are properly laid. All mine holes kept dry and pumped out daily if liable to be flooded. All leads, fuzes, detonators and primers are kept dry in a dry place and in good condition.

   (d) Both the sapper i/c and the reserve man are each in possession of the necessary fuzes, primers, etc., for firing the charge. Each coil of fuze, cut to length and jointed to detonator, with spare primers is labelled with name of sapper who is responsible for it.

   (e) Personal liaison is maintained with the various officers who have authority to order the mines to be blown. (This is essential owing to constant changes of garrisons of Strong Points and formations in the line.)

   (f) Arrangements are made whereby result of demolition, whether a success or failure, is reported at the earliest possible moment to O.C. Field Coy, who will in turn immediately report to Bde. H.Q. and to C.R.E.

DUTIES OF SAPPERS i/c DEMOLITIONS.
3. Sapper i/c Demolition.

As soon as the notification of the alarm reaches him, each sapper i/c of a demolition will

   (a) Report to Officer or N.C.O. i/c Demolitions at the billet in "Battle Order".

   (b) Proceed as quickly as possible to the demolition, taking with him all necessary fuzes, primers, detonators, exploder (where required) and a sharp knife.

   (c) Prepare charge for firing.

      (Where exploder is used leads will only be connected to terminals and the handle raised when the sapper receives the written order to blow or on approach of enemy.)

   (d) Keep a sharp lookout for runners bringing messages or for the approach of the enemy.

-2-

(c) Fire the charge on receipt of written orders to fire from any of the officers shewn in the table, or on seeing the enemy advancing and none of our own troops in danger of being cut off by the demolition.

Sapper in Reserve.

Each sapper in reserve as soon as the alarm reaches him will

(a) Report to Officer or N.C.O. i/c Demolitions.
(b) Collect his own kit and that of sapper i/c Mine.
(c) Stand by to take orders to the sapper i/c Mine.

N.B. When doing so, the reserve man will take with him the spare firing set.

[signature] Capt R.E.
for Lt.Col.R.E.
C.R.E. 31st Division.

5/7/18.

Copies to:- No 1. 31st Div.'G'.
2. C.E. XV Corps.(no map)
3-5. 210 Fd. Coy.
6-8. 211 Fd. Coy.
9-11. 223 Fd. Coy.
12-15. 92 Inf. Bde.
16-19. 93 Inf. Bde.
20-23. 94 Inf. Bde.
25. 12th K.O.Y.L.I.
26. O.C. LA MOTTE Defences.
27. O.C. PETIT SEC BOIS Defences.
28. C.R.E.
29. Adjt. (no map.)
30. File. " "
31-32. War Diary.(one map.)

DEMOLITIONS.

RIGHT BRIGADE AREA.

Group	Description.	Map location.	Demolition Party.	ORDERS FOR FIRING DEMOLITION The undermentioned are authorised to give orders to blow on their own responsibility. Orders must be in writing to Officer or N.C.O. i/c.
LA MOTTE.	1. Near CHATEAU. Road Bridge over Canal.	D.30.c.95.65.		1. G.O.C. RIGHT Infantry Brigade.
	2. Near CHURCH. Road Mine.	D.30.d.00.85.		2. Os.C. Battns. RIGHT Inf. Bdo.
	3. Near TOWER. Road Bridge over stream.	E.25.a.0.7.		3. O.C. LA MOTTE Defences.
	4. At Sawmills. Road Bridge over stream.	E.19.d.1.1.		4. R.E. Officer or N.C.O. i/c failing receipt of orders from any of
	5. Rails on Railway.	(D.30.b.55.30. (-D.24.d.6.1.	1 Officer, 1 N.C.O.	the foregoing on his own responsibility should he see the enemy
	6. Railway Bridge over stream.	D.24.d.6.1.	& 14 sappers	advancing in close proximity.
	7. Swing Bridge over canal.	D.30.a.6.3.	living in LA MOTTE.	5. G.O.C. Reserve Inf. Bds. if
	8. Bridge over Canal at FETTLE FARM.	D.24.c.7.9.	at D.30.d.0.3.	commanding any portion of Forward Area.
	9. Weldon Trestle Bridge over Canal.	D.18.c.7.2.		6. Os.C. Battns. Reserve Inf. Bde.
	10. Road Bridge over stream at SPOOK COTTAGE.	D.24.a.05.20.		if operating under their G.O.C. or attached to Forward Brigade.
	11. Road Mine near SPOOK COTTAGE.	D.24.a.1.1.		
	12. Road Bridge over stream at SCALLOP FARM.	D.23.c.95.55.		
	13. Road Bridge over Canal at PREAVIN.	K.1.c.7.2.	2 sappers in Rly. Embankment at K.1.c.8.4.	
PAPOTE GROUP.	1. Road Bridge over stream at PAPOTE.	D.16.d.2.2.	6 sappers at Coy. H.Q. at	
	2. Road Mine at PAPOTE.	D.16.d.2.2.	D.9.c.6.3.	
	3. Road Mine near MORBECQUE.	D.21.a.4.2.		

DEMOLITIONS.

LEFT BRIGADE AREA.

Group.	Description.	Map Location.	Demolition Party.	ORDERS for FIRING DEMOLITION. The undermentioned are authorised to give orders to blow on their own responsibility. Orders must be in writing to Officer or N.C.O. i/c.
Left Forward.	A. Road Mine.	1. E.9.a.4.4.	1 N.C.O. & 3 sappers at E.9.a.55.45. in touch with O.C. SEC BOIS Defences.	1. G.O.C. LEFT Infantry Brigade.
	do do	2. E.8.a.9.8.		2. Os-C. Battns. LEFT Inf. Bde.
	do do	3. E.8.c.6.6.		3. O.C. PT. SEC BOIS Defences.
	B. Road Bridge.	1. E.13.c.3.4.)	1 N.C.O. & 3 sappers at House at E.13.a.1.4.	4. R.E. Officer or N.C.O. i/c failing receipt of orders from any of the foregoing on his own responsibility should he see the enemy advancing in close proximity.
	do do	2. D.18.b.9.3.)		
	do do	3. D.12.d.5.0.)		5. G.O.C. Reserve Inf. Bde. if commanding any portion of Forward Area.
Left Rear.	Trestle Bridge.	1. D.17.b.9..) 2		6. Os-C. Battns. Reserve Inf. Bde. if operating under their G.O.C. or attached to forward Brigade.
	Road Bridge.	2. D.17.b.4.8.)		
	do do	3. D.11.d.2.0.)	1 Officer, 1 N.C.O. and 7 sappers in Camp at D.5.c.9.1.	
	do do	4. D.17.a.1.2.)		
	Trestle Bridge	5. D.11.a.4.3.)		
	Road Mine.	6. D.11.b.8.1.)		
	do do	7. D.16.b.9.6.)		

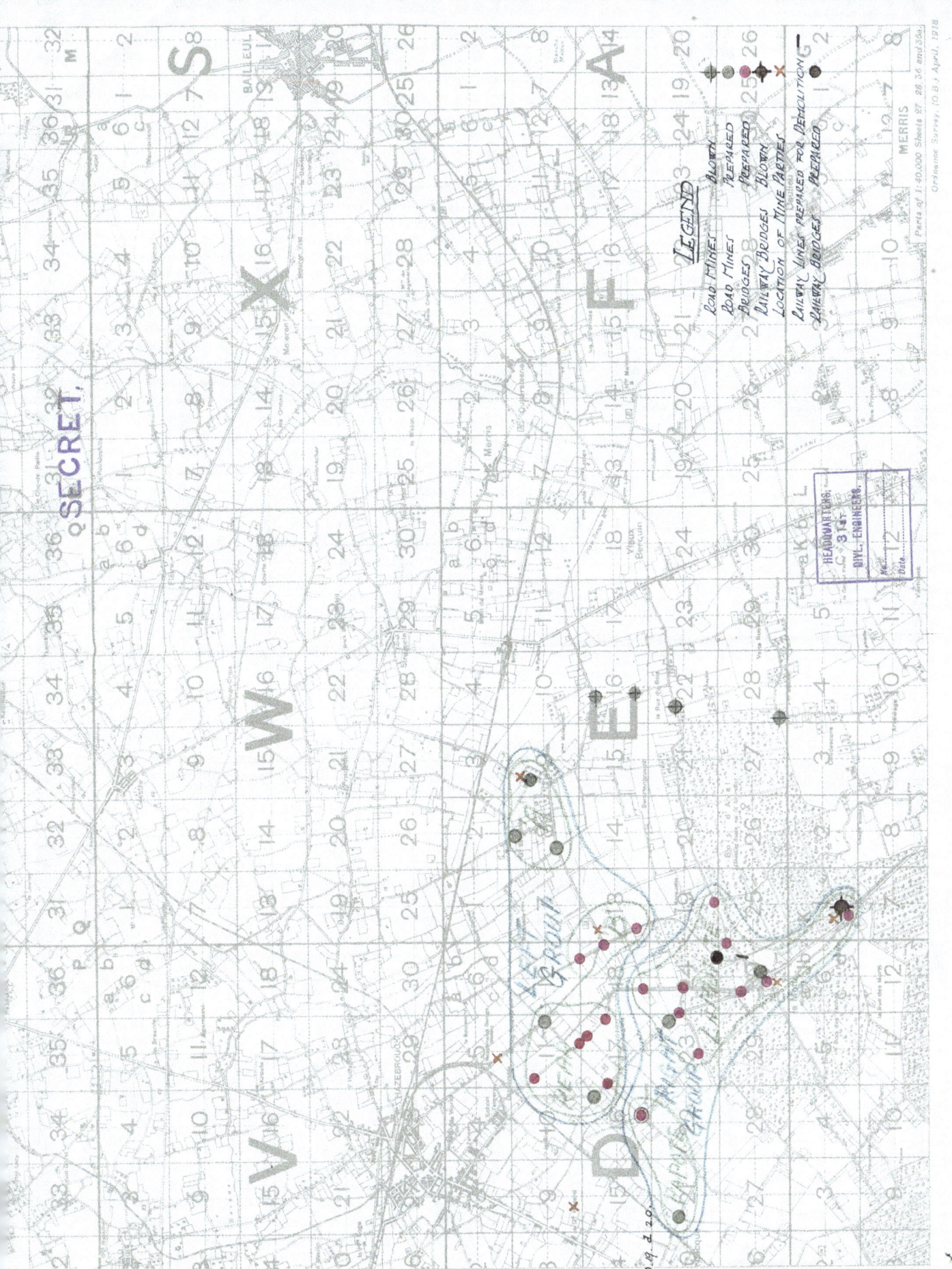

WAR DIARY

R.E. INSTRUCTIONS No 10.

SECRET.　　　　　　　　　　　　　　　　　　　　　　　Copy No 14

The following will be Programme of Work from 11th inst. inclusive.

I.

RIGHT COY in LINE.　223rd Field Coy. to whom RIGHT Brigade in line will apply for any small and immediate services.

    (a) 1 section on Concrete Pill Boxes for M.G's. in main line of resistance in AVAL Wood.

    (b) 1 section on 4.2 proof shelters at A.D.S. at D.18.a.5.3.

    (c) 1 section i/c Demolitions.

    (d) 1 section on FETTLE FARM Brigade H.Q.

    (e) Superintending hurdle and picket making by ½ Coy. K.O.Y.L.I. at Forestry Dump (E.25.d.9.4.)

  N.B. The 5 O.R. of the R.E. Forestry Coy. working here will also come under 223 Fd. Coy. for work and rations.

    (f) Upkeep of dryweather tracks, and roads and bridges generally in Right Bde. Area (NIEPPE Forest tracks excepted) with labour supplied by R.A.M.C.

LEFT COY. in LINE.　210th Field Coy.R.E. to whom LEFT Brigade in line will apply for any small and immediate services.

    (a) 1 section Bde. H.Q. at GD. MARQUETTE Farm.

    (b) 1 section on VOLLEY Farm - COBLEY COTTAGE Switch with 200 Infantry daily from Right Brigade.

    (c) 1 section on limber track from 'A' ride to LUG FARM.

    (d) 1 section on Demolitions.

    (e) Upkeep of dryweather tracks, bridges, and roads generally in Left Bde. Area with labour supplied by R.A.M.C.

RESERVE COY.　211th Field Coy.R.E.

    (a) 1 section on Battn. H.Q. at GRENADE Farm.

    (b) 1 section on Battn. H.Q. at FOREST Camp, E.25.d.9.4.

    (c) Completion of marking of tracks in AVAL Wood.

    (d) ½ Coy. on D.H.Q. accessory buildings.

    (e) 3 N.C.O. Instructors, 1 each for Battalions of 94 Bde, with one Officer superintending to give practical instruction to officers and O.R. in wiring and trench digging.

K.O.Y.L.I.　(a) 1 Coy.(garrison of Pt. SEC BOIS) less 1 platoon and Lewis Gun crews - work on main line of resistance from SANITAS CORNER to COBLEY COTTAGE improving trenches - assisted nightly by 100 men as working party from LEFT Brigade.

(2)

K.O.Y.L.I. (cont'd)

(b) 1 Coy. (garrison of SWARTENBROUCH) less 1 platoon and Lewis Gun crews - work on main line of resistance from VOLLEY FARM to VERTE RUE improving trenches - assisted nightly by 150 men as working party from RIGHT Brigade.

(c) 1 Coy. (garrison of LA MOTTE) less 1 platoon and Lewis Gunners -

   (i) $\frac{1}{2}$ Coy. under 223 Fd. Coy. making hurdles etc. at Forestry Dump, E.25.d.9.4.

   (ii) 1 platoon maintaining tram track and rides, and shooting trucks in AVAL Wood, East of River Track inclusive, and in the area enclosed by FETTLE FARM - LA MOTTE Station - SAW MILLS Bridge - E.19.a.4.7.

(d) In each case, (a),(b),(c), the Lewis Gun crews will work on improvement of trenches etc. of the Strong Points of which they form the garrison.

II GENERAL.

(a) Os.C. units concerned will arrange mutually for the necessary handing over reconnaissance to take place on 10th inst., and will take steps to get in touch with the various working parties, R.A., Infantry, and R.A.M.C. and with the formations and units supplying same.

(b) The handing over of all demolitions must receive especial attention.

(c) No change of camps or transport lines will take place.

F. Giles
Lt.Col. R.E.
C.R.E. 31st Division.

9/7/18.

Distribution:- Copy No 1. C.E. XV Corps.
               No 2. 31 Div.'G'.
               No 3. 92 Inf. Bde.
               No 4. 93   "   "
               No 5. 94   "   "
               No 6. 210 Fd. Coy.
               No 7. 211 "   "
               No 8. 223 "   "
               No 9. 12th K.O.Y.L.I.
               No 10. A.D.M.S.
               No 11. 31 Div. Arty.
               No 12. C.R.E.
               No 13. Adjt.
               No 14.)
               No 15.) War Diary. ✓
               No 16. File.

War Diary

ADDENDUM to R.E. INSTRUCTIONS No.11.

1. In order to obtain a continuous parapet throughout main line of resistance as quickly as possible, the earth for parados will not be thrown up until the whole of the parapet has been completed.

2. The parapet will only be made 6 ft thick at the top at first, but the distance of borrow pit from edge of trench will remain the same.

3. Gaps in the hurdle revetment of parados must be left every 20 yards to act as passage to living shelters in rear of parados.

20/7/18.

F. Giles.
Lieut-Colonel. R.E.
C.R.E. 31st Division.

Copies to all recipients of above instructions.

SECRET.

R.E. INSTRUCTIONS No 11.   Copy No 21

Reference S.G.83/547 of 2/7/18 :-

1. In view of approaching wet weather, it has been decided to make main line of resistance in accordance with following section -

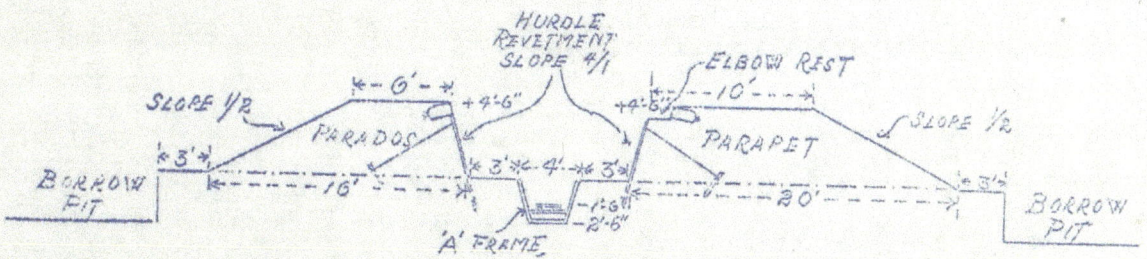

2. The division of labour in connection therewith is as follows :-

   (a) K.O.Y.L.I. Coys. erect hurdle and sandbag revetment and anchorages, and lay out tape to mark outting edge of front and rear borrow pit.

   (b) Infantry working parties (1 Coy. and 4 platoons Left Bde, 150 working party from Right Bde. with 3 Officers and necessary proportion of N.C.Os) under supervision of K.O.Y.L.I. throw up earth for parapet and parados.

   (c) R.E. insert 'A' frames and duckboards, and trim off interior of trench. Where time permits, they will also erect small elephant shelters behind parados.

3. (a) The work will be carried out between present posts occupied by Infantry. No portion of trench under construction is to be entered by Infantry garrison until duly handed over by O.C. K.O.Y.L.I. to the O.C. Battalion garrisoning the line.

   (b) As soon as all intervals are completed, and the Infantry are occupying the new posts thus made, the present posts will be renovated under arrangements to be made later.

4. Work, to commence with, will be concentrated on section from SANITAS CORNER, E.15.a.7.7. to CONDY COTTAGE, E.15.d.0.6. Left Brigade, and from VOLLEY FARM to VERTE RUE, Right Brigade.

F. Giles.
Lt.Col.R.E.
C.R.E. 31st Division.

15/7/18.

Distribution:- Copy No 1. C.E. XV Corps.
2. 31 Div.'G'.
3 - 6. 92 Bde.
7 - 10. 93 Bde.
11 - 14. 94 Bde.
15. 210 Fd. Coy.R.E.
16. 211 do do
17. 223 do do
18. 12 K.O.Y.L.I.
19. C.R.E.
20. Adjt.
21 - 22. War Diary.
23. File.

SECRET War Diary   Copy No. 14

R.E. INSTRUCTIONS No. 12.

Following will be programme of work from 23rd inst inclusive.

Right Coy. in Line. 223rd Field Coy. R.E. to whom Right Bde. in line will apply for any small and immediate service
(a) 1 section i/c Demolitions.
(b) ½ section on shelters at A.D.S. at D.18.a.5.3. with labour supplied by Field Ambulance.
(c) 1 section supervising and working on VOLLEY FARM – COBLEY COTTAGE Switch by day with 200 Infantry Working Party from Right Bde.
(d) 1 section supervising and working on line from VOLLEY FARM – VERTE RUE by night with 150 Infantry Working Party from Right Bde.
(e) Supervising erection of Left Battn. H.Q. E.27.a.3.3.
    Right Battn. H.Q. E.26.d.8.3.
labour supplied by Battns. concerned.
(f) Supervising completion of Arty. Bde. H.Q. Shelter at FETTLE FARM with labour supplied by R.A.
(g) Superintending hurdle and picket making by 1 platoon K.O.Y.L.I. Forestry Dump (E.25.d.9.4.) with 5 O.R. of the R.E. Forestry Coy.
(h) Upkeep of dry weather tracks, and roads and bridges generally in Right Bde. Area. (NIEPPE Forest Tracks excepted) with labour provided by R.A.M.C.

Left Coy. in Line. 210th Field Coy. R.E. to whom Left Bde. in line will apply for any small and immediate services.
(a) 1 Section i/c Demolitions.
(b) 1½ sections byday on line SANITAS Corner – COBLEY Cottage (both inclusive) fixing 'A' frames and X.P.M. hurdles in trench.
(c) 1 section hurdling by night on same line and supervising 300 Infantry supplied by Left Bde. employed on throwing up parapet.
(d) ½ section with 24 Infantry supplied by Left Bde. on Bde. H.Q. at GD. MARQUETTE Farm.
(e) Upkeep of dry weather tracks, bridges and roads generally in Left Bde Area with labour supplied by R.A.M.C.

Reserve Coy. 211th Field Coy. R.E.   E.20.b.8.0.
(a) 1 section on Battn. H.Q. at GRENADE Farm/ Loading party of 18 AU SOUVERAIN daily from Left Bde. and offloading party of 25 daily at E.20.b.8.0. from Right Bde.
(b) 1 section on Battn. H.Q. at FOREST Camp, E.25.d.9.4. with 20 Infantry from Reserve Battn. filling sandbags.
(c) ½ section on D.H.Q. accessory buildings.
(d) ½ section on work for Div. Arty.
(e) 1 section on general services in back Area.

K.O.Y.L.I.
(a) 1 Coy. (garrison of PETIT SEC BOIS) less 1 platoon and Lewis Gun crews – permanent wiring party by night on line from SEC BOIS to COBLEY Cottage.
(b) 1 Coy. (garrison of SWARTENBROUCH) less 1 platoon and Lewis Gun crews – permanent wiring party by night on line from VOLLEY Farm inclusive to Southern Divisional Boundary.
(c) 1 Coy. (garrison of LA MOTTE) less 1 platoon and Lewis Gun crews –

  (i) 1 platoon under 223 Fd. Coy. making hurdles, pickets etc at Forestry Dump, E.25.d.9.4.

  (ii) 2 platoons maintaining roads, rides, tracks and tram track in Forest of NIEPPE Area.

(d) In each case, (a), (b), and (c), the Lewis Gun crews will work on improvement of trenches etc. of the Strong Points of which they form garrison.

F. Giles.
Lieut-Colonel. R.E.
C.R.E. 31st Division.

22/7/18.

Distribution:- Copy No 1. C.E. XV Corps.
2. 31 Div. 'G'.
3. 31 Div. Arty.
4. 92 Inf. Bde.
5. 93 Inf. Bde.
6. 94 Inf. Bde.
7. 210 Fd. Coy.
8. 211 Fd. Coy.
9. 223 Fd. Coy.
10. 12 K.O.Y.L.I.
11. A.D.M.S.
12. C.R.E.
13. Adjt.
14.)
15.) War Diary.
16. File.

SECRET.   War Diary

                                                    Copy. No......

                    R.E. Instructions No. 13.

Map. Sheet 36 A. N.E.
Edition 7.A.

                1.   The 3rd Canadian Tunnelling Coy. will gradually
3rd Can. Tunnlg.   take over construction of reinforced concrete shelters
    Coy.   for H.Q. of Units and formations in this Divisional
                        Area.

                2.   To commence with a party of 1 Officer and 25 O.R's
Work of First   will begin work on 2nd August at proposed Bde. H.Q. at
Contingent &   GRAND MARQUETTE FARM.   This party will live with
Location of Camp.   the Loft Coy in line at D.5.c.9.1.

                3.   The work at GRAND MARQUETTE FARM consists in
Description   erection of 1 concrete block dugout Type 2 (arriving
of Work.   at AU SOUVERAIN Dump on night of 31 July- 1 August.)
                        and 3 English shelters (covered by monolithic
                        reinforced concrete.)

                4.   Transport, which can proceed at night time only,
                        consists of 5 G.S. Wagons from 31st D.A.C., doing
Transport.   two trips each.   Further transport in the
                        shape of lorries can be obtained by O.C. Det. Tunnelling
                        Coy. on application to Adjutant R.E.

                5. (a) Gravel Sand and Cement may be drawn from
                        AU SOUVERAIN Dump by O.C. Det. Tunnelling Coy. as
Materials.   required on authority from this office.
                   (b) Other R.E. Stores may be obtained on authority
                        from this office from Divisional R.E. Dump at CINQ
                        RUES

                6.   O.C. 210th Field Coy. R.E. (Left Coy. in line)
Plans, Drawings,   will hand over plans & drawings in connection with
Information &   the work and supply O.C. Det. Tunnelling Coy. with
Assistance.   all information and assistance he may require.

                7.   Careful and ample screening must be erected
Screening.   on S.E. & N.E. sides of the farm house before any
                        work is commenced by daylight and material must be dumped
                        under cover or else   camouflaged if deposited
                        in the open.

                8.   Empty cement barrels are to be loaded on to
Empty Cement   returning wagons and offloaded at AU SOUVERAIN
  Barrels.   Dump nightly.   On no account are they to be
                        broken up.

                9.   Infantry working party as required will be
Infy. Working   supplied as heretofore by Loft Bde. in line by
  Party.   arrangement direct between Bde. and O.C. Det. Tunnellg.
                        Coy.

                                            F. Giles.
                                              Lieut-Colonel. R.E.
        31/7/18.   C.R.E. 31st Division.

                                                            P.T.O.

Copies to :-

Copy. No. 1. C.E. XV Corps.
2. H.Q. 31st Division.'G'.
3. H.Q. 92nd Inf.Bde.
4. H.Q. 93rd Inf.Bde.
5. H.Q. 94th Inf.Bde.
6.)
7.) O.C. 3rd Canadian Tunnelling Coy.
8. O.C. 210th Field Coy.R.E.
9. O.C. 211th Field Coy.R.E.
10. O.C. 223rd Field Coy.R.E.
11. _ , C.R.E.
12. Adjutant.R.E.
13.)
14.) War Diary.
15. File.

ORIGINAL

CONFIDENTIAL

WAR DIARY

of

Headquarters, 31st Divisional Engineers.

From 1/8/18 to 31/8/18.

VOLUME XXXII

Army Form C. 2118.

H.Q. 31 Div. R.E.

WAR DIARY
or
INTELLIGENCE SUMMARY
(Erase heading not required.)

Instructions regarding War Diaries and Intelligence Summaries are contained in F.S. Regs, Part II. and the Staff Manual respectively. Title pages will be prepared in manuscript.

Place	Date	Hour	Summary of Events and Information	Remarks and references to Appendices
MERRIS Camp C.20.c.8.	1/8/18		Work continued in FOREST OF NIEPPE. 210 Fld Coy & Bde area. 223 Fld Coy in Rt Bde area working on 2 lines. 211 Fld Coy in reserve working on Brigade and Battalion H.Q. also at D.H.Q.	
	2/8/18		Casualties 10 R wounded LEMOTTE. 6/8/18 Capt CLARKE from 211 Fld Coy to Fld Coy	
	7/8/18		½ PAGET appointed 223 Fld Coy from hospital 8/8/18 Canadian 10 R killed	
	9/8/18		Maj MONSEL 211 Fld Coy return from leave to U.K. Lt MITCHELL joins 223 Fld Coy	
	11/8/18		211 Fld Coy relieved 210 Fld Coy as L Bde Sectn 210 Fld Coy into reserve.	
			Work in forward area continues as above.	
	10/8/18		Capt WALKER Adjutant to hospital sick. 2/Lt WAKEFORD on leave to U.K.	
	14/8/18		2/Lt BOOTH on leave to U.K. 190 Bde take over right Bde area	
	15/8/18		Major MONSEL awarded D.S.O. M.C. Lt ALDOUS & Lt FISHER awarded M.C.	
	18/8/18		MEUX BERQUIN and OUTTERSTEN Ridge occupied. Enemy gradually retiring	
			On a wide front. H.Q. moved to RENESCURE	
RENESCURE 23/9/18			Work in area continues. One to Field Coys of 40th Division and work taken	
	24/9/18			over from Field Coys of 9th Divisn in METEREN Sector.	
	29/9/18			H.Q. moves from RENESCURE to Camp near SPOYPETRE CAPPEL	

Army Form C. 2118.

H.Q. 31 Div. R.E.

WAR DIARY
or
INTELLIGENCE SUMMARY.
(Erase heading not required.)

Instructions regarding War Diaries and Intelligence Summaries are contained in F. S. Regs., Part II. and the Staff Manual respectively. Title pages will be prepared in manuscript.

Place	Date	Hour	Summary of Events and Information	Remarks and references to Appendices
Q. SYLVESTRE CAPEL	2/8/17		Arrived Ans Glon at Major CAPEL. Companies working on new Z Line through METEREN and conferring accommodation	
	3/8/17		2/Lt. BUSH MAKFORD returned from leave U.K. 2/Lt. ROWE proceed on leave U.K. Enemy retired beyond BAILLEUL. HQ moved to PRUDE HOUSE on CENTRE METEREN ROAD	
PRUDE HOUSE	3/8/17		Companies all moved forward and worked on bridges & craters on METEREN BAILLEUL ROAD and clearing streets in BAILLEUL	

M. Inglauw
Major
31st DIVISIONAL ENGINEERS
for Lt. Col. CRE 31 Div.

SECRET.

Map Ref: 1/40,000.
Sheets 27 & 36.A.

WAR DIARY

31st Divisional Engineers.

OPERATION ORDER No 33.

Copy No 18

**HANDING-OVER.
31 Division
to
40 Division.**

1. (a) 31st Division will hand over Right Divisional Sector of XV Corps front to 40th Division on 23rd, 24th and 25th August.

    (b) Attached Table 'A' gives relief of Field Coys. and Pioneers.

    (c) Reconnaissance parties from 229th and 231st Field Coys. and 17th Worcester R. (40th Division) will rendezvous at Hd. Qrs. 223rd and 210th Field Coys. and 12th K.O.Y.L.I. (31st Division) respectively at 10 a.m. on 22nd inst., and of 224th Field Coy. at Hd. Qrs. of 211th Field Coy. at 10 a.m. on 23rd inst.

    (d) All R.E. stores, tools, machinery, dumps, maps, sketches, plans, gumboots, photos, works reports, demolition schemes, etc., will be handed over complete, and receipts obtained and carefully filed.

    (e) The 100 rounds S.A.A. per dismounted man extra to Mob. Tables will be handed over by Field Coys. and amount so handed over reported to this office at same time as completion of relief.

    (f) The Det. Land Drainage Coy. will continue to work on ditches and drains in Bois d' AVAL as heretofore.

    (g) The Det. 3rd Canadian Tunnelling Coy. will continue to work on Bde. H.Q. at GRAND MARQUETTE FARM as heretofore, but under C.R.E. 40th Division.

    (h) H.Q. R.E. will close at MEADOW CAMP, (U.30.c.0.7.) at 2 p.m. and open at Brewery, RENESCURE at same hour on 22nd inst.

P.T.O.

(2)

TAKING OVER.
31st Division
from
9th Division.

2. (a) 31st Division will take over Left Divisional Sector of XV Corps Front from 9th Division on 23rd, 24th and 25th August.

(b) Attached Table "B" gives relief of Field Coys. and Pioneers.

(c) All R.E. stores, tools, machinery, dumps, maps, sketches, plans, photos, works reports, demolition schemes, etc. will be taken over and receipts given.

(d) H.Q. R.E. will close Brewery, PENESCURE at 12 noon and open at P.36.a.1.0. at same hour on 25th inst.

F. Giles.
Lt.Col.R.E.
C.R.E. 31st Division.

21/8/18.

Distribution :-

Copy No 1. C.E. XV Corps.
2. 31 Div.'G'.
3. 40th Div.'G'.
4. 9th Div.'G'.
5. 31st Div.'Q'.
6. 40th Div.'Q'.
7. 9th Div.'Q'.
8. C.R.E. 9th Div.
9. C.R.E. 40th Div.
10. 210 Fd. Coy.
11. 211 Fd. Coy.
12. 223 Fd. Coy.
13. 12 K.O.Y.L.I.
14. Det. 3rd Can. Tunnelling Coy.
15. Det. Land Drainage Coy.
16. C.R.E.
17. Adjt.
18) War Diary.
19)
20. File.

C.R.E's CIRCULAR No 3.

NOTES on SANDBAGS & REVETMENTS BUILT OF SAME.

DESCRIPTION. 1. SERVICE SANDBAG.

    Empty - 2'9" x 1'3"
    Filled - 20" x 10" x 5".
Packed in bales of 250 weighing 96 lbs. each bale.
Cost - 8½d each.

REVETMENT. 2. SANDBAG REVETMENT.

(a) Alternate header and stretcher.

(b) Begin with header at bottom, and foundation cut out at right angles to slope.

(c) Top course must always be headers.

(d) Stretcher always seam towards parapet.

(e) Header with choke (mouth) end towards parapet.

(f) Each course of sandbags must be laid so that, looked at in section, the sandbag is at right angles to face of slope.

(g) No two vertical joints in contiguous courses must fall over one another.

(h) Sandbag should be filled only ¾ full to ensure its "bedding" well.

(i) Parapet must be built up simultaneously with revetment and earth carefully rammed in behind sandbags.

ELEVATION

SECTION

CORRECT.

CORRECT SECTION

Foundation should be cut at right angles to slope and always brought to a solid bottom

PARAPET

WRONG (Joints not broken)

WRONG (Vertical)

ELEVATION   SECTION

WRONG (Seams and choked Ends of bags outward)

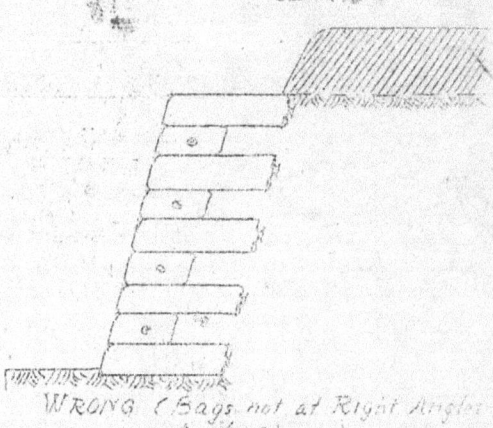
WRONG (Bags not at Right Angles to slope)

WRONG (all stretchers and no headers)

DATA for TASK WORK.   3.   Two men can <u>lay</u> 70 sandbags per hour.
Three men can fill 70 sandbags per hour.
Two men can carry 70 sandbags per hour.

N.B. Carriers must be increased if distance is great,
e.g. more than 15 yards,
i.e. 7 men can fill, carry, and lay 70 sandbags per hour, therefore

<u>ROUGH RULE for TASK for WORKING PARTY</u>

1 man per 10 sandbags per hour, to include filling, carrying, and laying.

CAUTION.   4.   It must always be borne in mind that

(a) The best built sandbag revetment or wall will not last more than 6 months at the outside.

(b) A sandbag wall, by itself, is useless for sustaining the weight of a roof or other heavy weight.

(c) No unsupported sandbag wall or revetment should ever be more than 3 feet high.

F. Giles.
Lt.Col.R.E.
C.R.E. 31st Division.

2/8/18.

Distribution :- 1 Copy.   31 Div. 'G'.   1 Copy.   223 Field Coy.
                30 Copies. 31 Div. Arty.   1 "   C.R.E.
                30 "   92 Bde.   1 "   Adjt.
                30 "   93 Bde.   1 "   File.
                30 "   94 Bde.   2 Copies. War Diary.
                 1 "   210 Field Coy.   1 Copy.   Spare.
                 1 "   211 Field Coy.

WAR DIARY

C.R.E's CIRCULAR No 4.

<u>NOTES on LARGE and SMALL ENGLISH SHELTERS and ERECTION of same.</u>

I. <u>LARGE ENGLISH SHELTERS.</u>

<u>DIMENSIONS.</u>
        Length.   - 17' 9"
        Height.   - 6' 5"
        Width at base. - 9' 0"

<u>DESCRIPTION.</u> The complete shelter consists of seven segments or arches, each composed of three sheets corrugated steel 2'9" wide, the centre sheet overlapping the two side sheets by 18", and each segment overlapping the next by half a corrugation. (3")

<u>ERECTION.</u> To commence erection, lay out the timber frame which consists of 8 pieces of 7" x 3" or 6" x 3" timber, 10'6" long, 4 bearer plates, 7" x 3" timber, 9'3" long, (4" being allowed for the halved joints on bearer plates) and eight 3" x 3" stringers, 9'1" long, as sketch below.

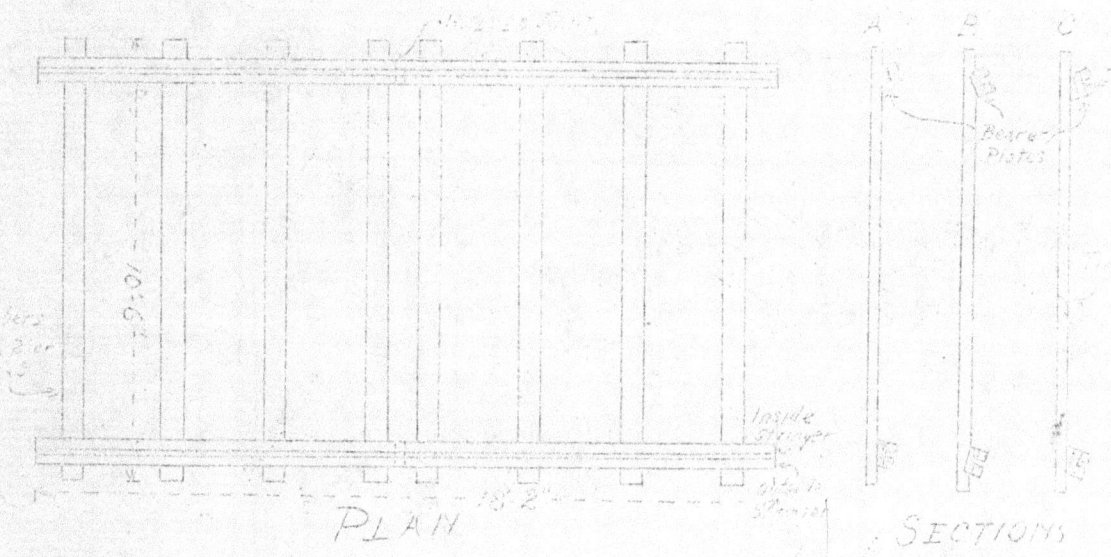

PLAN   SECTIONS

It will be noticed in Section 'A' that a wedge shaped or bevelled bearer is shown directly under the stringers. If there is any difficulty in obtaining or making those bevelled bearers, 7" x 2" timber may be substituted for 7" x 3" timber and same may be packed up with wedges for the full width of the 6" x 2" or 7" x 2" timber at each point where the bearers cross same. (See Section 'C'.) Another method is to notch the timber at a slant with the 7" x 3" framing. (See Section 'B'.)

After levelling up the frame and firmly nailing the bearer plates and inside stringers in position by 5" nails, the curved segments may be bolted together and placed in position, the inside stringers then being nailed down. It is not advisable to tighten up the bolts until the complete shelter is in position. Erection will be simpler, and bolt holes more easily pulled into position if this is attended to.

The shelter then only requires the ends finishing, which is done by putting in a light framework of 3" x 2" or 4" x 2" timber, and covering with X.P.M. or corrugated iron to take whatever material is used for splinter-proofing or protection against shelling.

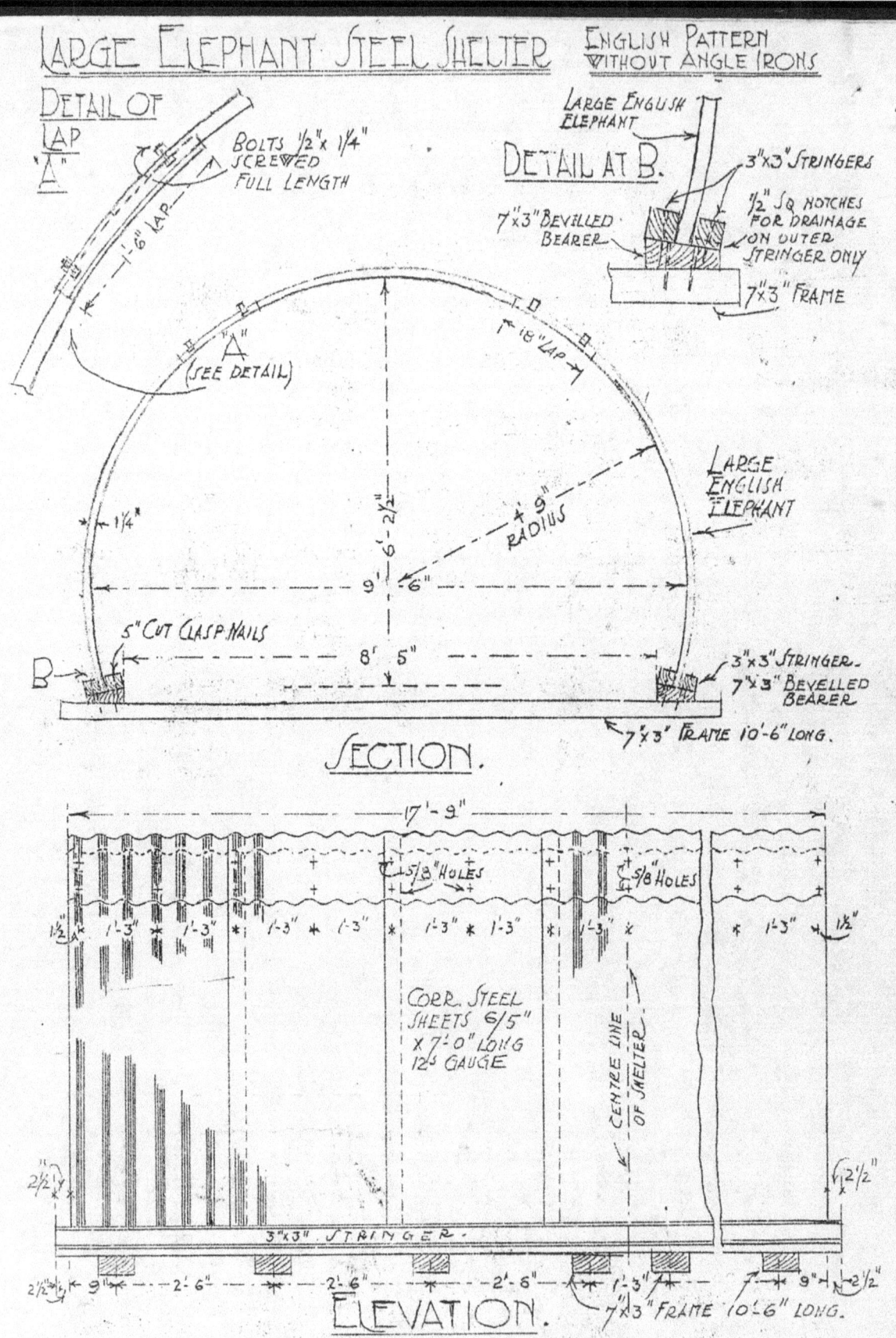

Quantities for One Shelter.
(7 segments.)

- 21 - curved sheets, 7' long, 6/5" corrugations, holed at each end for bolts.
- 60 - ½" bolts, 1¼" long, and nuts.
- 150 - 5" cut clasp nails.
- 8 - 3" x 3" stringers, 9'1" long.
- 4 - 7" x 3" bearers, 9'3" long, 4" allowed for halved joints.
- 8 - 7" x 3" timbers, 10'6" long.
- 2 - Podger spanners to suit above bolts.

II. SMALL ENGLISH SHELTERS.

DIMENSIONS.
- Length. — 12'9"
- Height. — 3'9"
- Width at base. — 5'0"

DESCRIPTION. The complete shelter consists of 5 segments or arches, each composed of 2 sheets, 2'9" wide, which overlap 12", and are fastened together by six ¼" bolts, 1¼" long, through holes drilled in the sheets for this purpose. Each segment overlaps the next by half a corrugation. (3")

ERECTION. The Small English Shelter is erected in exactly the same way as the large, angle irons being used instead of stringers on the bearer plates. These should be fastened down with the dog spikes before the segments are placed in position. (See sketches below.)

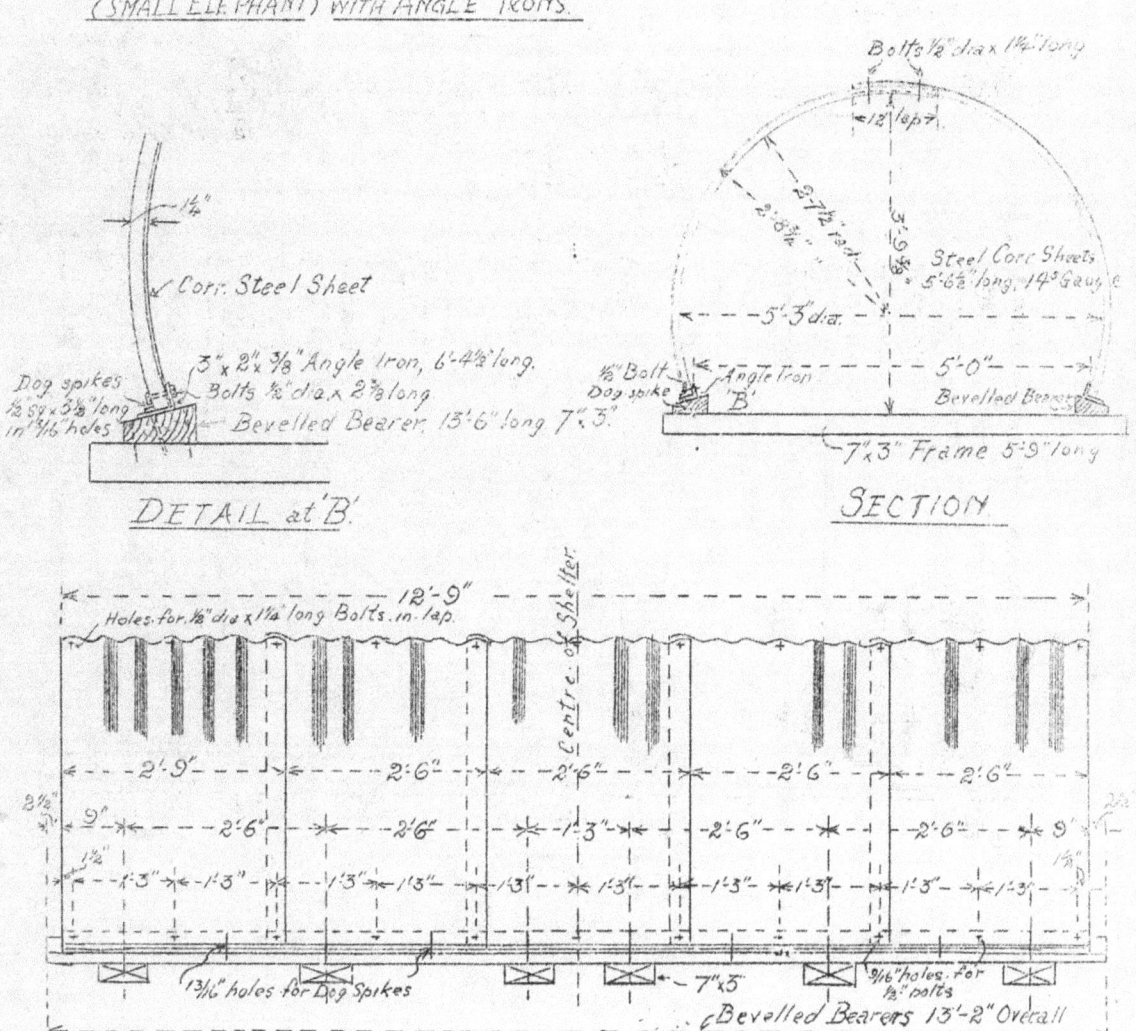

SMALL ENGLISH SHELTER.
(SMALL ELEPHANT) WITH ANGLE IRONS.

DETAIL at 'B'.   SECTION.

ELEVATION.

Quantities for One Shelter of 5 Sectors.

10 curved plates, 6/5" corrugations, 5'6½" long, 2'9" wide, 14 gauge, overlap 3", holed at each end for bolts.
4 3" x 2" x 3/8" angle irons, 6'4½" long.
22 ½" bolts, 1¼" long, and nuts.
22 ½" bolts, 2-3/8" long, and nuts.
10 dog spikes, ½" square, 3½" long, (2 spare)
6 timber frames, 7" x 3" x 5'9" long.
2 bevelled bearers, 13'6" long, (4" allowed for halved joints.)
2 Podger spanners to suit above bolts.
100 4" nails, cut clasp.

III. GENERAL.

A tabulated list is given shewing list of material for each type of shelter. Bolts and nails are packed separately in bags, and two spanners provided. When shelters are drawn from the R.E. Dump care must be taken that the full complement of bolts, spanners, spikes etc. are provided, and that the man drawing shelter is made responsible for delivery of same, as a large amount of time and labour is lost by shelters being drawn and taken to site, and then at the last minute it is discovered that the bolts have been lost or misplaced after drawing from the R.E. Dump.

J. Giles.
Lt.Col.R.E.
C.R.E. 31st Division.

5/8/18.

Distribution:—
1 Copy. 31 Div. 'G'.   7 Copies. 211 Fd. Coy.
20 Copies. 31 Div. Arty. 7   "   223   do
20   "   92 Bde.   1 Copy.   C.R.E.
20   "   93 Bde.   1   "   Adjt.
20   "   94 Bde.   2 Copies. War Diary.
20   "   121 Bde.   1 Copy.   File.
7   "   210 Fd. Coy.   18 Spare.

(2)

<u>12th K.O.Y.L.I.</u> (d) (i) One Coy. less 1 platoon, on Light Railways under 9th Foreways Coy.

(ii) One Coy. less 1 platoon, on roads and tracks etc. E. of COURTE CROIX - ROUKLOSHILLE Road, and completion of A.R.P. near EEKE with 20 men from D.A.C.

(iii) One Coy. less 1 platoon, on roads, tracks, etc. west of COURTE CROIX - ROUKLOSHILLE Road

(iv) One platoon from each of these Coys. at Battn. H.Q. training, bathing, etc.

F. Giles.

Lt.Col.R.E.
C.R.E. 31st Division.

28/8/18.

Distribution.
    Copy No 1. C.E. XV Corps.
           2. 31 Div. 'G'.
           3. 92 Inf. Bde.
           4. 93 Inf. Bde.
           5. 94 Inf. Bde.
           6. 210 Field Coy.
           7. 211 Field Coy.
           8. 223 Field Coy.
           9. 12th K.O.Y.L.I.
          10. 9th Foreways Coy.
          11. C.R.E.
          12. Adjt.
          13. Stores Officer.
          14. File.
          15) War Diary.
          16)

WAR DIARY

SECRET.

Copy No 15

R.E. INSTRUCTIONS No 17.

WORKS PROGRAMME.

GENERAL SCHEME
1. Each Field Coy. will have 3 sections, and each Pioneer Coy. 3 platoons on work.
Remaining Section and Platoon will be at their respective Transport Lines or Battn. H.Q. as the case may be, for bathing, training, etc.

RESPONSIBILITY for WORK.
2. (a) Infantry Bdes. in line are entirely responsible for all work or defences in front of "Z" Line - Any technical advice required will be supplied by the respective Field Coys. in the line.

(b) C.R.E. is responsible for all defence work up to and including "Z" Line - and also all roads and communications throughout the Divisional Area.

PROGRAMME of WORK.
3. Following will be programme of work from 28th inst. inclusive :-

RIGHT COY. in Line.
(a) 223 Field Coy. - to whom Right Bde. in line will apply for any small and immediate services, and for technical advice only on front line defences.

(i) 2½ sections on "Z" Line - wiring N. of METEREN Road, putting in shelters, draining, duckboarding, and 'A' Frames as necessary with 200 Infantry Working Party supplied by Right Bde.

(ii) ½ section i/c Demolitions.

(iii) 1 section at H.Q. making and painting notice boards for trenches and Right Bde area generally.

LEFT COY. in Line.
(b) 211 Field Coy. - to whom Left Bde. in line will apply for any small and immediate services, and for technical advice only on front line defences.

(i) 2 sections on "Z" Line - wiring, putting in shelters, draining, duckboarding and 'A' framing where required with 200 Infantry Working Party supplied by Left Bde. in Line.

(ii) 1 section duckboarding SCOTS ALLEY C.T. and C.T. from ROCKET Reserve Trench to RED HAND Reserve.

(iii) 1 section at Transport Lines making and painting notice boards for trenches and Left Bde. area generally.

(iv) A few sappers i/c Demolitions.

RESERVE COY.
(c) 210 Field Coy.

(i) Employed on erection of new Div. H.Q.

(ii) R.E. work for Div. Arty.

SECRET.

Copy No 13

R.E. INSTRUCTIONS No 16.

Until further notice, D & B Coys., K.O.Y.L.I. will work in conjunction with 211 Field Coy. R.E. on repair of MERE FARM and RUE du BOIS Roads respectively as far forward as LA PLATE BECQUE.

On completion, one platoon from each Coy. will remain as a maintenance gang, and remainder will return to work on 'Z' Line as laid down in para. 4, R.E. Instructions No 14.

J. Giles.
Lt. Col. R.E.
C.R.E. 31st Division.

18/8/18.

Distribution :- Copy No 1. C.E. XV Corps.
       2. 31st Div. 'G'.
       3. 92nd Inf. Bde.
       4. 93rd " "
       5. 94th " "
       6. 120th " "
       7. 210 Fd. Coy.
       8. 211 " "
       9. 223 " "
      10. 12 K.O.Y.L.I.
      11. C.R.E.
      12. Adjt.
      13)
      14) War Diary.
      15. File.

WAR DIARY

S E C R E T.   Copy No 12

R.E. INSTRUCTIONS No 15.

Reference 31st Division Order No 357 of 12/8/18, para 6.

On and after 14th inst,

1. 300 Infantry working party will be found by 120th Bde. to work by night on "Z" Line under 223rd Field Coy.R.E. from VOLLEY FARM exclusive, to Southern Divisional Boundary.

2. 150 Infantry working party will be found by 92nd Bde. to work by day on COBLEY COTTAGE Switch under 223rd Field Coy.R.E.

3. 150 Infantry working party will be found by 92nd Bde. to work by night on "Z" Line between COBLEY COTTAGE and SANITAS CORNER under 211th Field Coy.R.E.

4. 300 Infantry working party will be found by 94th Bde. to work by night on "Z" Line between SANITAS CORNER and N. Divisional Boundary under 211th Field Coy.R.E.

5. 12th K.O.Y.L.I. will work as laid down in para. 4 of R.E. Instructions No 14.

F. Giles.

Lt.Col.R.E.
C.R.E. 31st Division.

13/8/18.

Copy No 1. 31st Div.'G'.
2. 92 Bde.
3. 93 Bde.
4. 94 Bde.
5. 120 Bde.
6. 210 Field Coy.
7. 211 Field Coy.
8. 223 Field Coy.
9. 12 K.O.Y.L.I.
10. C.R.E.
11. Adjt.
12) War Diary.
13)
14. File

(d) In each case (a) (b) and (c) the Lewis Gun Crews will
    work on improvement of trenches etc of the Strong
    Points of which they form garrison.

F. Giles.

Lieut-Colonel. R.E.

10/8/18. C.R.E. 31st Division.

          Copy No.1. to C.E. XV Corps.
                   2   H.Q. 31st Division.'G'
                   3   H.Q. 31st Divisional Artillery.
                   4   H.Q. 92nd Inf.Bde.
                   5   H.Q. 93rd Inf.Bde.
                   6   H.Q. 94th Inf.Bde.
                   7   H.Q. 121st Inf.Bde.
                   8   O.C. 210th Field Coy.R.E.
                   9   O.C. 211th Field Coy.R.E.
                  10   O.C. 223rd Field Coy.R.E.
                  11   O.C. 12th K.O.Y.L.I. Bn.
                  12   C.R.E.
                  13   Adjutant.
                  14)
                  15)   War Diary.
                  16   Office File.

SECRET.　　　War Diary　　　Copy No. 14

R.E. INSTRUCTIONS No. 14.

Following will be programme of work from 12th inst. inclusive:—

1. **RIGHT COY. in LINE.** 223rd Field Coy. R.E. to whom Right Bde. in line will apply for any small or immediate service.

    (a) 1 section in charge of demolitions.
    (b) 1 section supervising and working on 'Z' line from VOLLEY FARM - COBBLEY COTTAGE by night and day with 200 Infy. from Right Bde.
    (c) 1 section supervising and working from VOLLEY FARM - VERTE RUE with 150 Infy. from Right Bde. by night.
    (d) 1 section employed
      (i) Supervising erection of Battn. H.Q. at BARRAGE BUILDINGS at E.27.a.3.3. off track 3.
      (ii) Completion of Reserve Battn. H.Q. at FOREST CAMP E.25.d.9.4.
      (iii) Superintending hurdle and picket making by 1 platoon K.O.Y.L.I. at FORESTRY DUMP (E.25.d.9.4.) with 5 O.R. of the R.E. Forestry Coy.
      (iv) Upkeep of dry weather tracks, roads and bridges generally in Right Bde. Area (NIEPPE FOREST Tracks excepted)
      (v) Completion of shelters for A.D.S. at CANAL CORNER (D.18.a.6.2.)
      (vi) Erection of large Elephant Shelter at FETTLE FARM.

2. **LEFT COY. in LINE.** 211th Field Coy. R.E. to whom Left and Centre Bdes. in Line will apply for any small and immediate services.

    (a) 1 section in charge of Demolitions.
    (b) 2 sections on 'Y' Line SANITAS CORNER to Engine Shed (E.10.a.6.5.) with 300 Infy. Working party supplied daily by 94 Bde. and 1 Coy. K.O.Y.L.I. (less 1 platoon and Lewis Gun crews)
    (c) 1 section on 'Z' line SANITAS CORNER to COBBLEY COTTAGE with 300 Infy. Working Party supplied daily by 121 Bde.
    (d) Upkeep of dry weather tracks, bridges and roads generally in Left Bde. Area.
    (e) Supervising erection of splinter proof protection at the several Battn. H.Q.
    (f) Strutting cellars at Bde. H.Q. at SEDIMENT HOUSE

3. **RESERVE COY.**

    (a) ½ section on work for Div. Arty.
    (b) 2 sections on general services back area.
    (c) ½ section erection of baths at D.18.c.8.3.
    (d) ½ section Training in Lewis Gun.

4. **12th K.O.Y.L.I. Bn.**

    (a) 1 Coy (garrison of PETIT SEC BOIS) less one platoon and Lewis gun crews on 'Z' Line Northwards from SANITAS CORNER, hurdling, clearing berm and widening trench for A Framing.
    (b) 1 Coy. (garrison SWARTENBROUCK) less 1 platoon and Lewis Gun Crews on 'Z' Line Southwards from VERTE RUE, hurdling clearing berm and widening trench for A Framing.
    (c) 1 Coy (Garrison of LA MOTTE) less 1 platoon and Lewis Gun Crews
      (i) 1 platoon making duckboard track from FETTLE FARM to SAWMILLS.
      (ii) 1 platoon under 223rd Fld. Coy. R.E. making hurdles, pickets, etc. at Forestry Dump E.25.d.9.4.
      (iii) 1 platoon maintaining roads, rides, tracks and tram tracks generally in Forest of NIEPPE Area.

TABLE "A".

Item No.	Date.	40th Div. relieve 31st Div.	Advance Parties. Numbers.	Rendezvous.	Time.	Locations for incoming Units. Billets.	Transport Lines.	31 Div. Units will be clear by
1.	23/8/18	223 Field Coy.R.E.	1 Officer & 1 Section. (Demolition party, store keepers)	D.9.b.5.4.	9 a.m.	D.9.b.5.4	D.1.d.8.8.	2 p.m.
2.	25/8/18	231 Field Coy.R.E.	1 N.C.O. and 3 men.	D.9.c.6.3.	9 a.m.	D.9.c.6.3.	D.1.d.8.6.	2 p.m.
3.	24/8/18	224 Field Coy.R.E.	1 Officer & 1 Section. (Demolition party and store-keepers.)	D.5.c.9.1.	9 a.m.	D.5.c.9.1.	V.25.d.0.7.	2 p.m.
4.	25 25/8/18	17th Worcesters.	Arrangements between inspective O.C's	D.2.c.9.1.	9 a.m.	D.2.c.9.1.	D.2.c.9.1.	2 p.m.
5.	22/8/18	H.Q. R.E.	R.S.M. 2 sappers & 18 Pioneers. (Dump.) 1 clerk.	V.19.c.8.7. U.30.c.0.7.	9 a.m. 12 noon	V.19.c.8.7. U.30.c.0.7.	— U.22.d.4.9.	*2 p.m.

TABLE "B"

Item No.	Date.	31 Div. relieve 9th Div.		Numbers.	Rendezvous.	Time.	New locations of 31st Div. Units.		9th Div. Units will be clear by
							Billets.	Transport Lines.	
1.	23/8/18	223 Field Coy.R.E.	90 Field Coy.R.E.	2 Officers. 8 O.R.	W.4.d.5.4.	9 a.m.	W.4.d.5.4.	P.36.b.5.5.	2 p.m.
2.	23/8/18	210 Field Coy.R.E.	63 Field Coy.R.E.	2 Officers. 4 O.R.	W.1.c.1.6.	9 a.m.	W.1.c.1.6.	V.10.b.7.6.	2 p.m.
3.	24/8/18	211 Field Coy.R.E.	64 Field Coy.R.E.	2 Officers. 8 O.R.	Q.36.b.1.2.	9 a.m.	Q.36.b.1.2.	P.36.b.7.0.	2 p.m.
4.	25/8/18	12th K.O.Y.L.I.	9th Seaforths.	Billetting parties to be arranged between Coys.	V.6.a.9.2. for H.Q.	9 a.m.		V.6.a.5.8.	2 p.m.
5.	24/8/18	Dump Staff.	Dump Staff	R.S.M. 2 sappers.	Q.32.d.9.8.	10 a.m.			
	25/8/18	H.Q. R.E.	H.Q. R.E.	1 clerk.	P.36.a.1.0.	12 noon.	P.36.a.1.0.	P.36.a.1.0.	12 noon.

ORIGINAL.

CONFIDENTIAL.

WAR DIARY

of

Headquarters, 31st Divisional Engineers.

From Sept. 1st to Sept.30th, 1918.

VOLUME XXXIII

Sheet 0

WAR DIARY
or
~~INTELLIGENCE SUMMARY~~
(Erase heading not required.)

Army Form C. 2118.

H.Q. 31 Div. R.E.

MONTH OF SEPTEMBER 1918

Place	Date	Hour	Summary of Events and Information	Remarks and references to Appendices
RYDE MORE N+d.11.c (Sheet 27)	1/9/18 to 2/9/18		Enemy retirement continues beyond BAILLEUL. Field Coys working on road and bridges in and around BAILLEUL. 210 Field Coy had two officers wounded. 228 Field Coy exploring water supply. 31 Div. R.E. are working under direction of C.R.E. 29 Div. until when 31 Div. relieves 29 Div.	
	3/9/18		210 Field Coy, keeping in touch with advancing Brigade, and repairing roads removes to 7.20 a.m. 223 Field Coy moves to S 27 Central. Work continued as above.	
GOUGH HOUT S.9/c (G 30 a + b)	4/9/18		31 Div H.Q. C.R.E. and C.R.E. move forward to GOUGH HOUSE. Routes of wheeled and tracked, killed work fast and m.t. during night. 223 Field Coy moving accommodation at GOUGH HOUSE for D.H.Q. 211 Field Coy relieves 210 Field Coy at T.25 a.1.1. 210 Field Coy returned to S 27 Central.	
PEUDE HOUSE N4.d.1.c	6/9/18		H.Q. R.E. moved next again to N4.d.1.8. 210 Ft. Coy exploring water supply in L. Brigade Area. 64" Field Coy R.E. (9" Div) attached to work of Driving RAVELSBERG ROAD. On whole Div an camps.	
	10/9/18		64" Field Coy (9" Div) withdrawn from Right Role area. 223 Fd Coy taking our Rue work. Work continues at above.	
	19/9/18		64" Field Coy R.E. (9" Div) withdrawn from road work on RAVELSBERG ROAD work.	

WAR DIARY
or
INTELLIGENCE SUMMARY.
(Erase heading not required.)

Army Form C. 2118.

H.Q. 31 Divn R.E.

Place	Date	Hour	Summary of Events and Information	Remarks and references to Appendices
RIDGE HOUSE N2 2118.	10/9/18		Being taken over by Brig. Romer (12. KOYLI). Bn. Hrs. held with our Bde. in line, other Bns. of Bailleul on Bde. in reserve at HONDEGHEM.	
	13/9/18		210 Hastings move back to CAESTRE.	
			211 Yeovil pulling in shelters in MEPPE system.	
	14/9/18		Lt. E.B. Flington R.E. reported from 34th Div. and a view to appointment as Adjutant.	
	15/9/18		Work continued as above.	
	16/9/18		252 Art Coy. work on Sout Rd. H.Q. Lappermne Fm. and support Bde. H. Bailleul	
	17/9/18		PLOEGSTEERT (remainder) work on road in neighbourhood of SOYER FARM.	
	18/9/18		Line advanced by 93rd Inf. Bde. in Nature of defence	
			C.R.E's O.O. No 36 issued. Capt. Ingham, Acting Adjutant, returns 1.5.210 Fd. Co. R.E.	
	20/9/18		Amendment No 1 to O.O. No 36 issued. Divisional Conference held at D.H.Q.	
	21/9/18		210 Fd. Co. relieve 211 Fd. Co. on line C.R.2 reconnoitring centres in	
	22/9/18		PLOEGSTEERT and HYDE PARK CORNER Roads.	
	23rd		Operations discussed in conference on 21st inst. postponed.	
	24th		Remain ready. Cuffled travels in PLOEGSTEERT & HYDE PARK CORNER Roads	
	25th		Defence of PLOEGSTEERT commenced by 1 Company of 12 KOYLI, 9 R Inf. Bde. relieved in line by 92nd Inf. Bde.	

WAR DIARY
or
INTELLIGENCE SUMMARY.
(Erase heading not required.)

Army Form C. 2118.

Place	Date	Hour	Summary of Events and Information	Remarks and references to Appendices
CAESTRE	26th		R.E. H.Q. moved to CAESTRE to form D.H.Q. who had already moved. Scanning of road from T.10.a.8.4. to T.16.b.6.6. and T.11.c.9.3. commenced by 2 companies of Pioneers. Forward dumps of road refouning material established by 210th Fd. Co. R.E. at UNDERHILL FARM T.16.d.6.3. and by 223rd Fd. Co. at LE DON 3.4.b.4.4.	
	27th		Tunnelled dugouts in Trench 6's observed to be 210th Fd.Co.R.E. Bde. in line side slipped Northwards on night of 26th/27th STEENWERCK church handed over to 1/40th Division. Rt. of Divisional front taken over by 93rd Bde from 92nd Bde on night 27th/28th	
	28th		Attack on N. commenced. 92nd Bde; attack at 3 p.m. 93rd Bde; to Plovers, accompanied by 2 sections of 223rd Fd. Co. Adv. D.H.Q. opened at BOUGH HOUSE Reconny. 2 sections of 223rd move up to S.30.b.i.2, 210th Fd. Co. Eve 1 sectn in H.P.G's dugouts	
	29th		2.11th Fd.Co. move from CAESTRE to S.27.c.7.7. Work in progress on cratch at BAVERLEY X roads, ROSSIGNOL Road and road from PLOEGSTEERT to BERGERS X roads via HYDE PARK Corner.	
	30th		Orders issued for establishment of Div front along Rd. Rue S. from WARNETON then W. along WARNAVE to C.I. central	to Capt R.F... 4A Co.... Capt R.F... C.R.E. 23rd...

SECRET.

WAR DIARY

Copy No 12.

R.E. INSTRUCTIONS No 18.

Work for 2nd September.

1. 210th Field Company.R.E.

   If and when situation permits, make good for lorry traffic the main BAILLEUL - ARMENTIERES Road from S.28. eastwards.

2. 211th Field Company.R.E.

   (a) ½ Coy. completing bridge at BARRIERE CAEVERDANS, work commencing 7 a.m.

   (b) ½ Coy. as above commencing 2 p.m.

3. 223rd Field Company.R.E.

   (a) ½ Coy. improving avoiding road W. and S. of BAILLEUL, work commencing 7 a.m.

   (b) ½ Coy. erecting stand for canvas water tank at S.25.b.9.4.

4. 12th K.O.Y.L.I.

   (a) One Coy. working in conjunction with 210th Field Coy.R.E.

   (b) (i) ½ Coy. working in conjunction with 211th Field Coy.R.E. making approaches to bridge at BARRIERE CALVERDANS. Rendezvous there 7 a.m.

   (ii) ½ Coy. as above report at same rendezvous at 2 p.m. for same work.

   (c) One Coy. completing clearing of roads in BAILLEUL in conjunction with 211 Field Coy. Report at BARRIERE CALVERDANS to an officer of 211 Field Coy.R.E. at 7 a.m.

5. ACKNOWLEDGE. (F Coys + KOYLI only)

HEADQUARTERS,
31st
DIVL. ENGINEERS.
No.
Date 1/9/18.

W. Duglan
Capt. R.E.
for. Lt.Col.R.E.
C.R.E. 31st Division.

Issued at 8.15 p.m.

Distribution:- Copy No 1. C.E. XV Corps.
2. 31 Div.'G'.
3. 210 Field Coy.R.E.
4. 211 do   do
5. 223 do   do
6. 12 K.O.Y.L.I.
7. C.R.E. 29th Div.
8. C.R.E. LE PEUPLIER Switch.
9. C.R.E.
10. Adjt.
11. File.
12) War Diary.
13)

SECRET.

WAR DIARY

Copy No 13

R.E. INSTRUCTIONS No 19.

Work for 3rd September.

1. **210th Field Company.R.E.**

    (a) Make good for lorry traffic the main BAILLEUL - ARMENTIERES Road up to De Seule.

    (b) Thence for field guns along DE SEULE - NEUVE EGLISE Road to T.25.d.5.4. thence along CONNAUGHT ROAD to T.28.c.2.3. thence to T.27.d.9.9. thence East to T.28.b.5.8. thence N. to T.22.d.3.4. thence eastwards to HYDE PARK CORNER, U.19.b.3.7.

    (c) Close liaison with Infy. Bdes. of 29th Division must be maintained to keep touch with the situation and push on as fast as possible.

2. **211th Field Company.R.E.**

    Completing bridge at BARRIERE CALVERDANS in two reliefs, 7 a.m. and 2 p.m.

3. **223rd Field Company.R.E.**

    (a) Making plank road round craters on road to STEENWERCK at S.27.central., work commencing at 7 a.m. and 2nd relief 2 p.m.

    (b) Work on tank stand at S.25.b.9.4. to cease. A representative of F.E. Water, XV Corps will call in at Coy. H.Q. at X.14.a.3.1. and take over canvas water tank and all particulars tomorrow.

4. **12th K.O.Y.L.I.**

    (a) One Coy. working in conjunction with 210th Field Coy. on road as in 1.(b).

    (b) One Coy. working on approaches to bridge at BARRIERE CALVERDANS in two reliefs, 7 a.m. and 2 p.m.

    (c) One Coy. completing clearing of BAILLEUL Town Streets. Report BARRIERE CALVERDANS to Officer of 211th Field Coy, 7 a.m.

5. ACKNOWLEDGE. (Field Coys. and K.O.Y.L.I. only.)

Issued at 9-45 p.m.

2/9/18.

Capt R.E. for Lt.Col.R.E.
C.R.E. 31st Division.

Distribution:- No 1. C.E. XV Corps.
2. F.E. Water, XV Corps.
3. 210 Field Coy.
4. 211 do do
5. 223 do do
6. 31 Div.'G'
7. 12 K.O.Y.L.I.
8. C.R.E. 29 Div.
9. C.R.E.
10. Adjt.
11. File.
12)
13) War Diary.

WAR DIARY

SECRET.　　　　　R.E. INSTRUCTIONS No 20.　　　　Copy No 12

Work for 4th September.

1.　210th Field Company.R.E.

　　Making good road as described in para 1 (b) of R.E. Instructions No 19 as far forward as possible, and reconnoitring condition of all roads in that area.

2.　211th Field Company.R.E.

　　Completing bridge at BARRIERE CALVERDANS in two reliefs, 7 a.m. and 2 p.m.

3.　223rd Field Company.R.E.

(a)　Improving plank road and bridges round crater at S.29.central to take all classes of heavy traffic on a two-way road. Two reliefs, 7 a.m. and 2 p.m.

(b)　Reconnoitring only roads forward in Right Bde. area.
N.B. 29th Div.R.E. are still working on these roads.

(c)　Supplying immediate demands for small services from 92nd Bde.

4.　12th K.O.Y.L.I.

(a)　One Coy. working in conjunction with 210 Field Coy.

(b)　One Coy. working on approaches to bridge at BARRIERE CALVERDANS in two reliefs, 7 a.m. and 2 p.m.

(c)　(i) ½ Coy. filling in shell-holes in road from S.27. central to STEENWERCK and LA CRECHE.

　　(ii) ½ Coy. in Reserve.

5.　ACKNOWLEDGE. (Field Coys. and K.O.Y.L.I. only.)

　　　　　　　　　　　　　　　　　Capt.R.E.
3/9/18.　　　　　　　　　A/Adjt. for C.R.E. 31st Division.

Issued at 7-30 p.m.

Distribution :- Copy No 1. C.E. XV Corps.
　　　　　　　　　　2. 210 Field Coy.
　　　　　　　　　　3. 211　do　do
　　　　　　　　　　4. 223　do　do
　　　　　　　　　　5. 31 Div.'G'.
　　　　　　　　　　6. 12 K.O.Y.L.I.
　　　　　　　　　　7. C.R.E. 29 Div.
　　　　　　　　　　8. 92 Bde.
　　　　　　　　　　9. C.R.E.
　　　　　　　　　10. Adjt.
　　　　　　　　　11. File.
　　　　　　　　　12)
　　　　　　　　　13) War Diary.

WAR DIARY

SECRET.   31st Divisional Engineers.   Copy No 16

OPERATION ORDER No 34.

RELIEF.   1. (a)   31st Division will relieve 29th Division
                      in the line and will take over Right Bde. Sector
                      of 29th Division with 92nd Infantry Bde. tonight.

             (b)   Relief of Left Bde. Sector which will be
                      carried out by 94th Bde. will be notified later.

BOUNDARIES. 2.   29th Divisional Boundary is at present
                      as follows :-

                      <u>N. Boundary.</u> (also boundary between XV
                                          and X Corps.)

                      S.22.c.0.0. to CUSTOM HOUSE in T.20.c.
                      thence to WHITE GATES in T.18.a. to
                      GABION FARM in U.2.c. and thence S. of
                      MESSINES.

                      <u>S. Boundary.</u>

                      A.16.a.0.0. due east along grid line
                      inclusive of NIEPPE Village.

                      <u>Inter-Brigade Boundary.</u>

                      E. and W. grid lines between squares
                      T. and B.

RIGHT FLANK 3.   121 Brigade, 40th Division is on our right.
BRIGADE.   H.Q. at A.20.b.3.3.

LOCATION of 4.   For the present, H.Qrs. will probably be
INFANTRY H.Q.   as follows :-

                      92 Bde.H.Q.   A.6.d.9.5.
                      Leading Battn.(10 E. Yks.R.)   B.8.b.3.3.
                      Support Battn.(11 E. Lancs.R.)   A.3.a.1.2.
                      Reserve Battn.(11 E. Yk.R.)   not yet fixed.

LOCATIONS   5. (a)   210th Field Company.R.E. will remain in
and MOVES of   present camp, S.27.c.9.6. but must keep in touch,
FIELD COYS. &   through Left Bde., with Infantry situation and be
K.O.Y.L.I.   prepared to move forward as close behind the
                      Infantry as possible, notifying any change of
                      location to Div. R.E. H.Q.

             (b)   211th Field Company.R.E. will remain
                      at BESACE FARM until further orders.

             (c)   223rd Field Company.R.E. will move up to
                      camp at about S.27.c.9.6., leaving heavy
                      vehicles and horses at about X.16.d.8.6.

             (d) (i) H.Q. K.O.Y.L.I. will remain at W.12.c.3.5.

                (ii) One Coy. working in conjunction with 210
                      Field Coy. will move forward today to about
                      T.25.

               (iii) Two Coys. will move forward early on 4th
                      Sept. to camp at about S.27.d.2.6.

                                                              P.T.O.

-2-

ADVANCED R.E. DUMP.	6.	An advanced R.E. Dump has been opened at S.26.a.2.5.
LOCATION of DIVSL. H.Q.	7.	31 Div. H.Q. will remain for the present at W.5.c.3.6. and 31 Div. R.E. H.Q. at W.4.d.1.8. (Sheet 27)
ARRIVAL.	8. (a)	Completion of moves of Field Coys. together with exact locations will be notified by Code word "STAND at (here give location) at (here give time of completion)"
	(b)	O.C. K.O.Y.L.I. will notify Div.R.E. H.Q. of exact location of the Coys. as early as possible after move completed.
	9.	ACKOWLEDGE.

F. Iles.
Lt.Col.R.E.
C.R.E. 31st Division.

3/9/18.

Issued at 7-30 p.m.

Distribution:-   Copy No 1. 31 Div.'G'.
                         2. 31 Div.'Q'.
                         3. 29 Div.'G'.
                         4. 29 Div.'Q'.
                         5. C.E. XV Corps.
                         6. C.R.E. 29 Div.
                         7. 92 Bde.
                         8. 93 Bde.
                         9. 94 Bde.
                        10. 210 Field Coy.
                        11. 211   do do
                        12. 223   do do
                        13. 12 K.O.Y.L.I.
                        14. C.R.E.
                        15. Adjt.
                        16. War Diary.
                        17. "   "
                        18. File.

WAR DIARY

SECRET. R.E. INSTRUCTIONS No 21. Copy No. 14

Work for 5th September.

1. **210th Field Company. R.E.**

    Making good roads in Left Bde. Area as close behind Infantry as possible, and reconnoitring forward for any bridging or crater work.

2. **211th Field Company. R.E.**

    (a) Move forward to new camp and reconnoitre all roads in Left Bde. Area.

    (b) 1 section erecting notice boards in BAILLEUL.

    (c) Supplying immediate demands for small services to Left (94th Infantry) Bde.

3. **223rd Field Company. R.E.**

    (a) Commence filling in crater at S.29.central, two reliefs.

    (b) Keep in touch with Right Bde. and carry out any small immediate services required.

    (c) Erect office and store for R.E. Divisional Dump at S.26.a.2.5.

4. **12th K.O.Y.L.I.**

    (a) One Coy. working in conjunction with 210 Field Coy.

    (b) One Coy. making good road from BAILLEUL Station, (S.26.a.4.7.) to S.20.d.9.5.

    (c) One Coy. clearing streets in BAILLEUL to full width.

5. ACKNOWLEDGE. (Field Coys. and K.O.Y.L.I. only.)

                                        F. Giles.
                                        Lt.Col.R.E.
4/9/18.   C.R.E. 31st Division.

Issued at 8.30 p.m.

Distribution :- Copy No 1. C.E. XV Corps.   No 9. C.R.E. 29 Div.
                        2. 210 Field Coy.   10. C.R.E.
                        3. 211 do   do   11. Adjt.
                        4. 223 do   do   12. File.
                        5. 92 Inf. Bde.   13.)
                        6. 94 Inf. Bde.   14.) War Diary.
                        7. 31 Div.'G'.
                        8. 12 K.O.Y.L.I.

SECRET.   Copy No. 15

R.E. INSTRUCTIONS No. 22.

Work for 7/9/18.

1. **210th Field Company. R.E.**

    Locate and exploit all sources of water supply in Left Bde. area, both drinking and horses, including new Northern Divisional Boundary, sending samples to be tested at Main Dressing Station, BAILLEUL, and notice boarding wells, etc. in accordance with Medical Instructions.

    Locations to be reported daily to this office with full details.

2. **211th Field Company. R.E.**

    (a) Repairing and making good roads in forward LEFT Bde. area to take guns and limbers - concentrating especially on the ROMARIN - HYDE PARK CORNER - MESSINES Road.

    Daily report to state class of traffic each road will take, wet or dry weather, as well as extent worked on.

    Special attention to be paid to WATERLOO Road, S.17.d.8.9. - T.20.a.9.0.

    (b) Supplying any immediate small services required by 94th Bde. with whom the O.C. will keep in touch.

3. **223rd Field Company. R.E.**

    (a) Improving, camouflaging and fencing advanced D.H.Q. at GOUGH HOUSE.

    (b) Supplying any immediate small services required by 92 Bde. with whom the O.C. will keep in touch.

4. **12th K.O.Y.L.I.**

    (a) One Coy. working in conjunction with 211 Field Coy.

    (b) Two Coys. working on RAVELSBURG Road from BAILLEUL - NEUVE EGLISE.

5. **64th Field Coy. (9th Division.)**

    Erecting road screen on RAVELSBURG Road between BAILLEUL and NEUVE EGLISE to afford protection from view from East and S.E. as necessary.

6. **General.**

    One section of each Field Coy. and one platoon of each Pioneer Coy. will remain in camp until further orders as a reserve against any sudden call or emergency.

    N.B. This does not apply to 64th Field Coy.

7. ACKNOWLEDGE. (Field Coys. and K.O.Y.L.I. only.)

                                                     W. Tigham
                                                     Capt. R.E.
                                              for   Lt.Col.R.E.
6/9/18.   C.R.E. 31st Division.

Issued at 4.45 p.m.   P.T.O.

Distribution :-

    Copy No 1. C.E, XV Corps.
           2. 210 Field Coy.
           3. 211   do   do
           4. 223   do   do
           5. 64   do   do
           6. 92 Inf. Bde.
           7. 93 "   "
           8. 94 "   "
           9. 31 Div.'G'.
          10. 31 Div.'Q'.
          11. 12 K.O.Y.L.I.
          12. C.R.E. 29 Div.
          13. C.R.E.
          14. Adjt.
          15)
          16) War Diary.
          17. File.

WAR DIARY

SECRET.   Copy No 15

R.E. INSTRUCTIONS No 23.

Work for 8/9/18.

1. **210th Field Company.R.E.**

    (a) Exploit water supply.

    (b) Supervise further clearing of streets in BAILLEUL, especially main road from Grande Place to ARMENTIERES, and filling up of shell-holes in Grande Place.
    Infantry working party of 2 Coys. with shovels reporting at 9 a.m. Mairie, S.13.d.5.0.

2. **211th Field Company.R.E.**

    (a) Repairing and making good roads in forward Left Bde. Area, concentrating especially on :-

    (i) ROMARIN - HYDE PARK CORNER - MESSINES.
    (ii) NEUVE EGLISE - WHITE GATES - LE ROSSIGNOL.
    (iii) WATERLOO Road.

    (b) Supplying any small and immediate services required by 94th Bde. with whom O.C. will keep in touch.

3. **223rd Field Company.R.E.**

    (a) Improving camouflaging and fencing advanced D.H.Q. at GOUGH HOUSE

    (b) Supplying any small and immediate services required by 92 Bde. with whom O.C. will keep in touch.

    (c) Repair decking and ribands to plank road round crater at S.29.central.

4. **64th Field Company.R.E. (9th Division.)**

    Erecting road screens on RAVELSBURG and WATERLOO Roads.

5. **12th K.O.Y.L.I.**

    (a) One Coy. working in conjunction with 211th Field Coy.

    (b) Two Coys. working on RAVELSBURG Road.

6. ACKNOWLEDGE. (Field Coys. and K.O.Y.L.I. only.)

                                                    W. Dunham
                                                    Capt. R.E.
                                                    for Lt.Col.R.E.
                                                    C.R.E. 31st Division.

7/9/18.

Issued at 8 p.m.

Distribution :-

Copy No			No	
1.	C.E. XV Corps.		9.	31 Div.'G'.
2.	210 Field Coy.		10.	12 K.O.Y.L.I.
3.	211 do do		11.	C.R.E. 29 Div.
4.	223 do do		12.	C.R.E.
5.	64 do do		13.	Adjt.
6.	92 Inf. Bde.		14)	War Diary.
7.	93 Inf. Bde.		15)	
8.	94 Inf. Bde.		16.	File.

WAR DIARY

SECRET.   Copy No 14

R.E. INSTRUCTIONS No 24.

Work for 9/9/18.

1. 210th Field Company.R.E.

   (a)   Exploit water supply in Left Bde. Area.

   (b)   Make good horse troughs and standings at South Side WESTHOF Farm, notice board same, put in a pump, and report completion on daily progress report of 9/9/18.

   (c)   Repair shell-holes etc., on main BAILLEUL - ARMENTIERES Road between S.20.b.0.5. and S.27.central.

2. 211th Field Company.R.E.

   (a)   Repairing and making good and draining roads in forward Left Bde. Area, especially

        (i)   ROMARIN - HYDE PARK CORNER - MESSINES.
        (ii) WESTHOF Farm Road from S.30.b.5.4. northwards.
        (iii) WATERLOO Road on steep pitch at about T.19.b.2.6.

   (b)   Supplying any small and immediate services required by 94th Bde. with whom O.C. will keep in touch.

3. 223rd Field Company.R.E.

   (a)   Completing advanced D.H.Q. at GOUGH HOUSE and filling in holes in approach road thereto.

   (b)   Supplying any small and immediate demands of 92nd Bde. with whom O.C. will keep in touch.

4. 64th Field Company.R.E. (9th Division.)

   Erecting screening on road BAILLEUL - RAVELSBURG - WATERLOO Road.

5. 12th K.O.Y.L.I.

   (a)   One Coy. working in conjunction with 211th Field Coy.

   (b)   One Coy. working on RAVELSBURG Road.

   (c)   One Coy. working on drains and shell-holes on WATERLOO Road between S.17.b.9.1. and T.19.a.7.7.

6. ACKNOWLEDGE. (Field Coys. and K.O.Y.L.I. only.)

8/9/18.   Lt.Col.R.E.
Issued at 5.35 p.m.   C.R.E. 31st Division.

Distribution :-
          Copy No 1. C.E. XV Corps.   No 9. 31 Div.'G'.
                 2. 210 Field Coy.   10. 12 K.O.Y.L.I.
                 3. 211 do   do   11. C.R.E. 29 Div.
                 4. 223 do   do   12. C.R.E.
                 5. 64 do   do   13. Adjt.
                 6. 92 Inf. Bde.   14.) War Diary.
                 7. 93 Inf. Bde.   15.)
                 8. 94 Inf. Bde.   16. File.

SECRET.

R.E. INSTRUCTIONS No 25.

Copy No. 15

Work for the 10th will be as in R.E. Instructions No 24 with the following exception.

The Reserve Section of each Field Coy., together with the Platoon of Pioneers at Batt. H.Q. will be employed on filling in the road crater at S.27.c.8.9. under the direction of O.C. 210th Field Company.R.E.

Work to commence at 8 a.m.

Transport to be found by 210th Field Coy.R.E.

On completion of filling in of crater, the road to the Company Transport Lines will be made good.

Lt.Col.R.E,
C.R.E. 31st Division.

9/9/18.

Issued at 6.15 p.m.

Distribution:-   Copy No 1. C.E. XV Corps.
                        2. 210 Field Coy.
                        3. 211   do   do
                        4. 223   do   do
                        5. 64   do   do
                        6. 92 Inf. Bde.
                        7. 93 Inf. Bde.
                        8. 94 Inf. Bde.
                        9. 31 Div.'G'.
                       10. 12 K.O.Y.L.I.
                       11. C.R.E. 29 Div.
                       12. C.R.E.
                       13. Adjt.
                       14) War Diary.
                       15)
                       16. File.

WAR DIARY

SECRET.

Copy No 15

R.E. INSTRUCTIONS No 26.

Work for the 11th September will be the same as in R.E. Instructions No's 24 and 25 with the following exception.

O.C. 223rd Field Coy. will arrange for an Officer to report at H.Q. 455 Field Coy. R.E. A.10.d.4.6. at 8-30 a.m. tomorrow morning to take over the work 455 Field Coy. have in hand.

223rd Field Coy. (less Reserve Section employed under O.C. 210 Field Coy.) will work on filling in crater at A.4.c. and repairing road between S.27.central and A.4.c.

ACKNOWLEDGE. (Field Coys. and K.O.Y.L.I. only.)

Capt. R.E.

10/9/18.

A/Adjt. for C.R.E. 31st Division.

Issued at 9-15 p.m.

Distribution :-

      Copy No 1. C.E. XV Corps.
             2. 210 Field Coy.
             3. 211 Field Coy.
             4. 223 Field Coy.
             5. 64 Field Coy.
             6. 92 Inf. Bde.
             7. 93 Inf. Bde.
             8. 94 Inf. Bde.
             9. 31 Div.'G'.
           10. 12 K.O.Y.L.I.
           11. C.R.E. 29 Div.
           12. C.R.E.
           13. Adjt.
           14)
           15) War Diary.
           16. File.

SECRET.

WAR DIARY

Copy No 15

R.E. INSTRUCTIONS No 27.

Work for 12/9/18.

1. **210th Field Company.R.E.**

    Commence work on new D.H.Q. at CAESTRE.

2. **211th Field Company.R.E.**

    (a) Work to continue as before on roads.
    No working party will be available, but 4 G.S. wagons will report at BAILLEUL Dump at 9 a.m.

    (b) Supplying any small and immediate services required by Left Bde. with whom O.C. will keep in touch.

3. **223rd Field Company.R.E.**

    (a) Completing horse watering point at TROIS ARBRES, B.13.b.2.6.

    (b) Complete filling in of crater at A.4.c.

    (c) Complete dump of sleepers for crater on PONT d' ACHELLES — PLOEGSTEERT Road.

    (d) Supplying any small and immediate services required by Right Bde. with whom O.C. will keep in touch.

4. **64th Field Coy.R.E.**

    (a) Continue work o screening of WATERLOO Road.
    Screening of RAVELSBURG Road will not be continued East of road junction S.17.b.8.1.

5. **12th K.O.Y.L.I.**

    (a) 1 Coy. on filling shell-holes and draining road between S.27.central and A.4.c. 4 D.A.C. wagons will report at S.27.central at 8 a.m. for collecting rubble.

    (b) 1 Coy. working in conjunction with 211th Field Coy.

    (c) 1 Coy. filling in shell-holes and draining RAVELSBURG – WATERLOO Road.

6. **General.**

    Reserve Sections of Field Coys. and Platoon of K.O.Y.L.I. will complete filling in crater at S.27.c.8.9. and making good road to Coy. lines.

7. ACKNOWLEDGE. (Field Coys. and K.O.Y.L.I. only.)

Capt.R.E.

11/9/18.   A/Adjt. for C.R.E. 31st Division.

Issued at 6-45 p.m.

Distribution :- Copy No 1. C.E. XV Corps.   No 9. 31 Div.'G'.
                        2. 210 Field Coy.   10. 12 K.O.Y.L.I.
                        3. 211   do   do   11. C.R.E. 29 Div.
                        4. 223   do   do   12. C.R.E.
                        5. 64   do   do   13. Adjt.
                        6. 92 Inf. Bde.   14)
                        7. 93 Inf. Bde.   15) War Diary.
                        8. 94 Inf. Bde.   16. File.

WAR DIARY

SECRET.
※=※=※=※=※

Copy No 10

31st Divisional Engineers.

OPERATION ORDER No 35.

210th Field Company.R.E. will move on the morning of the 12th inst. from their present location (S.27.c.9.8.) to billets at CAESTRE, for work on the new I.H.Q.

One Officer with advanced party will report at 10 a.m. on the 12th inst. at Area Commandant's Office at W.5.d.2.3. to arrange billetting.

After Coy. is billetted an Officer will report at H.Q. R.E. for instructions as to work to be carried out on following day.

F. Giles.
Lt.Col.R.E.

11/9/18.

C.R.E. 31st Division.

Issued at 6.45 p.m.

Distribution :- Copy No 1. 31 Div. 'G'.
2. 31 Div. 'A'.
3. C.E. XV Corps.
4. 210 Field Coy.
5. 211   do   do
6. 223   do   do
7. 12 K.O.Y.L.I.
8. C.R.E.
9. Adjt.
10.) War Diary.
11.)
12. File.

WAR DIARY

SECRET.   R.E. INSTRUCTION No 28.   Copy No 13

Work for 13/9/18.

1. **210th Field Company.R.E.**

    D.H.Q. CAESTRE.

2. **211th Field Company.R.E.**

    Shelters and Drying Rooms for Brigade in NIEPPE System.

3. **223rd Field Company.R.E.**

    (a) Complete dump of sleepers for craters on PONT d' ACHELLES - PLOEGSTEERT Road.

    (b) Make winter accommodation for a Field Coy. at S.27.c.7.5.

    (c) Making good road from S.27.c.8.9. to S.27.c.7.5. with Reserve Section of 211th and 223rd Field Coys. and Reserve Platoon of K.O.Y.L.I. - 2 D.A.C. Wagons at 8 a.m. at S.27.c.8.9.

4. **12th K.O.Y.L.I.**

    (a) One Coy. screening WATERLOO Road.

    (b) One Coy. making good road from S.27.c.8.9. to A.4.c.7.6. - 2 D.A.C. Wagons at 8 a.m. at S.27.c.8.9.

    (c) One Coy. draining and clearing RAVELSBURG and WATERLOO Roads.

5. ACKNOWLEDGE. (Field Coys. and K.O.Y.L.I. only.)

                                            F. Giles.
                                            Lt.Col.R.E.
12/9/18.   C.R.E. 31st Division.

Issued at 8.30 p.m.

        Distribution :- Copy No 1. C.E. XV Corps.
                                2. 210 Field Coy.
                                3. 211 do   do
                                4. 223 do   do
                                5. 92 Inf. Bde.
                                6. 93 Inf. Bde.
                                7. 94 Inf. Bde.
                                8. 31 Div.'G'.
                                9. 12 K.O.Y.L.I.
                               10. C.R.E.
                               11. Adjt.
                               12.)
                               13.) War Diary.
                               14. File.

SECRET.

WAR DIARY

R.E. INSTRUCTIONS No 29.

Work for 14/9/18.

Copy No 13

1. **210th Field Company.R.E.**

    D.H.Q. CAESTRE.

2. **211th Field Company.R.E.**

    (a) Shelters and Drying Rooms for Brigade in NIEPPE System.

    (b) Duckboarding Coy. Posts, and making good and revetting firebays in same.

3. **223rd Field Company.R.E.**

    (a) Complete dump of sleepers for craters on PONT d' ACHELLES - PLOEGSTEERT Road.

    (b) Make winter accommodation for a Field Coy. at S.27.c.7.5.

    (c) Additions to Bde. H.Q. at GOUGH HOUSE.

    (d) Make good road from S.27.c.8.9. to S.27.c.7.5. with Reserve Sections of 211th and 223rd Field Coys. and Reserve Platoon of K.O.Y.L.I.

4. **12th K.O.Y.L.I.**

    (a) One Coy. screening WATERLOO Road.

    (b) One Coy. draining and clearing RAVELSBURG and WATERLOO Roads.

    (c) One Coy. making good road from S.27.c.8.9. to A.4.c.7.6. and from S.27.d.9.2. to A.3.a.3.2.

5. ACKNOWLEDGE. (Field Coys. and K.O.Y.L.I. only.)

for Lt.Col.R.E.
C.R.E. 31st Division.

13/9/18.

Issued at 6 p.m.

Distribution:- Copy No 1. C.E. XV Corps.
2. 210 Field Coy.
3. 211 do do
4. 223 do do
5. 92 Inf. Bde.
6. 93 Inf. Bde.
7. 94 Inf. Bde.
8. 31 Div.'G'.
9. 12 K.O.Y.L.I.
10. C.R.E.
11. Adjt.
12.)
13.) War Diary.
14. File.

WAR DIARY

SECRET.

Copy No 13

R.E. INSTRUCTIONS No 30.

Work for 15/9/18.

1. 210th Field Company.R.E.

    D.H.Q. CAESTRE.

2. 211th Field Company.R.E.

(a) Shelters and Drying Rooms for Brigade in NIEPPE System.

(b) Duckboarding Coy. Posts, and making good firebays, etc.

(c) Reserve Section building Coy. Horse Standings.

3. 223rd Field Company.R.E.

(a) Erecting shelters for Brigade H.Q. at LAMPERNISSE Farm, (B.3.a.0.4.)

(b) Making winter accommodation for a Field Coy. at S.27.c.7.5. including horse standings.

(c) Complete sleeper dump for PONT d' ACHELLES - PLOEGSTEERT Road.

4. 12th K.O.Y.L.I.

(a) One Coy. screening WATERLOO Road.

(b) One Coy. clearing out drains and making good RAVELSBURG and WATERLOO Roads.

(c) One Coy. clearing out drains, and making good roads from S.27.c.8.9. to A.4.c.7.6. and also S.27.d.9.2. to A.3.a.3.2.

5. ACKNOWLEDGE. (Field Coys. and K.O.Y.L.I. only.)

F. Giles.
Lt.Col.R.E.
C.R.E. 31st Division.

14/9/18.

Issued at 6.15 p.m.

Distribution:- Copy No 1. C.E. XV Corps.
2. 210 Field Coy.
3. 211 do do
4. 223 do do
5. 92 Inf. Bde.
6. 93 Inf. Bde.
7. 94 Inf. Bde.
8. 31 Div.'G'.
9. 12 K.O.Y.L.I.
10. C.R.E.
11. Adjt.
12.)
13.) War Diary.
14. File.

SECRET.

WAR DIARY

Copy No 12

R.E. INSTRUCTIONS No 31.

Work for 16/9/18.

1. **210th Field Company.R.E.**

    (a) D.H.Q. CAESTRE.

    (b) Gas-proofing R.A. Bde. and Battery H.Q.

2. **211th Field Company.R.E.**

    (a) Shelters and Drying Rooms and gas-proofing for Brigade in NIEPPE System.

    (b) Duckboarding posts, and making good firebays.

    (c) Building Coy. Horse Standings.

    (d) Improvement of camp at T.25.

3. **223rd Field Company.R.E.**

    (a) Making winter accommodation for a Field Coy. at S.27.c.7.5. including Horse Standings.

    (b) Completing sleeper dump for craters on PONT d' ACHELLES - PLOEGSTEERT Road.

    (c) Erecting shelters for H.Q. of Bde. in line at LAHPERNISSE Farm.

    (d) Erecting Nissen Huts for Support Bde. H.Q. on BAILLEUL - STRAZEELE Road about S.19.a.

4. **12th K.O.Y.L.I.**

    (a) One Coy. screening WATERLOO and DE SEULE - NEUVE EGLISE Roads

    (b) One Coy. clearing drains and making good WATERLOO Road eastwards of T.19.a.7.7.

    (c) One Coy. clearing drains and making good roads from S.27.central to A.4.c. and from S.27.d.9.2. to A.3.a.3.2.

5. ACKNOWLEDGE. (Field Coys. and K.O.Y.L.I. only.)

Lt.Col.R.E.
C.R.E. 31st Division.

15/9/18.

Issued at 8-5 p.m.

Distribution :- Copy No 1. C.E. XV Corps.
2. 210 Field Coy.
3. 211 do do
4. 223 do do
5. 92 Inf. Bde.
6. 93 Inf. Bde.
7. 94 Inf. Bde.
8. 31 Div.'G'.
9. 12 K.O.Y.L.I.
10. C.R.E.
11. Adjt.
12) War Diary.
13)
14. File.

SECRET.

WAR DIARY

Copy No 12

R.E. INSTRUCTIONS No 32.

Work for 17/9/18.

1. 210th Field Company.R.E.

    (a)   D.H.Q. CAESTRE.

    (b)   Gas-proofing R.A. Bde. and Battery H.Q.

2. 211th Field Company.R.E.

    (a)   Shelters, Drying Rooms, and gas-proofing for Brigade in NIEPPE System.

    (b)   Building Coy. Horse Standings.

    (c)   Improvement of Camp at T.25.

3. 223rd Field Company.R.E.

    (a)   Making winter accommodation for a Field Coy. at S.27.c.7.5. including Horse Standings.

    (b)   Erecting shelters for H.Q. of Brigade in line round LAMPERNISSE Farm.

    (c)   Erecting huts for H.Q. of Support Brigade at S.19.a.

4. 12th K.O.Y.L.I.

    (a)   One Coy. screening Waterloo Road.

    (b)   One Coy. clearing drains and making good roads from S.27.central to A.4.c. and from S.27.d.9.2. to A.3.a.3.2.

    (c)   One Coy. duckboarding and making good firebays in NIEPPE System in conjunction with 211 Field Coy.

    (d)   Reserve platoon of Coy. as at (b) salving German screening material.

5. ACKNOWLEDGE.(Field Coys. and K.O.Y.L.I. only)

Lt.Col.R.E
C.R.E. 31st Division.

16/9/18.

Issued at 6 p.m.

Distribution:- Copy No 1. C.E. XV Corps.
2. 210 Field Coy.
3. 211   do   do
4. 223   do   do
5. 92 Inf. Bde.
6. 93 Inf. Bde.
7. 94 Inf. Bde.
8. 31 Div.'G'.
9. 12th K.O.Y.L.I.
10. C.R.E.
11. Adjt.
12) War Diary.
13)
14. File.

WAR DIARY

SECRET.
　　　　　　　　　　　　　　　　　　　　　　　　　　　　Copy No 13

R.E. INSTRUCTIONS No 33.
Work for 18/9/18.

Work will be continued as laid down in R.E. Instructions No 32 of the 16th inst.

ACKNOWLEDGE. (Field Coys. and K.O.Y.L.I.)

　　　　　　　　　　　　　　　　　　　E. J. Wilkington Lt.R.E.
　　　　　　　　　　　　　　　　　　　　for Lt.Col.R.E.

17/9/18.　　　　　　　　　　　　　　　　C.R.E. 31st Division.

Issued at 7-30 p.m.

　　Distribution :-
　　　　　　　　Copy No 1. C.E. XV Corps.
　　　　　　　　　　　　 2. 210 Field Coy.
　　　　　　　　　　　　 3. 211 Field Coy.
　　　　　　　　　　　　 4. 223 Field Coy.
　　　　　　　　　　　　 5. 92 Inf. Bde.
　　　　　　　　　　　　 6. 93 Inf. Bde.
　　　　　　　　　　　　 7. 94 Inf. Bde.
　　　　　　　　　　　　 8. 31 Div. 'G'.
　　　　　　　　　　　　 9. 12 K.O.Y.L.I.
　　　　　　　　　　　　10. C.R.E.
　　　　　　　　　　　　11. Adjt.
　　　　　　　　　　　　12.)
　　　　　　　　　　　　13.) War Diary.
　　　　　　　　　　　　14. File.

WAR DIARY

SECRET.

Copy No 12

R.E. INSTRUCTIONS No 34.

Work for 19/9/18.

Work will be continued as laid down in R.E. Instructions No 32 of the 16th inst.

ACKNOWLEDGE. (Field Coys. and K.O.Y.L.I. only)

E. Belkington Lt. R.E.
for Lt.Col.R.E.
C.R.E. 31st Division.

18/9/18.

Issued at 8-45 p.m.

Distribution:- No 1. C.E. XV Corps.
2. 210 Field Coy.
3. 211 Field Coy.
4. 223 Field Coy.
5. 92 Inf. Bde.
6. 93 Inf. Bde.
7. 94 Inf. Bde.
8. 31 Div. 'G'.
9. 12 K.O.Y.L.I.
10. C.R.E.
11. Adjt.
12)
13) War Diary.
14. File.

WAR DIARY

SECRET.

Copy No 12

R.E. INSTRUCTIONS No 35.

Work for 20/9/18.

Work will be continued as laid down in R.E. Instructions No 32 of the 16th inst.

ACKNOWLEDGE. (Field Coys. and K.O.Y.L.I. only.)

Lieut. R.E.

19/9/18.   for C.R.E. 31st Division.

Issued at ____ p.m.

Distribution :- Copy No 1. C.E. XV Corps
2. 210 Field Coy.
3. 211 do do
4. 223 do do
5. 92 Inf. Bde.
6. 93 Inf. Bde.
7. 94 Inf. Bde.
8. 31 Div. 'G'.
9. 12 K.O.Y.L.I.
10. C.R.E.
11. Adjt.
12) War Diary.
13)
14. File.

WAR DIARY

SECRET.　　　　　　　　　　　　　　　　　　　　　　Copy No 13

R.E. INSTRUCTIONS No 36

Work for 21/9/18.

Work will be continued as laid down in R.E. Instructions No 32 of the 16th inst.

ACKNOWLEDGE. (Field Coys. and K.O.Y.L.I. only.)

E. B. Elkington.
Lieut. R.E.
for C.R.E. 31st Division.

20/9/18.
Issued at 8·45 p.m.

Distribution :- Copy No 1. C.E. XV Corps.
2. 210 Field Coy.
3. 211 do do
4. 223 do do
5. 92 Inf. Bde.
6. 93 Inf. Bde.
7. 94 Inf. Bde.
8. 31 Div. 'G'.
9. 12 K.O.Y.L.I.
10. C.R.E.
11. Adjt.
12)
13) War Diary.
14. File.

SECRET.

Copy No 13

WAR DIARY

31st Divisional Engineers.

OPERATION ORDER No 36.

1. On September 22nd, 210th Field Coy.R.E. will take over the work of 211th Field Coy.R.E. in the line, and the latter will become reserve Field Coy., leaving one section at Transport Lines to construct Horse Standings.

2. Necessary reconnaissance will be carried out between Coys. on September 21st, and all maps, plans, works reports, etc. will be handed over complete.

3. (a) Four lorries for dismounted personnel of 210th Field Coy. will be at CAESTRE Church at 7 a.m. on 22/9/18. They will convey them to Camp at T.25. and bring back dismounted personnel of 211th Field Coy. to same place.

   (b) Transport will march by road under Company arrangements.

4. O.C. 210th Field Coy. will see that work is on no account interrupted in the forward area, and will direct parties to proceed to work after arrival at T.25.

5. ACKNOWLEDGE. (210 and 211 Field Coys. only.)

F. Giles.
Lt.Col.R.E.
C.R.E. 31st Division.

20/9/18.

Issued at ____ p.m.

Distribution :- Copy No 1. 31 Div. 'G'.
2. 31 Div. 'Q'.
3. 92 Inf. Bde.
4. 93 Inf. Bde.
5. 94 Inf. Bde.
6. 210 Field Coy.
7. 211 do do
8. 223 do do
9. 12 K.O.Y.L.I.
10. C.R.E.
11. Adjt.
12.) War Diary.
13.)
14. File.

War Diary

SECRET.   Copy No 7

51st Divisional Engineers.
Amendment No 1 to Operation Order No 56.

For para 2 (a) read :-

A decauville train for the dismounted personnel of 210th
Field Company will be at the point where the track crosses
the main CAESTRE - FLETRE Road, W.3.b.5.2. at 7 a.m. on
22/9/18.
It will convey them to the point where the track crosses
the BLOUNT FARM Road, T.25.c.5.5., arriving there at
9-30 a.m., will turn round in CONNAUGHT Sidings, and
return to CAESTRE with the dismounted personnel of 211th
Field Company.R.E.

                                                    Lt.Col.R.E.
21/9/18.   C.R.E. 51st Division.

Issued at 11.25 a.m.

        Distribution :-

                Copy No 1. 51st Div.'Q'.
                       2. 210 Field Coy.
                       3. 211 Field Coy.
                       4. C.R.E.
                       5. Adjt.
                       6.)
                       7.) War Diary.
                       8. File.

War Diary

SECRET.   Copy No 13

R.E. INSTRUCTIONS No 37.

Work for 22/9/18.

1. **210th Field Coy.** to whom Bde. in line will apply for any small and immediate services.

    (a) Shelters, Drying Rooms, and Gas-proofing for Posts in NIEPPE System with assistance of Infantry garrison.

    (b) Shelters for Right Battn. H.Q. at B.10.b.6.2.

    (c) Gas-proofing R.A. Bde. and Battery H.Q.

    (d) Gas-proofing M.G. Coy. and Section H.Q. in T.28.

2. **211th Field Coy.**

    (a) 3 Sections on D.H.Q. CAESTRE.

    (b) 1 Section building Horse Standings for a Field Coy. at A.3.a.9.6.

3. **223rd Field Coy.**

    (a) Making winter accommodation and horse standings for a Field Coy. at S.27.c.7.5.

    (b) Erecting shelters for H.Q. of Bde. in line at LAMPERNISSE Farm.

    (c) Completing Nissen Huts for Support Bde. H.Q. at S.19.a.

4. **12th K.O.Y.L.I.**

    (a) One Coy. screening DE SEULE - NEUVE EGLISE Road.

    (b) One Coy. clearing drains and making good road from S.27.d.9.2. to A.3.a.3.2.

    (c) One Coy. duckboarding and making good firebays in NIEPPE System in conjunction with 210th Field Coy.

    (d) Reserve Platoon of Coy. as at (b) salving German screening material and transporting same to site of new work.

5. ACKNOWLEDGE. (Field Coys. and K.O.Y.L.I. only.)

                                            F. Giles.
                                            Lt.Col.R.E.
21/9/18.   C.R.E. 31st Division.

Issued at 2.30 p.m.

            Distribution :- Copy No 1. C.E. XV Corps.
                                    2. 210 Field Coy.
                                    3. 211 Field Coy.
                                    4. 223 Field Coy.
                                    5. 92 Inf. Bde.
                                    6. 93 Inf. Bde.
                                    7. 94 Inf. Bde.
                                    8. 31 Div.'G'.
                                    9. 12 K.O.Y.L.I.
                                    10. C.R.E.
                                    11. Adjt.
                                    12.)
                                    13.) War Diary.
                                    14. File.

WAR DIARY

SECRET. Copy No 14

R.E. INSTRUCTIONS No 38.

Work for 23/9/18.

1. **210th Field Coy.R.E.**

   (a) Carting material for and making plank deviation round crater at T.23.b.6.1. Night work.

   (b) Collecting material for plank roads from back area and stacking at about T.26.d.1.3.

   (c) Gas-proofing M.G. Coy. and Section H.Q. in T.28.

2. **211th Field Coy.R.E.**

   D.H.Q. CAESTRE.

3. **223rd Field Coy.R.E.**

   (a) Carting material for and making plank deviations round craters at T.29.d.3.4. and T.30.c.45.55, - night work.

   (b) Completing huts at Support Bde. H.Q. at S.19.a.

   (c) Completing shelters for H.Q. of Bde. in line at LAPERNISSE FARM.

4. **12th K.O.Y.L.I.**

   (a) One Coy. working in conjunction with 210 Field Coy. on crater at T.23.b.6.1.

   (b) One Coy. working in conjunction with 223 Field Coy. on craters at T.29.d.3.4. and T.30.c.45.55.

   (c) One Coy. working on road from S.27.d.9.2. to A.3.a.3.2. and salving screening material.

5. ACKNOWLEDGE. (Field Coys. & K.O.Y.L.I. only)

J. Giles Lt.Col.R.E.
C.R.E. 31st Division.

22/9/18

Issued at 8 p.m.

Distribution :- Copy No 1. C.E. XV Corps.
2. 210 Field Coy.
3. 211 do do
4. 223 do do
5. 92 Inf. Bde.
6. 93 Inf. Bde.
7. 94 Inf. Bde.
8. 31 Div.'G'.
9. 12 K.O.Y.L.I.
10. 31 Bn. M.G.C.
11. C.R.E.
12. Adjt.
13.)
14.) War Diary.
15. File.

SECRET.   WAR DIARY   Copy No 14

R.E. INSTRUCTIONS No 39.

Work for 24/9/18.

1. **210th Field Company.R.E.**

   (a)   Carting material for plank roads from back area and stacking at about T.26.d.1.3.

   (b)   Gas-proofing M.G. Coy. and Section H.Q. in T.28.

   (c)   Completing deviation round crater at T.23.b.6.1. Night Work.

2. **211th Field Company.R.E.**

   D.H.Q. CAESTRE.

3. **223rd Field Company.R.E.**

   (a)   Completing deviations round craters at T.29.d.3.4. and T.30.c.45.55. Night work.

   (b)   Completing huts at Support Bde. H.Q. at S.19.a.

   (c)   Completing shelters for H.Q. of Bde. in line at LAMPERNISSE Farm.

4. **12th K.O.Y.L.I.**

   (a)   One Coy. working in conjunction with 210 Field Coy. on crater at T.23.b.6.1.

   (b)   One Coy. working in conjunction with 223 Field Coy. on craters at T.29.d.3.4. and T.30.c.45.55.

   (c)   One Coy. wiring and making good inner defences of PLOEGSTEERT.

5. ACKNOWLEDGE. (Field Coys. and K.O.Y.L.I. only.)

                                                            Lt.Col.R.E.
23/9/18.   C.R.E. 31st Division.

Issued at 7.30 p.m.

              Distribution :- Copy No 1. C.E. XV Corps.
                                      2. 210 Field Coy.
                                      3. 211   do   do
                                      4. 223   do   do
                                      5. 92 Inf. Bde.
                                      6. 93 Inf. Bde.
                                      7. 94 Inf. Bde.
                                      8. 31 Div.'G'.
                                      9. 12 K.O.Y.L.I.
                                     10. 31 Bn.M.G.C.
                                     11. C.R.E.
                                     12. Adjt.
                                     13.)
                                     14.) War Diary.
                                     15. File.

WAR DIARY

SECRET.   Copy No ___13___

R.E. INSTRUCTIONS No 40.

Work for 25/9/18.

1. **210th Field Company.R.E.** to whom Bde. in line will apply for small and immediate services.

   (a)   Gas-proofing M.G. Coy. and Section H.Q. in T.28.

   (b)   Carting material for plank roads from back area, and stacking at about T.26.d.1.3.

   (c)   Erecting shelters and making firebays in Posts in NIEPPE System.

2. **211th Field Company.R.E.**

   D.H.Q. CAESTRE.

3. **223rd Field Company.R.E.**

   (a)   Erecting Nissen Huts at Bde. H.Q. at S.19.a.

   (b)   Completing shelters for Bde. H.Q. at LAMPERNISSE Farm.

   (c)   Making winter accommodation and horse standings for a Field Coy. at S.27.c.7.5.

4. **12th K.O.Y.L.I.**

   (a)   One Coy. screening WATERLOO and DE SEULE - NEUVE EGLISE Roads.

   (b)   One Coy. working in conjunction with 210 Field Coy. on Posts in NIEPPE System.

   (c)   One Coy. wiring and making good inner defences of PLOEGSTEERT.

5. ACKNOWLEDGE. (Field Coys. and K.O.Y.L.I. only.)

                                              F.Giles.
                                              Lt.Col.R.E.
24/9/18.   C.R.E. 31st Division.

Issued at 7.30 p.m.

    Distribution :- Copy No 1. C.E. XV Corps.
                           2. 210 Field Coy.
                           3. 211   do   do
                           4. 223   do   do
                           5. 92 Inf. Bde.
                           6. 93 Inf. Bde.
                           7. 94 Inf. Bde.
                           8. 31 Div.'G'.
                           9. 12 K.O.Y.L.I.
                          10. 31 Bn.M.G.C.
                          11. C.R.E.
                          12. Adjt.
                          13) War Diary.
                          14)
                          15. File.

SECRET.

WAR DIARY

Copy No 14

R.E. INSTRUCTIONS No 41.

Work for 26/9/18.

1. **210th Field Company.R.E.**

   (a) Salving and carting material for plank roads and forming dump at about T.18.d.3.3. (Night work.)

   (b) Gas-proofing M.G. Coy. and Section H.Q. in T.28.

   (c) Clearing out dugouts in HILL 63. (Night work.)

2. **211th Field Company.R.E.**

   D.H.Q. CAESTRE.

3. **223rd Field Company.R.E.**

   (a) Erecting Armstrong Huts and shelters at GOUGH HOUSE.

   (b) Erecting accommodation for Bde. H.Q. personnel, and supervising sandbagging Bde. H.Q. shelters with Infantry assistance at LAMPERNISSE FARM.

   (c) Construction of forward camp for A Coy. at about T.25.

4. **12th K.O.Y.L.I.**

   (a) 2 Coys. on screening from observation from ARMENTIERES of road running from T.10.a.8.4. to T.16.c.7.8. and thence to about T.11.c.9.3. (Night work)

   (b) One Coy. assisting 210 Field Coy. in collection of plank road material.

5. ACKNOWLEDGE. (Field Coys. and K.O.Y.L.I. only.)

G. Giles.
Lt.Col.R.E.
C.R.E. 31st Division.

25/9/18.

Issued at 8.15 p.m.

Distribution :- Copy No 1. C.E. XV Corps.
2. 210 Field Coy.
3. 211 Field Coy.
4. 223 Field Coy.
5. 92 Inf. Bde.
6. 93 Inf. Bde.
7. 94 Inf. Bde.
8. 31 Div. 'G'.
9. 31 Div. Arty.
10. 12 K.O.Y.L.I.
11. 31 Bn.M.G.C.
12. C.R.E.
13. Adjt.
14.) War Diary.
15.)
16. File.

SECRET. **WAR DIARY** Copy No 13

R.E. INSTRUCTIONS No 42.

Ref. 31st D.O. No 395, para 10.

1. Os.C. Coys. must use their own initiative in keeping touch with the Infantry advance, and maintaining the closest liaison with Inf. Bdes. and Battalions.

2. At the same time it is absolutely essential that all information as to requirements for stores and material, as well as location and nature of sources of water supply should reach Divl. R.E. H.Q. at the earliest possible moment.

3. Since it is certain that there will be heavy traffic on the forward telephone lines, and in order to supplement this means of communication the following arrangements will be made -

4. On "J" day and following days, a runner from Divl. R.E. H.Q. will be at Camp at T.25.a.0.2. at noon, at 4 p.m. and at 8 p.m.
Os.C. Coys. will see that all reports on the situation, so far as they are concerned, reach this point at half an hour previously; the H.Q. runner will then return with reports to C.R.E's Office.

5. In any case, Os.C. Coys. will send a report on the general situation daily by their own runners, to reach C.R.E's Office by 6 p.m. and 8 a.m. without fail.

6. The main points to bear in mind are :-

   (a) <u>Roads</u> - to be kept open for <u>limbers</u> (reports to be sent where much work for <u>H.A.</u> is required to enable C.E. Corps to be informed.)

   (b) <u>Water Supply</u> - Only location of <u>suitably tested</u> wells, etc. required. Horse Water Points to be opened up where possible.

   (c) <u>Forward Reconnaissance by Officers or reliable N.C.O.</u> - essential to give O.C. Coy. sufficient time to make necessary preparations for any engineering work and getting forward R.E. Stores.

   (d) <u>Keep a reserve</u> of at least one section or platoon per Coy. in hand each day to meet any unforeseen calls of which there are sure to be many.

   (e) <u>Be prepared to move forward</u> sections and platoons at a moment's notice without reference to Divl. R.E. H.Q. but report new location as early as possible

   (f) <u>Liaison with Div. Arty.</u> to be maintained.

7. 210 and 223 Field Coys. will each arrange for a trestle wagon with one Weldon Trestle and two bays superstructure to be parked at the advcd. Coy. Dumps at UNDERHILL FARM and LE DON FARM respectively by daylight on "J" day. These will be used in case a gap is met wider than an "Arty" Bridge can span.

F. Giles.
Lt.Col.R.E.

26/9/18.

Issued at 7-15 p.m.

C.R.E. 31st Division.

Distribution:- Copy No 1. C.E. XV Corps.   No 9. 31 Div. Arty.
              2. 210 Field Coy.   10. 12 K.O.Y.L.I.
              3. 211 Field Coy.   11. C.R.E.
              4. 223 Field Coy.   12. Adjt.
              5. 92 Inf. Bde.   13) War Diary.
              6. 93 Inf. Bde.   14)
              7. 94 Inf. Bde.   15. File.
              8. 31 Div.'G'.

WAR DIARY

SECRET.   Copy No 14

R.E. INSTRUCTIONS No 43.
Work for 27/9/18.

Work will be continued as laid down in R.E. Instructions No 41 except for para 4, read

12th K.O.Y.L.I.

(a) 2 Coys. screening NEUVE EGLISE Road from T.14.d.4.0. to T.15.a.0.3.

(b) 1 Coy. assisting 210 Field Coy. in collecting plank road material.

ACKNOWLEDGE (Field Coys. and K.O.Y.L.I. only.)

26/9/18.

Issued at 7-15 p.m.

Lt.Col.R.E.
C.R.E. 31st Division.

Distribution :-   Copy No 1. C.E. XV Corps.
                          2. 210 Field Coy.
                          3. 211 Field Coy.
                          4. 223 Field Coy.
                          5. 92 Inf. Bde.
                          6. 93 Inf. Bde.
                          7. 94 Inf. Bde.
                          8. 31 Div. 'G'.
                          9. 31 Div. Arty.
                         10. 12 K.O.Y.L.I.
                         11. 31 Bn.M.G.C.
                         12. C.R.E.
                         13. Adjt.
                         14) War Diary.
                         15)
                         16. File.

WAR DIARY

SECRET.

Copy No 15

R.E. INSTRUCTIONS No 44.

Work for 28/9/18.

Work will be continued as laid down in R.E. Instructions No 43 of the 26th inst.

ACKNOWLEDGE.(Field Coys. and K.O.Y.L.I. only.)

[signature]

Lt.Col.R.E.
C.R.E. 31st Division.

27/9/18.

Issued at 8.30 p.m.

Distribution:- Copy No 1. C.E. XV Corps.
2. 210 Field Coy.
3. 211 Field Coy.
4. 223 Field Coy.
5. 92 Inf. Bde.
6. 93 Inf. Bde.
7. 94 Inf. Bde.
8. 31 Div.'G'.
9. 31 Div. Arty.
10. 12 K.O.Y.L.I.
11. 31 Bn. M.G.C.
12. C.R.E.
13. Adjt.
14) War Diary.
15)
16. File.

ORIGINAL.

CONFIDENTIAL.

WAR DIARY

of

Headquarters, 31st Divisional Engineers.

From 1/10/18 to 31/10/18.

VOLUME XXXIV

Army Form C. 2118.

WAR DIARY
or
INTELLIGENCE SUMMARY.

(Erase heading not required.)

Month of OCTOBER Sheet-(1)

Place	Date	Hour	Summary of Events and Information	Remarks and references to Appendices
CAESTRE	1st		C.R.E and A.A & Q.M.G visit MESSINES and reconnoitre forward roads in the vicinity of ASH Crater. Work in progress on the Crater at BAKERY Crossroads. Craters at LA HUTTE on the BAKERY Cross Roads. - HYDE PARK Corner road taken over by 3rd Canadian Tunnelling Company.	
	2nd		Reconnaissance made of the Tramway Systems in Squares U.11.c, U.17.a, U.16.b and U.22.a, b & c with a view to Reg adoption and a main line of Resistance. Fd. Coys instructed to reconnoitre all hedgerows and equipment at the selected Company Headquarters. C.R.E. visits Carpenter & Pioneer in evening. Bakery Cross Roads Craters to	
	3rd		1st Div. Come in and take over "Rossignol" road as at forward as WHITE GATES. Enemy interferes with work and sit-order and damage roadway somedays already laid	
	4th		211 F.Coy. C. R.Z. move forward as indicated in O.O. No 37. Attempt made to cross the LYS on raft and other improvised rafts. No success on account of enemy occupation of the further bank. Intelligible return from Raiders duty with french parks. C.R.Z visits Army Bridging Stores and obtains particulars of the sort of the LYS at balloon bends 2 pontoons carried as with a light type of German foothridge found at PONT DE NIEPPE	

Army Form C. 2118.

Reel (2)

WAR DIARY
or
INTELLIGENCE SUMMARY.
(Erase heading not required.)

Place	Date	Hour	Summary of Events and Information	Remarks and references to Appendices
CAESTRE	6.12		Experiments carried with an improvised Aldwin footbridge. 94. Infy. Bde. 3 Bde. relieve 93rd Bde. in the line, taking over the whole of the Divl. front.	
	7.12		Demonstration at WEST HOF Farm of various types of footbridges. 120 ft in all constructed. Pioneer companies the duying operations. Pocked under orders of Fld. Co. Commanders. Came under direct control of O.C. 12th KOYLI	
	8.12		ance more. Appointment of Lt. (a/Capt.) E.S. ELKINGTON to be Adjutant R.E. 31st Divn. approved by A.G. BAILLEUL Dumb compiled into an advanced Corps PARK. To remain under control of C.R.E. 31st Divn. but stores required by 14th and 40th Divisions to be sent up here also	
	9.12		Chief Engineer X.12 Corps inspects improvised Aldwin bridge. Maj: Mansel 211th Fld. Co. returns from leave	
	10.12		Maj: Mansel takes over from Col: Gibbs and goes round the works	
	11.12		Col: Gibbs goes on a month's leave. Maj: Spruyle (210) returns from leave	
	12.12		92nd Bde. relieve 94th in the line.	
	13.12		Lt. Partridge 12th KOYLI returns from leave	
	14.12		Combined British, Belgian & French attack starts N. of NEERWICQ. Good progress reported.	

Army Form C. 2118.

WAR DIARY
or
INTELLIGENCE SUMMARY.
(Erase heading not required.)

Sheet (3)

Instructions regarding War Diaries and Intelligence
Summaries are contained in F.S. Regs., Part II.
and the Staff Manual respectively. Title pages
will be prepared in manuscript.

Place	Date	Hour	Summary of Events and Information	Remarks and references to Appendices
	15.10.18.		92nd Bde push patrols across the R. Lys on rafts constructed by 21st Fld. Co. and a floating Bridge at the SUGAR REFINERY built by 210 Fld. Co.	
	16.10.18.		Enemy in full retreat towards the SCHELT. QUESNOY occupied. Bridge over Lys at WARNETON for Pack transport completed at 6.30 pm. Track for Pack mules built across river at PONT ROUGE. D/A.Q. moved from COMINES to German camp at HILL 63.	
U.13.c.60.	17th		LINDELLES cratered cross roads repaired. Rough towing Bridge for Pack transport completed at PONT ROUGE. Advanced RE Dump commenced at LE GHEER.	
	18th		C.R.E. & Intelpieder go forward to TOURCOING. 210th Fd Co. move forward in advance of 102. 92 Bde. 211 Fd Co. move to QUESNOY & 223 Fd Co. to WARNETON. Lieuy Lodge and DEVLE reinforced by 2/10 at QUESNOY. Work commenced on new D.H.Q. at 24 CROIX BLANCHE.	
CROIX BLANCHE	19th		D.H.Q. move to CROIX BLANCHE. from HILL 63. Lieut Caldwell. 3rd Can. Tun. Cy. and B.O.R. reports for duty to be attd CRE. for work on mines. Capt. Ellenglin goes on 14 days leave. Div. RE dump Bailleul handed over to CRE Cdn. Troops, permanent move to Le Gheer dump. The Division	

T2134. Wt. W708—776. 500000. 4/15. Sir J.C. & S.

WAR DIARY or INTELLIGENCE SUMMARY

Army Form C. 2118.
Sheet 4

Place	Date	Hour	Summary of Events and Information	Remarks and references to Appendices
CROIX BLANCHE	20th		Side slope to the Pont Jibeur we from 40th Div. 59th Div is on our right. Damaged bridge over Pheam between TOURCOING & ROUBAIX opened for horse by 210 Fd Coy R.E. Box car reported on loan. Early this a.m. infantry ente. BAILLEUL & ESTAIMBOURG, ably evening held western bank of R. ESCAUT. 210 Fd Coy R.E. completed bridge over Canal de ROUBAIX, also bridge for horse over Pheam S. of WATTRELOS. 211 Fd Coy R.E. completed bridge for 'A' Loads over R. DEULE at QUESNOY. Two bridges over Canal in ROUBAIX Completed by 223 Fd Coy 17/10, all loads respectively.	
LANNOY	21st		Enemy established post on Eastern bank of R. ESCAUT. Reconnaissance made by 2/Lt ROGERS, R.E. of bridge over R. ESCAUT. D.H.Q. moved to LANNOY, enthusiastic reception by inhabitants. Counter attack by enemy on our post E. side of river repulsed. Trestle bridge at PONT ROUGE dismantled by 211 Fd Coy R.E.	
"	22nd		Gun post E. of R. L'ESCAUT attacked & withdrawn to W. bank of river. Bridge over Canal de ROUBAIX finished for horse by 210 Fd Coy R.E. Corps preparing & collecting material for bridging L'ESCAUT B.S.M. Holloway & men from dump report from GHEER dump & proceed to dump E. of ROUBAIX.	
"	23rd		Detachment from 3rd Can. Tun. Coy returns to their unit in ROUBAIX. No change in situation.	
"	24th		40th Div is to relieve 31 Div. 31 Div is to relieve 29 Div. 210 & 211 Fd Coy R.E. move to COURTRAI area	
"	25th		is to relieve Fd Coy of 29 Div.	

Army Form C. 2118.

Sheet 5

WAR DIARY
or
INTELLIGENCE SUMMARY.
(Erase heading not required.)

Instructions regarding War Diaries and Intelligence Summaries are contained in F. S. Regs., Part II. and the Staff Manual respectively. Title pages will be prepared in manuscript.

Place	Date	Hour	Summary of Events and Information	Remarks and references to Appendices
LANNOY	26th		3rd Div. takes over R.E. Div. front of II Corps. 92 Inf. Bde. relieves Bde. of 3rd Divn. front line tonight.	
COURTRAI	27th		D.H.Q. moves to COURTRAI	
	28th		Maj. Cochran goes on two weeks leave. 93rd Inf. Bde., 223 Fd. Coy. RE. & Divl Pioneers arrive in STACEGHEM from MOUSCRON	
	29th		Divl. RE dump formed in old enemy dump 3 mile E. of Courtrai. Divl. Pioneers take over found roads from 2nd Div. Pioneer. All Coys. R.E. preparing bridging material.	
	30th		Work same as yesterday. COURTRAI heavily shelled at night.	
	31st		Attack launched at dawn by 94 Inf. Bde. in conjunction with lent Divs. on flanks. All objectives gained, casualties light. 3 guns & over 600 prisoners captured.	

T. O. Kemp Capt. R.E.
Offg. for C.R.E. 31st. Divn.

T2134. Wt. W708—776. 500000. 4/15. Sir J. C. & S.

SECRET.   WAR DIARY   Copy No 13

R.E. INSTRUCTIONS No 45.

Work for 1/10/18.

1. **210th Field Coy. R.E.**

    (a) Make N. to S. deviation round crater at BAKERY Cross Roads, U.14.a.5.4. and then assist in making road East of this road passable for limbers.

    (b) Exploit water supply in forward area.

2. **211th Field Coy. R.E.**

    (a) Make good PLOEGSTEERT - WARNETON Road for heavy traffic as far forward as the situation permits.

    (b) Make good screening on NEUVE EGLISE Road from T.20.central to T.15.a.0.3.

3. **223rd Field Coy. R.E.**

    Make good for limbers

    (a) Road from BAKERY Cross Roads Eastwards as far as situation permits.
    In this work, 210 Field Coy. will assist as soon as the BAKERY Cross Roads deviation is completed. (See 1 (a) above.)
    Details to be arranged between Os.C. Coys. concerned as regards division of work.

    (b) Road from U.15.b.3.8. Southwards to junction with PLOEGSTEERT - WARNETON Road at LE GHEER (U.21.d.0.7.)

4. **12th K.O.Y.L.I.**

    (a) One Coy. working in conjunction with 210 Field Coy.

    (b) One Coy. working in conjunction with 211 Field Coy.

    (c) One Coy. working in conjunction with 223 Field Coy.

5. ACKNOWLEDGE. (Field Coys. & K.O.Y.L.I. only)

F. Giles.
Lt.Col. R.E.

30/9/18.

Issued at 7-45 p.m.

C.R.E. 31st Division.

Distribution :- Copy No 1. C.E. XV Corps.
2. 210 Field Coy.
3. 211 Field Coy.
4. 223 Field Coy.
5. 92 Inf. Bde.
6. 93 Inf. Bde.
7. 94 Inf. Bde.
8. 31 Div. 'G'.
9. 31 Div. Arty.
10. 12 K.O.Y.L.I.
11. C.R.E.
12. Adjt.
13.) War Diary.
14.)
15. File.

SECRET.

WAR DIARY

Copy No 14

R.E. INSTRUCTIONS No 46.

Work for 2/10/18.

1. **210th Field Coy.R.E.** to whom 92 Inf. Bde. will apply for any small and immediate services.

   (a) Work on road East of BAKERY Cross Roads.

   (b) Exploit water supply in forward area.

2. **211th Field Coy.R.E.**

   (a) Make good PLOEGSTEERT - WARNETON Road for heavy traffic as far forward as the situation permits.

   (b) Make good screening on NEUVE EGLISE Road from T.20.central to T.15.a.0.3.

   (c) Make office and shelters for Advcd. R.E. Dump at CONNAUGHT Sidings.

3. **223rd Field Coy.R.E.**

   Work on road East of BAKERY Cross Roads; to be fit for wheeled traffic as early as possible.

4. **12th K.O.Y.L.I.**

   (a) Two Coys. working on road East of BAKERY Cross Roads in conjunction with 210th and 223rd Field Coys.

   (b) One Coy. working in conjunction with 211th Field Coy. on PLOEGSTEERT - WARNETON Road.

5. ACKNOWLEDGE. (Field Coys. and K.O.Y.L.I. only.)

Capt. R.E.

1/10/18.

Issued at 6.30 p.m.

for C.R.E. 31st Division.

Distribution :- Copy No 1. C.E. XV Corps.
2. 210 Field Coy.
3. 211 Field Coy.
4. 223 Field Coy.
5. 92 Inf. Bde.
6. 93 Inf. Bde.
7. 94 Inf. Bde.
8. 31 Div.'G'.
9. 31 Div. Arty.
10. 12 K.O.Y.L.I.
11. C.R.E.
12. Adjt.
13.) War Diary.
14.)
15. File.

SECRET.

WAR DIARY

Copy No 13

R.E. INSTRUCTIONS No 47.

1. Reference R.E. Instructions No 46, para. 3 :-

    Application should be made to 223rd Field Coy. for any small and immediate services required by 93 Inf. Bde.

2. Work for 3/10/18 will be continued as laid down in R.E. Instructions No 46 of 1/10/18.

3. A Field Coy. 14th Division, has taken over upkeep of road from T.10.central to "HITE GATES,T.18.a.5.8. and thence to T.24.a.8.9. road junction.
    No further work on this portion will be done by Units of 31st Division.

4. ACKNOWLEDGE. (Field Coys. and K.O.Y.L.I. only.)

2/10/18.

Issued at 18·00

Capt.R.E.
for C.R.E. 31st Division.

Distribution :-
        Copy No 1. C.E. XV Corps.
               2. 210th Field Coy.
               3. 211th Field Coy.
               4. 223rd Field Coy.
               5. 92 Inf. Bde.
               6. 93 Inf. Bde.
               7. 94 Inf. Bde.
               8. 31 Div. 'G'.
               9. 31 Div. Arty.
              10. 12 K.O.Y.L.I.
              11. C.R.E.
              12. Adjt.
              13)
              14) War Diary.
              15. File.

SECRET.

WAR DIARY

Copy No 14

R.E. INSTRUCTIONS No 48

Work for 4/10/18.

1. **210th Field Coy.R.E.** to whom 92 Inf. Bde. will apply for any small and immediate services.

   (a) Work on road between WHITE GATES, T.18.a.5.8. and ASH CRATERS, U.15.b.2.8.

   (b) Exploiting water supply.

2. **211th Field Coy.R.E.**

   (a) Preparing bridging material and forming dump of same near LE GHEER, U.21.d.7.0.
   N.B. Close liaison to be kept with Battn. in line to ascertain where bridges are required by Infantry.

   (b) Forming forward camp at farm, T.29.d.9.3.

   (c) Completing deviation round LANCASHIRE COTTAGE (T.26.b.7.3.) as may be necessary.

3. **223rd Field Coy.R.E.** to whom 93 Inf. Bde. will apply for any small and immediate services.

   (a) Preparing bridging material and forming dump of same.

   (b) Reconnoitring River LYS for suitable place to form pontoon bridge where required.

   (c) Standing by to push bridges across River LYS wherever required by the Infantry.

4. **12th K.O.Y.L.I.**

   (a) One and a half Coys. working in conjunction with 210 Field Coy. on WHITE GATES - ASH CRATER Road.

   (b) ½ Coy. with 223 Field Coy. to assist in making approaches to any bridges required.

   (c) 1 Coy. making good PLOEGSTEERT - WARNETON Road, and road from LE GHEER, U.21.d.7.0. southwards as far forward as situation permits, under direct control of O.C. 12th K.O.Y.L.I.

5. ACKNOWLEDGE. (Field Coys. and K.O.Y.L.I. only.)

3/10/18

Issued at 18.30

Capt.R.E.
for C.R.E. 31st Division.

Distribution:- Copy No 1. C.E. XV Corps.
2. 210 Field Coy.
3. 211 Field Coy.
4. 223 Field Coy.
5. 92 Inf. Bde.
6. 93 Inf. Bde.
7. 94 Inf. Bde.
8. 31 Div.'G'.
No 9. 31 Div. Arty.
10. 12 K.O.Y.L.I.
11. C.R.E.
12. Adjt.
13) War Diary.
14)
15. File.

WAR DIARY

SECRET. Copy No 13

31st Divisional Engineers.

OPERATION ORDER No. 37.

1. 211th Field Coy. R.E. will move on early morning of 4/10/18 two sections to forward camp at T.29.d.9.3. and all transport will move up from present camp at S.27.c.6.4. which will be vacated, to camp at S.30.b.5.2.

2. ACKNOWLEDGE. (211 Field Coy. only.)

J. Giles.

3/10/18.

Issued at 18-30

Lt.Col.R.E.
C.R.E. 31st Division.

Distribution :-

Copy No 1. 31 Div. 'G'.
2. 31 Div. 'Q'.
3. 92 Inf. Bde.
4. 93 Inf. Bde.
5. 94 Inf. Bde.
6. 210 Field Coy.
7. 211 Field Coy.
8. 223 Field Coy.
9. 12 K.O.Y.L.I.
10. C.R.E.
11. Adjt.
12)
13) War Diary.
14. File.

SECRET.   Copy No 14

R.E. INSTRUCTIONS No 49.

Work for 5/10/18.

1. **210th Field Company.R.E.** to whom Brigade in line will apply for any small and immediate services.

   (a)   Work on road between WHITE GATES, T.18.a.5.8. and ASH CRATERS, U.15.b.2.8.

   (b)   Exploiting water supply.

   (c)   Standing by to carry out any bridging work required on N. half of Divisional front from WARNETON up to SUGAR REFINERY (exclusive.)

2. **211th Field Company.R.E.**

   (a)   Standing by to carry out any bridging work required in S. half of Divisional front from SUGAR REFINERY (inclusive) to S. Divisional boundary.

   (b)   Forming forward camp at T.29.d.9.3.

   (c)   Repairing cuts in L.R. between COURT DREVE, T.24.a. central and front edge of PLOEGSTEERT WOOD. All particulars from A.D.S. at COURT DREVE.

3. **223rd Field Company.R.E.**

   Repairing German huts on HILL 63 for a Bde. or Div. H.Q.

4. **12th K.O.Y.L.I.**

   (a)   2 Coys. working in conjunction with 210 Field Coy. on WHITE GATES - ASH CRATERS Road, and standing by to assist in making any approaches for bridges required.

   (b)   1 Coy. on PLOEGSTEERT - WARNETON Road, and on road from LE GHEER Southwards.

5.   ACKNOWLEDGE. (Field Coys. and K.O.Y.L.I. only.)

                                                    Capt.R.E.
4/10/18
Issued at 17.00   for C.R.E. 31st Division.

   Distribution:- Copy No 1. C.E. XV Corps.
                          2. 210 Field Coy.
                          3. 211   do   do
                          4. 223   do   do
                          5. 92 Inf. Bde.
                          6. 93 Inf. Bde.
                          7. 94 Inf. Bde.
                          8. 31 Div. 'G'.
                          9. 31 Div. Arty.
                         10. 12 K.O.Y.L.I.
                         11. C.R.E.
                         12. Adjt.
                         13) War Diary.
                         14)
                         15. File.

SECRET. *War Diary* Copy No 14

R.E. INSTRUCTIONS No 50.

Work for 6/10/18.

Work will be continued as laid down in R.E. Instructions No 49 of 4/10/18.

Acknowledge. (Field Coys. and K.O.Y.L.I. only.)

F. Giles.

5/10/18.
Issued at 20.00

Lt.Col.R.E.
C.R.E. 31st Division.

Distribution :-

Copy No 1. C.E. XV Corps.
2. 210 Field Coy.
3. 211 do do
4. 223 do do
5. 92 Inf. Bde.
6. 93 Inf. Bde.
7. 94 Inf. Bde.
8. 31 Div. 'G'.
9. 31 Div. Arty.
10. 12 K.O.Y.L.I.
11. C.R.E.
12. Adjt.
13.)
14.) War Diary.
15. File.

SECRET.   War Diary   Copy No 14

R.E. INSTRUCTIONS No 51.

Work for 7/10/18.

1. **210th Field Coy.** to whom Bde. in line will apply for any small and immediate services.

   (a) Standing by for bridging work on N. half of Div. Front from BAS WARNETON to SUGAR REFINERY (exclusive.)

   (b) Preparing light cork pier bridge.

   (c) Exploiting water supply.

2. **211th Field Coy.**

   (a) Standing by for bridging work on S. half of Div. Front from SUGAR REFINERY (inclusive) to S. Div. boundary.

   (b) Forming forward camp at T.29.d.9.3.

   (c) Making and placing notice boards in forward area.

   (d) Repairing L.R. between COURT DREVE Farm and Eastern edge of PLOEGSTEERT WOOD.

   (e) Preparing oil drum Infantry bridge.

3. **223rd Field Coy.**

   Repairing German huts on HILL 63 for a Bde. or Div.H.Q.

4. **12th K.O.Y.L.I.**

   (a) One Coy. on PLOEGSTEERT - WARNETON Road, and on road from LE GHEER Southwards.

   (b) Two Coys. on road from WHITE GATES - BAKERY Cross Roads - ASH CRATERS - WARNETON.

   (c) These Coys. will now work directly under O.C. K.O.Y.L.I. who will be responsible for all supervision and communication of instructions.

5. ACKNOWLEDGE. (Field Coys. and K.O.Y.L.I. only.)

                                                    E.B Whiting
                                                    Capt.R.E.
6/10/18.
Issued at 19.00   for C.R.E. 31st Division.

Distribution :-   Copy No 1. C.E. XV Corps.
                              2. 210 Field Coy.
                              3. 211 Field Coy.
                              4. 223 Field Coy.
                              5. 92 Inf. Bde.
                              6. 93 Inf. Bde.
                              7. 94 Inf. Bde.
                              8. 31 Div.'G'.
                              9. 31 Div. Arty.
                             10. 12 K.O.Y.L.I.
                             11. C.R.E.
                             12. Adjt.
                             13) War Diary.
                             14)
                             15. File.

SECRET.

War Diary

Copy No 14

R.E. INSTRUCTIONS No 52.
Work for 8/10/18.

Work will be continued as laid down in R.E. Instructions No 51 of 6/10/18.

ACKNOWLEDGE. (Field Coys. and K.O.Y.L.I. only.)

7/10/18.

Issued at 20.30

Capt. R.E.

for C.R.E. 31st Division.

Distribution :-

        Copy No 1. C.E. XV Corps.
               2. 210 Field Coy.
               3. 211 Field Coy.
               4. 223 Field Coy.
               5. 92 Inf. Bde.
               6. 93 Inf. Bde.
               7. 94 Inf. Bde.
               8. 31 Div.'G'.
               9. 31 Div. Arty.
              10. 12 K.O.Y.L.I.
              11. C.R.E.
              12. Adjt.
              13)
              14) War Diary.
              15. File.

SECRET.   War Diary   Copy No 14

R.E. INSTRUCTIONS No 53.

Work for 9/10/18.

1. 210th Field Company.R.E.

    (a)   Improving accommodation at Battn. H.Q. in line.

    (b)   Preparing cork bridge pier.

    (c)   Exploiting water supply.

    (d)   Standing by for bridging work on LYS.

2. 211th Field Company.R.E.

    (a)   Making and placing notice boards in forward area.

    (b)   Making oil drum Infantry Bridges.

    (c)   Standing by for bridging work on LYS.

3. 223rd Field Company.R.E.

          Repairing German huts on HILL 63 for Bde. or Div. H.Q.

4. 12th K.O.Y.L.I.

    (a)   One Coy. on roads PLOEGSTEERT - WARNETON, and communications S. of this.

    (b)   One Coy. maintaining road BAVERY Cross Roads to WARNETON (including repair of plank road where and when necessary.)

    (c)   One Coy. maintaining and repairing road WHITE GATES to BAVERY Cross Roads.

    (d)   All these Coys. will work directly under O.C. K.O.Y.L.I. who is responsible for all supervision and communication of instructions.

5. ACKNOWLEDGE. (Field Coys. and K.O.Y.L.I. only.)

                                                E. Pilkington
8/10/18.   Capt.R.E.

Issued at _____   Adjt. for C.R.E. 31st Division.

Distribution :-   Copy No 1. C.E. XV Corps.
                           2. 210 Field Coy.
                           3. 211 Field Coy.
                           4. 223 Field Coy.
                           5. 92 Inf. Bde.
                           6. 93 Inf. Bde.
                           7. 94 Inf. Bde.
                           8. 31 Div.'G'.
                           9. 31 Div. Arty.
                          10. 12 K.O.Y.L.I.
                          11. C.R.E.
                          12. Adjt.
                          13)
                          14) War Diary.
                          15. File.

SECRET.   WAR DIARY   Copy No 14

R.E. INSTRUCTIONS No 54.

Work for 10/10/18.

Work will be continued as laid down in R.E. Instructions No 53 of 8/10/18 except,

Delete para 4 (b) and substitute :-

"One Coy. maintaining road ASH CRATERS - WARNETON, excluding plank road."

ACKNOWLEDGE. (Field Coys. and K.O.Y.L.I. only.)

9/10/18.

Issued at _____

Capt. R.E.
Adjt. for C.R.E. 31st Division.

Distribution:-   Copy No 1. C.E. XV Corps.
2. 210 Field Coy.
3. 211 Field Coy.
4. 223 Field Coy.
5. 92 Inf. Bde.
6. 93 Inf. Bde.
7. 94 Inf. Bde.
8. 31 Div. 'G'.
9. 31 Div. Arty.
10. 12 K.O.Y.L.I.
11. C.R.E.
12. Adjt.
13) War Diary.
14)
15. File.

WAR DIARY

SECRET.   Copy No 14

R.E. INSTRUCTIONS No 55

Work for 11/10/18.

Work will be continued as laid down in R.E. Instructions
No 54 of 9/10/18.

Acknowledge. (Field Coys. and K.O.Y.L.I. only.)

                                        E.B.Elkington
10/10/18.   Capt.R.E.
Issued at 1900   Adjt. for C.R.E. 31st Division.

        Distribution :- Copy No 1. C.E. XV Corps.
                            No 2. 210 Field Coy.
                            No 3. 211 Field Coy.
                            No 4. 223 Field Coy.
                            No 5. 92 Inf. Bde.
                            No 6. 93 Inf. Bde.
                            No 7. 94 Inf. Bde.
                            No 8. 31 Div.'G'.
                            No 9. 31 Div. Arty.
                            No 10. 12 K.O.Y.L.I.
                            No 11. C.R.E.
                            No 12. Adjt.
                            No 13) War Diary.
                            No 14)
                            No 15. File.

WAR DIARY

SECRET.   Copy No 14

R.E. INSTRUCTIONS No 56.

Work for 12/10/18.

Work will be continued as laid down in R.E. Instructions
No 54 of 9/10/18.

Acknowledge. (Field Coys. and M.O.Y.L.I. only.)

                                                    [signature]
11/10/18.   Capt.R.E.
Issued at 1900   Adjt. for C.R.E. 31st Division.

Distribution :- As R.E. Instructions No 54.

SECRET.   WAR DIARY   Copy No 14

R.E. INSTRUCTIONS No 57.

Work for 13/10/18.

1. **210th Field Company.R.E.**

    (a)   Exploiting water supply.

    (b)   Carrying out small services required by Bde. in the line.

2. **211th Field Company.R.E.**

    (a)   Making and placing notice boards in forward area.

    (b)   Making light Infantry bridges.

    (c)   Standing by for bridging work on the LYS.

3. **223rd Field Company.R.E.**

    Repairing German Huts on HILL 63 for Bde. or Div. H.Q.

4. **12th K.O.Y.L.I.**

    (a)   One Coy. on roads PLOEGSTEERT - WARNETON, and communications S. of this.

    (b)   One Coy. maintaining road BAKERY Cross Roads to WARNETON, and also repairing duckboard track from UNCIVIL POST to THATCHED COTTAGE (U.15.c.4.9. to U.16.a.5.6.)

    (c)   One Coy. maintaining and repairing road WHITE GATES to BAKERY Cross Roads.

5. ACKNOWLEDGE. (Field Coys. and K.O.Y.L.I. only.)

12/10/18.

Issued at 1900

Capt. R.E.
Adjt. for C.R.E. 31st Division.

Distribution:- Copy No 1. C.E. XV Corps.
              2. 210 Field Coy.
              3. 211 Field Coy.
              4. 223 Field Coy.
              5. 92 Inf. Bde.
              6. 93 Inf. Bde.
              7. 94 Inf. Bde.
              8. 31 Div.'G'.
              9. 31 Div. Arty.
              10. 12 K.O.Y.L.I.
              11. C.R.E.
              12. Adjt.
              13.)
              14.) War Diary.
              15. File.

SECRET.

WAR DIARY

Copy No 14

R.E. INSTRUCTIONS No 58.

Work for 14/10/18.

1. **210th Field Company.R.E.**

   (a) Exploiting water supply.

   (b) Carrying out small services required by Bde. in line.

   (c) Standing by for bridging work on the LYS.

2. **211th Field Company.R.E.**

   (a) Making and placing notice boards in forward area.

   (b) Making light Infantry bridges.

   (c) Standing by for bridging work on the LYS.

3. **223rd Field Company.R.E.**

   (a) Repairing German huts on HILL 63 for Bde. or Div. H.Q.

   (b) Repairing D.A.D.O.S. Store at LA CRECHE.

   (c) Repairing roof of Clean Clothing Stores on DE SEULE - NEUVE EGLISE Road.

4. **12th K.O.Y.L.I.**

   (a) One Coy. on roads PLOEGSTEERT - WARNETON, and communications South of this.

   (b) One Coy. maintaining road BAKERY Cross Roads to WARNETON and also repairing duckboard track from UNCIVIL POST to THATCHED COTTAGE, (U.15.c.4.9. to U.16.a.5.6.)

   (c) One Coy. maintaining and repairing road WHITE GATES to BAKERY Cross Roads.

5. ACKNOWLEDGE. (Field Coys. and K.O.Y.L.I. only.)

13/10/18.

Issued at 2000

Capt.R.E.
Adjt. for C.R.E. 31st Divsn.

Distribution :- Copy No 1. C.E. XV Corps.
2. 210 Field Coy.
3. 211 Field Coy.
4. 223 Field Coy.
5. 92 Inf. Bde.
6. 93 Inf. Bde.
7. 94 Inf. Bde.
8. 31 Div.'G'.
9. 31 Div.Arty.
10. 12 K.O.Y.L.I.
11. C.R.E.
12. Adjt.
13.) War Diary.
14.)
15. File.

SECRET.

Copy No. 13

31st Divisional Engineers.

OPERATION ORDER No. 38

In the event of an enemy retirement on the front of this Division, the following arrangements will be made for bridging the River LYS, and opening up the roads up to and forward of the River :-

1. 210th Field Company.R.E. and one Coy. of 12th Bn. K.O.Y.L.I. will co-operate in the Left Battalion Area (North of the SUGAR REFINERY), and will carry out the following work :-

   (a) Speedy erection of light bridges to take the Infantry across the river.

   (b) Repair of the bridge in U.12.d. to take first line transport, and if possible, 3-ton lorries.

   (c) Repair of the road through WARNETON.

   (d) Repair of the WARNETON - QUESNOY Road.

   (e) Reconnaissance of, and if necessary, work on other roads within the Divisional Area North of the WARNETON - QUESNOY Road.

   The 210 Field Coy. will carry out paras (a) and (b), and will ask the O.C. K.O.Y.L.I. Coy. for any assistance which may be required.

   The Coy. K.O.Y.L.I. will carry out paras (c), (d) and (e) and will give O.C. Field Coy. any assistance which he may require.

   O.C. Field Coy. and O.C. Coy. K.O.Y.L.I. will get into touch as early as possible to arrange details, and will reconnoitre forward camps in the neighbourhood of WARNETON.

2. 211th Field Company.R.E. and one Coy. 12th Bn. K.O.Y.L.I. will co-operate in the Right Battalion Area (South of the SUGAR REFINERY) and will carry out the following work :-

   (a) Speedy erection of light bridges to take the Infantry across the river.

   (b) Repair of the PONT ROUGE Bridge in U.29.b. to take 1st line transport, and if possible, 3-ton lorries.

   (c) Repair of the road U.23.a.8.9. - PONT ROUGE - QUESNOY.

   (d) Repair of bridge at U.30.b.2.4. to take 1st line Transport, and if possible, 3-ton lorries.

   (e) Repair of the road U.30.c.15.65. through DEULEMONT to the WARNETON - QUESNOY Road

   The 211 Field Coy. will carry out paras (a), (b) and (d), and will ask O.C. K.O.Y.L.I. Coy. for any assistance which may be required.

   The Coy.,K.O.Y.L.I. will carry out paras (c) and (e) and will give O.C. Field Coy. any assistance which he may require.

   O.C. Field Coy. and O.C. Coy.,K.O.Y.L.I. will get into touch as early as possible to arrange details, and will reconnoitre forward camps in the neighbourhood of PONT ROUGE.

3. 223 Field Coy. and one Coy. 12th Bn. K.O.Y.L.I. will be in reserve and will be ready to move at short notice.

4. 211 Field Coy. are making light Infantry bridges which will be kept at the Transport Lines at T.25.a.0.2.

P.T.O.

(2)

5. 210 and 211 Field Coys. will move their trestle wagons which are now at 211 Field Coy. Forward Camp to T.25.a.0.2. These will be unloaded, and the pontoons and equipment stacked near the road in wagon loads conveniently for re-packing.

6. 210 and 211 Field Coys. will each keep their three trestle wagons at T.25.a.0.2. unloaded and ready to move up bridging materials as required.

7. Wherever possible bridges over the LYS should be constructed at one side and clear of the original bridge, but this should not be done if it would involve considerable delay.

8. In the event of Divisional Headquarters moving forward, the C.R.E. will move to the present Bde. H.Q. at HYDE PARK CORNER. Urgent messages regarding operations will be sent to HYDE PARK CORNER. Pending arrival of C.R.E. the O.C. 223 Field Coy. will arrange to collect and forward any messages sent to HYDE PARK CORNER.

12th Battn. K.O.Y.L.I. are similarly moving forward their Headquarters to the PIGGERIES.

9. It is most important that both R.E. and K.O.Y.L.I. Companies should send in as early as possible any information which they may obtain regarding work to be done, progress of work, the general situation, etc.

10. The above order will be carried out on receipt of the message "Carry out R.E. Operation Order No. 38."

11. ACKNOWLEDGE. (Field Coys. and K.O.Y.L.I. only.)

R A Mansel

Major. R.E.

13/10/18.

Issued at 0000

A/C.R.E. 31st Division.

Distribution:- Copy No 1. 31 Div.'G'.
2. 31 Div.'Q'.
3. 92 Inf. Bde.
4. 93 Inf. Bde.
5. 94 Inf. Bde.
6. 210 Field Coy.
7. 211 Field Coy.
8. 223 Field Coy.
9. 12 K.O.Y.L.I.
10. C.R.E.
11. Adjt.
12)
13) War Diary.
14. File.

SECRET.   WAR DIARY   Copy No 7

61st Divisional Engineers.

OPERATION ORDER No 59.

Operations on our left may result in the Corps on our left pushing forward on to the Canal N.E. of WARNETON on the 14th inst.

In conjunction with this, 92 Bde. are undertaking, if possible, to form bridgeheads across the River LYS.

Os.C. 210 and 211 Field Coys. should keep in close touch with 92 Bde. with a view to erecting one or two light floating bridges after the bridgeheads are formed.

No more of this light bridging work should be done than is absolutely necessary, as if the operation results in an enemy retirement it will be necessary to carry on as quickly as possible with the remainder of R.E. Operation Order No 58, particularly as regards the bridges at WARNETON and PONT ROUGE, and the roads leading up to them.

Should the enemy retire 210th and 211th Field Coys. will each detail a party to search for, test, and notice board sources of supply of drinking water.

The dividing line between Companies for this purpose will be the WARNETON - QUESNOY Road, (QUESNOY inclusive to 211th Field Coy.)

One R.A.M.C. man is being sent to 211th Field Coy. to assist in this work.

ACKNOWLEDGE.

13/10/18.
Issued at 2000

Major.R.E.
A/C.R.E. 61st Division.

Distribution:- Copy No 1. 210 Field Coy.
2. 211 Field Coy.
3. 222 Field Coy.
4. 12 K.O.Y.L.I.
5. C.R.E.
6. Adjt.
7)
8) War Diary.
9. File.

SECRET.   Copy No. 14

R.E. INSTRUCTIONS No. 59.

Work for 17/10/18.

1. **210th Field Company.R.E. and 1 Coy. K.O.Y.L.I.** ('B' Company.)

   (a) Continue work on WARNETON Bridge and approaches.

   (b) Draw mine under road at V.19.central.

   (c) R.E. Party to search for, test, notice board, and report sources of water supply in the captured area North of the WARNETON - QUESNOY Road (excluding QUESNOY).

   (d) Supervise 2 Coys. of infantry working on the WARNETON - QUESNOY Road.
   These infantry will rendezvous at V.19.central at 1200.
   223rd Field Company.R.E. will deliver 50 picks and 350 shovels at V.19.central by 1100.
   O.C. 210th Field Company.R.E. will arrange to take over these tools.

   (e) K.O.Y.L.I. Coy. will supervise infantry party on the road (para 4) and any of this Coy. not required on the WARNETON Bridge can work on this road.

2. **211th Field Company.R.E. and 1 Coy. K.O.Y.L.I.** ('C' Company.)

   (a) Continue work on PONT ROUGE Bridge and approaches to it.

   (b) R.E. Party to search for, test, notice board, and report sources of water supply South of the WARNETON - QUESNOY Road (LE QUESNOY inclusive to 211th Field Coy.).

   (c) Party of K.O.Y.L.I. not required at bridge (at least 1 platoon) repairing the PONT ROUGE - LE QUESNOY Road.

   Note. O.C. 211th Field Coy.R.E. will report as early as possible on the bridges across the DEULE in LES ECLUSES and QUESNOY, giving full details.

3. **223rd Field Company.R.E.**

   (a) Supervising 1 Battalion of infantry on PLOEGSTEERT - WARNETON Road.
   Rendezvous at 1200 at LE GHEER U.21.d.7.0.
   O.C. 223rd Field Coy.R.E. will arrange tools.

   (b) Carting tools to V.19.central. (350 shovels, 50 picks).

   (c) Continue work on D.H.Q.

4. **1 Coy. K.O.Y.L.I.** ('D' Coy.).

   (a) Work on QUESNOY - LINSELLES road (QUESNOY inclusive) and report on this road.

(b) Reconnoitre and report on roads:-
   (i) LE BLATON W.15.c. - LA VIGNE E.9.a. to Div Boundary
      E.15.a.2.0.
  (ii) ST MARGUERITE - D.12.contral - E.13.a.

1°/10/18.

Issued at 2030.

                                                    Capt.R.E.

                    Adjt. for C.R.E. 31st Divn.

Distribution :- Copy No. 1. C.E. XV Corps.
                          2. 210 Field Coy.
                          3. 211 Field Coy.
                          4. 223 Field Coy.
                          5. 92 Inf. Bde.
                          6. 93 Inf. Bde.
                          7. 94 Inf. Bde.
                          8. 31 Div 'G'.
                          9. 31 Div. Arty.
                        10. 12 K.O.Y.L.I.
                        11. C.R.E.
                        12. Adjt.
                        13.)
                        14.) War Diary. ✓
                        15. File.

S E C R E T.   Copy No. 14

R.E. INSTRUCTIONS No. 66.
Work for 18/10/18.

1. **210th Field Company, R.E.**

   (a) Hand over WARNETON Bridge to 223rd Field Coy. R.E.

   (b) Reconnoitre billets near W.25.c. and move whole Coy. with its transport to this point.

   (c) Send forward one section to work on new D.H.Q. at CHATEAU DE LA CROIX, BLANCHE F.1.c.2.2.
   This section must be at the CHATEAU by 1100.
   One Coy. of infantry will report to 210th Field Coy.R.E. at
   (d) the CHATEAU at 1100.

   (d) Keep in close touch with G.O.C. 92nd Inf. Bde and reconnoitre forward with a view to opening up communications through TOURCOING

2. **211th Field Company, R.E.**

   (a) Move whole company including transport to some convenient part on S. side of River DEULE at QUESNOY.

   (b) Commence work on a bridge to take lorry traffic over the DEULE at QUESNOY. Work in shifts continuously till the bridge is finished.

   (c) Reconnoitre and report on the best lorry route from the PONT DE NIEPPE through ARMENTIERES to QUESNOY.

   (d) Leave a small party at PONT ROUGE to look after the PONT ROUGE Bridge and hand it over to 223rd Field Coy.R.E. when they arrive.

3. **223rd Field Company, R.E.**

   (a) Send 500 shovels to V.19.central to be there by 1100

   (b) Take over 210th Field Coy.R.E. Billets and transport lines at WARNETON.

   (c) Take over charge of WARNETON and PONT ROUGE Bridges.

   (d) Take charge of the WARNETON - PLOEGSTEERT and WARNETON - PONT ROUGE Roads with working party of 1 Battalion of infantry.

4. **12th K.O.Y.L.I.**

   (a) 1 Coy. Working on the WARNETON - QUESNOY Road and roads through QUESNOY.
   This Coy. will supervise 2 Battalion of infantry working on this road in accordance with the attached Working Party Table.
   O.C. 223rd Field Coy.R.E. is arranging to dump 500 shovels at V.19.central by 1100

   (b) 1 Coy.
   (i) Assisting 211th Field Coy.R.E. on approaches to lorry bridge over the River DEULE at QUESNOY.

   (ii) Repairing road QUESNOY (exclusive) - D.6.c.3.3.- W.26.d.3.3. - LA VIGNE.

   1 Coy.
   (i) Repairing road LA VIGNE - E.10.b.8.9. - E.23.b.7.2.

   (ii) Making good crater at BONDUES Church E.17.d.4.1.

   Continued.

5.   ACKNOWLEDGE. (Field Coys. and K.O.Y.L.I. only.)

[signature]

17/10/18.   Major. R.E.

Issued at 2100.   A/C.R.E. 31st Division.

    Distribution:- Copy No. 1. C.E. XV Corps.
                                      2. 210 Field Coy.
                                      3. 211 Field Coy.
                                      4. 223 Field Coy.
                                      5. 92nd Inf. Bde.
                                      6. 93rd Inf. Bde.
                                      7. 94th Inf. Bde.
                                      8. 31st Div 'G'.
                                      9. 31st Div. 'O'.
                                    10. 12th K.O.Y.L.I.
                                    11. 31st Div. Arty.
                                    12. C.R.E.
                                    13. Adjt.
                                    14.)
                                    15.) War Diary.
                                    16. File.

SECRET.   Copy No. 14

R.E. INSTRUCTIONS No. 61.

Work for 19/10/18.

1. **210th Field Company.R.E.**

   (a)   Keep in close touch with leading Brigade (92nd) and carry out any work required.

   (b)   Repair road culvert at A.14.b.3.4.

2. **211th Field Company.R.E.**

   (a)   Continue work on bridge to carry 'A' loads across the DEULE at QUESNOY.

   (b)   Send an officer to make a detailed report on the best site for a bridge to carry 'A' loads over the DEULE at WARBRECHIES, giving details regarding stores available etc.

3. **223rd Field Company.R.E.**

   (a)   Reconnoitre billets in the neighbourhood of CROIX BLANCHE, approx F.7. and move into them with whole company including transport.

   (b)   Leave a small party at PONT ROUGE and WARNETON bridges to hand over these bridges to C.R.E. Corps Troops who is sending 1 N.C.O. and 6 Sappers to each bridge to take them over.

4. **12th K.O.Y.L.I.**

   (a)   One company to assist 211th Field Coy.R.E. on bridge over River DEULE at QUESNOY and to repair the QUESNOY - PREVOTE Road.

   (b)   H.Qrs and 2 Companies to reconnoitre and move into billets in the area approx ~~F.15.a. and b.~~ L.9
   Before moving the company at BONDUES should repair the crater at BONDUES ~~and the cross roads at LA VIGNE~~.

5. ACKNOWLEDGE. (Field Coys and K.O.Y.L.I only).

                                                      R A Mansel
18/10/18   Major.R.E.

Issued at 2200   A/C.R.E. 31st Division.

   Distribution :-   Copy No. 1.C.E. XV Corps.
                             2.210 Field Coy.
                             3.211 Field Coy.
                             4.223 Field Coy.
                             5.92 Inf. Bde.
                             6.93 Inf. Bde.
                             7.94 Inf. Bde.
                             8.31st Div.'G'
                             9.31st Div.'Q'
                             10.12th K.O.Y.L.I.
                             11.31st Div. Arty.
                             12.C.R.E.
                             13.Adjt.
                             14)
                             15)War Diary.
                             16 File.

War Diary

SECRET.   Copy No. 14

R.E. INSTRUCTIONS No. 62.
Work for 20/10/18.

1. **210th Field Coy.R.E.**

   (a) Keep in close touch with 92 Brigade and carry out any urgent work required.

   (b) Construct bridge to carry wheeled tra[nsport] over Canal DE ROUBAIX at about A.29.d.

2. **211th Field Coy.R.E. and one company K.O.Y.L.I..**

   (a) Completing details to bridge at QUESNOY which is now through for traffic.

   (b) Coy.R.E. move with transport to point East of Canal at about L.3.
   Coy. K.O.Y.L.I. reconnoitre and move into billets at about L.9., near present K.O.Y.L.I. Headquarters.

   (c) R.E. and K.O.Y.L.I. improve bridge at L.8.a.5.7. to take 'A' loads and reconnoitre and commence bridge to take wheeled transport.

3. **223rd Field Coy.R.E..**

   (a) Make two bridges across the canal in F.17.d. to take all classes of traffic.

   (b) Reconnoitre canal between A.13.d. and A.20.a. with a view to constructing a bridge to take horsed transport and commence construction as early as possible.

4. **12th K.O.Y.L.I.**

   (a) **1 Company.**
   (i) Move into the area A.27. and select billets there.

   (ii) Send Officer to report to R.E. Officer of 210th Field Coy.R.E. at bridge at A.28.c.3.4. at 0830 for instructions regarding work.
   Remainder of the Coy. will be at A.28.c.3.4. at 1000 to commence work.
   No tools will be required.

   (b) **1 Company.**
   (i) Reconnoitring and clearing roads from bridge at L.8.a.5.3. to LANNOY.
   Work is required particularly at L.9.a.1.6. where the railway bridge has been dropped onto the road.

   (c) **1 Company.**
   (i) Assisting 211th Field Coy.R.E. on bridges at L.8.a.5.3. and QUESNOY.
   This Coy. will move up from QUESNOY to billets near present K.O.Y.L.I. Headquarters.

5. ACKNOWLEDGE. (Field Coys and K.O.Y.L.I. only).

19/10/18.

Issued at 2200.

[signature]
Major.R.E.
A/C.R.E. 31st Division.

Distribution :-   Copy No. 1. C.E. XV Corps.
                            2. 210th Field Coy.R.E.
                            3. 211th Field Coy.R.E.
                            4. 223rd Field Coy.R.E.
                            5. 92nd Inf. Bde.
                            6. 93rd Inf. Bde.
                            7. 94th Inf. Bde.
                            8. 31st Div. 'G'.
                            9. 31st Div. 'Q'.
                           10. 12th K.O.Y.L.I.
                           11. 31st Div Arty.
                           12. C.R.E.
                           13. Adjt.
                           14.)
                           15.) War Diary.
                           16. File.

<u>223rd Field Company.R.E.</u> (continued).

Add to previous instructions para

(c)   Send one section to keep in close touch with Right Brigade (93rd Bde).
      This section will carry out any immediate work which the Brigade may require and forward   all information obtained to O.C. 223rd Field Coy.R.E.
      (93rd Brigade are at present in LANNOY.

SECRET.   Copy No. 10

R.E. INSTRUCTIONS No. 63.
Work for 21/10/18.

1. **210th Field Company.R.E. and 1 Coy. K.O.Y.L.I.**

   (a) Complete bridge at A.29.d.7.3.

   (b) Commence bridge at B.21.c.7.1. to take 3 ton lorries.

   (c) Repair road TOURCOING - WATTRELOS - LEERS for lorry traffic.

2. **211th Field Company.R.E.**

   (a) Move in accordance with attached order.

   (b) Detail party to search for, test, notice board and report sources of water supply within the Divisional Area East of the North and South Grid Line between A.G. and B.H.

   (c) Commence making oil drum or petrol tin bridge for light briding operations.

3. **223rd Field Company.R.E.**

   (a) Move in accordance with attached order.

   (b) Complete bridge at A.26.a.5.5. to take 3 ton lorries.

   (c) Carry out as early as possible a reconnaissance of L'ESCAUT between WARCOING and PECQ (both inclusive) with a view to ascertaining damage done to existing bridges and best sites for temporary bridges.

4. **12th K.O.Y.L.I.**

   (a) 1 Company.
   (i) Assisting 210th Field Coy.R.E. on TOURCOING - WATTRELOS - LEERS Road and on bridges at A.29.d. and B.21.c.

   (b) H.Q.rs and 2 Companies move to area about G.10. 11. 16 in accordance with attached instructions.

   1 Company.
   (i) Reconnoitre and clear road LANNOY - NECHIN - ESTAIMBOURG - PECQ.

   1 Company.   clear
   (i) Reconnoitre and/road G.8.b.8.6. - G.3.d.3.9. - LEERS - LEERS NORD - B.22.d.9.6. - C.25.a.4.7. - WARCOING.
   This road is at present blocked at G.3.d.3.9. by railway bridge debris.

5. ACKNOWLEDGE. (Field Coys and K.O.Y.L.I. only).

20/10/18.

Issued at 2100

Major.R.E.
A/C.R.E. 31st Division.

Distribution :- Copy No. 1. C.E. XV Corps
2. 210th Field Coy.R.E.
3. 211th Field Coy.R.E.
4. 223rd Field Coy.R.E.
5. 92nd Inf. Bde.
6. 93rd Inf. Bde.
7. 94th Inf. Bde.
8. 31st Div. 'G'.
9. 31st Div. 'Q'.
10. 12th K.O.Y.L.I
11. 31st Div. Arty.
12. C.R.E.
13. Adjt.
14.)
15.) War Diary.
16. File.

SECRET.   Copy No. -- 14

R.E. INSTRUCTIONS NO. 64
Work for 22/10/18.

1. **210th Field Company.R.E. and One Coy. K.O.Y.L.I.** working in conjunction.

   (a) Move to the vicinity of LEERS NORD.

   (b) Prepare material and make forward dumps with a view to constructing a lorry bridge over the L'ESCAUT at PECQ.

2. **211th Field Company.R.E.**

   (a) Collecting light bridging materials and bringing forward bridging equipment from the PONT ROUGE Bridge.

3. **223rd Field Company.R.E.**

   (a) Move sections with section transport forward to area about H.8.,9.,14.,15.,.

   (b) Stand by for putting a Weldon Trestle and Pontoon Bridge across L'ESCAUT River.
       Keeping in close touch with advanced Brigade (93rd Bde.) so as to be able to commence work as soon as the situation permits.
       One Coy of K.O.Y.L.I. will work in conjunction with 223rd Field Coy.R.E.

   (c) One section attached to 93rd Bde. to assist in getting the infantry across the river L'ESCAUT by light bridging.

4. **12th K.O.Y.L.I.**

   (a) One company now at NECHIN to assist forward Brigade in light Bridging Operation as required.
       When light bridging is completed this Coy. will stand by ready to assist in bridging operations.

   (b) One Coy. working in conjunction with 211th Field Coy. and moving tomorrow 22nd to the vicinity of LEERS NORD.

   (c) One Coy. will move tomorrow 22nd to area about H.8.,9.,14.,15. and stand by to assist 223rd Field Coy.R.E. in bridging operations.

                                                    R.A.F. Mansel.
                                                        Major.R.E.
21/10/18.
Issued at 2030.   A/C.R.E. 31st Division.

Distribution :-   Copy No. 1. C.E. XV Corps.
                           2. 210th Field Coy.R.E.
                           3. 211th Field Coy.R.E.
                           4. 223rd Field Coy.R.E.
                           5. 92nd Inf. Bde.
                           6. 93rd Inf. Bde.
                           7. 94th Inf. Bde.
                           8. 31st Div. 'G'.
                           9. 31st Div. 'Q'.
                          10. 12th K.O.Y.L.I.
                          11. 31st Div. Arty.
                          12. C.R.E.
                          13. Adjt.
                          14.) War Diary.
                          15.)
                          16. File.

SECRET. *War Diary* Copy.No. 14

R.E. INSTRUCTIONS No. 65.

Work for 23/10/18.

1. **210th Field Company,R.E. and 1 Coy. K.O.Y.L.I.**

   (a) Continue forming dump of bridging materials at H.10.a.&.9. with transport as under.
   - 3 Coy. Trestle Wagons.
   - 3 lorries.
   - 1 Box car.
) Reporting at factory A.18.a.9.2. at 0900

2. **211th Field Company.R.E.**

   (a) Throughly overhaul, clean and repair Trestle Wagons and bridging equipment and when completed hand over to 223rd Field Coy.R.E.

3. **223rd Field Company.R.E.**

   (a) Stand by for bridging work on the River L'ESCAUT.

4. **12th K.O.Y.L.I.**

   (a) One Coy. assisting 210th Field Coy.R.E. forming forward dump.

   (b) Two Coys. standing by for bridging work on River L'ESCAUT.

5. ACKNOWLEDGE. (Field Coys and K.O.Y.L.I. only.).

22/10/18.

Issued at 1900.

R A Hansel
Major.R.E.
A/C.R.E. 31st Division.

Distribution:- Copy No.
1. C.E. XV Corps.
2. 210th Field Coy.R.E.
3. 211th Field Coy.R.E.
4. 223rd Field Coy.R.E.
5. 92nd Inf. Bde.
6. 93rd Inf. Bde.
7. 94th Inf. Bde.
8. 31st Div. 'G'.
9. 31st Div. 'Q'.
10. 12th K.O.Y.L.I.
11. 31st Div. Arty.
12. C.R.E.
13. Adjt.
14.) War Diary.
15.)
16. File.

SECRET.   *War Diary*   Copy No. 12

31st Divisional Engineers.

OPERATION ORDER No. 41.

Moves will be carried out as under:-

1. **211th Field Coy. R.E.**

    Move tomorrow 25th inst. to CUERNE via AELBEKE - MARCK - and bridge at G.36.a.5.3. Coy. will march independently via bridge at A.29.a. to WATTRELOS (A.16.d.6.4.), head of column will reach A.16.d.6.4. at 1110. and join 92nd Brigade at this point.
    Billeting party should be sent on ahead to report to 92 Bde. H.Q.
    223rd Field Coy. R.E. will arrange to return 211th Field Coy. R.E. Pontoon Wagons by 0800. (See 223rd Field Coy. R.E. Order.)

2. **210th Field Coy. R.E.**

    Move tomorrow to MOUSCRON via WATTRELOS. Head of column will cross bridge in A.29.d. at 1200. Billeting parties should be sent in advance to report to 94th Bde H.Q.
    1 Trestle wagon will be sent to MECHIN tomorrow morning to take over 2 Weldon Trestles with superstructure and equipment from 223rd Field Coy. R.E.

3. **223rd Field Company. R.E.**

    Will probably move to MOUSCRON about the 27th inst. after handing over to Field Coy. R.E. 40th Division.

4. <u>Bridging Equipment will be dealt with as under.</u>

    (a) 2 Weldon Trestles with equipment complete will be handed over to 210th Field Coy. R.E. tomorrow morning 25th inst.

    (b) 1 Trestle Wagon of 211th Field Coy. R.E. will be loaded with 2 Weldon Trestles and equipment complete, remaining 2 trestles will be unloaded. These 3 vehicles will be sent by 223rd Field Coy. R.E. to G.11.a.3.1. and handed over to 211th Field Coy. R.E. by 0800 tomorrow 25th inst.

    (c) 1 Pontoon with superstructure and equipment will be dumped at 223rd Field Coy. R.E. Horse Lines and subsequently handed over to Field Coy. R.E. of 40th Division.

    (d) The remainder of bridging equipment (2 Weldon Trestles and superstructure, 1 pontoon and) will be taken by 223rd Field Coy. R.E. when they move.

5. **12th K.O.Y.L.I.**

    All 3 Coys. will be concentrated tomorrow the 25th inst. in LANNOY and LYS, as near as possible to present H.Q. of 12th K.O.Y.L.I.

6. **Pontoon Equipment.**

    The pontoon equipment of Field Coys. R.E. will probably be completed by taking 5 pontoons out of bridge N.E. of COURTRAI in H.21.b.and d.
    Further orders will be issued about this.

24/10/18.

Issued at 2330.

Major. R.E.
A/C.R.E. 31st Division.

Distribution:- Copy No. 1. 31st Div. 'G'.
                          2. 31st Div. 'Q'.
                          3. 92nd Inf. Bde.
                          4. 93rd Inf. Bde.
                          5. 94th Inf. Bde.
                          6. 210th Field Coy.R.E.
                          7. 211th Field Coy.R.E.
                          8. 223rd Field Coy.R.E.
                          9. 12th K.O.Y.L.I.
                         10. C.R.E.
                         11. Adjt.
                         12.)
                         13.) War Diary.
                         14. File.

SECRET   Copy No. 16

War Diary

R.E. INSTRUCTIONS No. 66.   Work for 29-10-18.

1. **210th Field Company. R.E.**

   (a) Dismantle Pontoon Bridge, H.21.c.60.
   Lay out stores for Companies in accordance with F.S.Manual, by 1100 as under:-

211th Field Co. R.E.	No.1. Pontoon Wagon.
	No.2. " "
223rd Field Co. R.E.	No.1. Pontoon Wagon.
	No.2. " "
	Trestle Wagon.

   Balance of stores will be loaded on 210th Field Co. Wagons and list of deficiencies sent into this office by 4 p.m.

   (b) Repair Baths at I.20.d.4.2.

   (c) Patrol Bridges over River LYS.

2. **211th Field Company. R.E.**

   (a) Send two Trestle Wagons to H.21.c.60. at 1100 to take over Pontoon Equipment. Report all deficiencies in Bridging Equipment to this office by 4 p.m.

   (b) Withdraw party from Bridge H.21.c.60.

   (c) Examine and deal with mines at VICHTE STATION.

   (d) Arrange to have light infantry footbridges dumped as under:-
   One Bridge 130ft long, with forward section at VICHTE.
   Two Bridges, each 130 ft long at 31st Divisional R.E.Dump, which is being formed tomorrow in the Corps Dump at I.20.d.4.2.

3. **223rd Field Company. R.E.**

   (a) Send three Trestle Wagons to H.21.c.60. at 1100 to take over Pontoon Equipment. Report all deficiencies in Bridging Equipment to this office by 4 p.m.

   (b) Prepare materials for plank roads, and dump same in 31st Divisional R.E.Dump, which is being formed tomorrow in the Corps Dump at I.20.d.4.2.

   (c) Give R.S.M.Holloway any assistance required in constructing shelters for the Dump Staff, and in moving stores into new 31st Divisional R.E.Dump, I.20.d.4.2.

4. **12th K.O.Y.L.I.**

   (a) One Coy working on road DEERLYCK - VICHTE - INGOYGHEM.

   This Coy should reconnoitre for billets in the area about I.15,16,17, 22,23, and if accomodation can be found should move into this area.

   (b) One Coy working on road STACEGHEM - STEENBRUGGE - I.20.d.62 - VICHTE.

   (c) One Coy working on road H.27.d.99 - STACEGHEM - HARLEBEKE.

   NOTE. Work required on above roads is :-
   (a) Dig out ditches.
   (b) Repair shell holes as far forward as possible.
   (c) Where water can lie in pools, drain off into the ditches.
   On no account should the mud be cleared off between the Pavé and the ditches. There is no metalling on this part of the road, and the

(2)

removal of the mud only results in the pave being left standing above the general level of the road.

5. ACKNOWLEDGE. (Field Coys and K.O.Y.L.I. only.)

[signature]
Major. R.E.
A/C.R.E. 31st Division.

28-10-18.

Issued at 2200.

Distribution :- Copy No. 1. C.E. XV Corps.
2. 210th Field Co. R.E.
3. 211th Field Co. R.E.
4. 223rd Field Co. R.E.
5. 92nd Inf. Bde.
6. 93rd Inf. Bde.
7. 94th Inf. Bde.
8. 31st Div. 'G'.
9. 31st Div. 'Q'.
10. 12th K.O.Y.L.I.
11. 31st Div. Arty.
12. C.R.E.
13. Adjt.
14.) War Diary.
15.)
16. File.

SECRET.   Copy No. 14

War Diary

R.E. INSTRUCTIONS. No. 67

Work for 30-10-18.

1. 210TH FIELD COMPANY. R.E.

   (a) Dismantle Pontoon Bridge at B.30.b.9.3. Deficiencies in Bridging Equipment of all three Field Companies will be replaced from this Bridge and the balance of stores will be moved tomorrow, 30th inst by 210th Field Coy. R.E. to 31st Divisional R.E. Dump at I.20.d.2.2.

   (b) Repair Baths at I.20.d.2.2.

   (c) Move all broken parts of Bridging Equipment, (including broken peices of Weldon Trestles) from H.21.b.6.0. to I.20.d.2.2.

2. 211TH FIELD COMPANY. R.E.

   (a) Send Wagons at 1100, to Pontoon Bridge at B.30.b.9.3. and draw stores to make up any deficiencies in Bridging Equipment.

   (b) Continue preparing and practicing with light infantry footbridges.

3. 223RD FIELD COMPANY. R.E.

   (a) Send Wagons at 1100 to Pontoon Bridge at B.30.b.9.3. and draw stores to make up any deficiencies in Bridging Equipment.

   (b) Continue work at 31st Divisional R.E. Dump. I.20.d.4.2.

4. 12TH. K.O.Y.L.I.

   Continue work as in R.E.Instructions. No. 66.

5. ACKNOWLEDGE. (Field Companies and K.O.Y.L.I. only)

29-10-18.

Issued at _____

R.O.Mansell.
Major.R.E.
A/C.R.E. 31st Division.

Distribution:- Copy No.1. C.E. 2nd Corps.
                         2. 210th Field Co. R.E.
                         3. 211th Field Co. R.E.
                         4. 223rd Field Co. R.E.
                         5. 92nd Inf.Bde.
                         6. 93rd Inf.Bde.
                         7. 94th Inf.Bde.
                         8. 31st Div.'G'.
                         9. 31st Div.'Q'.
                        10. 12th K.O.Y.L.I.
                        11. 31st Div.Arty.
                        12. C.R.E.
                        13. Adjt.
                        14.) War Diary.
                        15.)
                        16. File.

Index

SUBJECT.

No.	Contents.	Date.

(23,360). Wt.28,121—60. 2000. 9/17. Gp.132. A.&E.W.
(26,250). ,, 10,082—13. 5000. 12/17. ,, ,,

CONFIDENTIAL.

WAR DIARY

of

Headquarters, 31st Divisional Engineers.

From 1/11/18 to 30/11/18.

VOLUME XXXV

Army Form C. 2118.

WAR DIARY
or
INTELLIGENCE SUMMARY.
(Erase heading not required.)

Original

Month of November 1918

Instructions regarding War Diaries and Intelligence Summaries are contained in F. S. Regs., Part II. and the Staff Manual respectively. Title pages will be prepared in manuscript.

Place	Date	Hour	Summary of Events and Information	Remarks and references to Appendices
COURTRAI	1st		Infantry make a further advance to R. L'ESCAUT without opposition. 211 Sel. G/RE keep in touch with advancing Bde. No any necessary work. AUSTRIA sign an armistice.	
	2nd		31st Div is being relieved by 41st French Div. 94 Bde (front line) handed over during last night.	
HALLUIN	3rd		Division moved back to ROUNCQ - HALLUIN area. D.H.Q opens at ROUNCQ. R.E.H.Q all three Fld. Coys & Pioneer Battalion at HALLUIN.	
	4th 5th		Divisional conference. Training programme drawn up. Capt. ELKINGTON returns from leave. Warning orders received to be prepared to move forward. C.R.E visits C. Engrs. Corps & C.R.E. 16th Div. to obtain information concerning the SCHELDT at AVELGHEM and the supply of bridging material.	
	6th		223 Fld. Coy moves forward to STEEN'S'RUGGER & 210 Fld Coy to COURTRAI to commence preparing improved bridging material. 211 Fld Coy remains in HALLUIN. R. Fusrs Coys take over fatigues from the other 2 Companies & stand by for hurrying.	
	7th		Construction of light bridging material continues. Demarcation of new avant postes Fells at Mouske at 8 p.m. 92nd Bde relieved a Bde of 30th Div. in the line on the QUEGHEM front. See Place list. 31st/11; now R. Div. of 15th Corps.	

WAR DIARY
or
INTELLIGENCE SUMMARY.
(Erase heading not required.)

Army Form C. 2118.

Place	Date	Hour	Summary of Events and Information	Remarks and references to Appendices
SWEVEGHEM	8th		D.H.Q. moved forward from HALLUIN to SWEVEGHEM. 210 Fd. Co. 2nd section forward to KATTESTRAAT, 211 Fd. Co. 1 section to O.2. central, & 223 Fd Co. 1 section to OOTEGHEM. Transport of bridging material to forward billets commenced. D.O. No 483 received. Field news received of German withdrawal from L'ESCAUT. 210th & 223rd Fd. Cos moved up at dusk to billets.	
	9th		Other respective advanced sections Bridging equipment concentrated at OOTEGHEM. Footbridge pushed across the river at RUGGE and pontoon bridge built. 7a/ 7b passing over at 6.30 p.m. 210 & 223 Fd. Cos. left moved to RUGGE. 211th Fd Co. march from HALLUIN to SWEVEGHEM and are taken on by lorry to SWEVEGHEM. LT PARTRIDGE and convoy of lorries taking up bridging material from STEEN BRUGGE to the RUGGE bridge approach road.	
RUYEN.	10th		D.H.Q. moves across the river and billets for the night at RUYEN. 211/12 Fd. Co. move up to MOIGNIES. 210/15 to ORROIR. 1 Sect. to work on roads. 223rd Fd Co. remain at RUGGE bridge and start operating light lorry material. News received that the Armistice is signed.	
RENAIX	11th		D.H.Q. moved to RENAIX. Authorgraphic censation by eurhernies. Hostilities	

WAR DIARY
or
INTELLIGENCE SUMMARY

Army Form C. 2118.

Place	Date	Hour	Summary of Events and Information	Remarks and references to Appendices
RENAIX	12th		Ceased at 11 a.m. 92nd Inf. Bde. now occupying defence line on R. SAMBRE. 210th & 211th Fld. Coys. both move up into RENAIX	
	13th		Orders received that no troops are to move further East. 210th Fld. Co. who had started for EVERBECQ turned back. Division is not to proceed to Germany. Bde. is to be moved to an area further W.	
	14th		Lt. Col. Giles returns from 2 months leave in England. Concerts and football matches. Interpreters deposits for 117TH DLOT PLATGE. 210th Fld. Co. moves into 93rd Bde group STAVELGHEM area. 211th Fld. Co. remaining behind is confined. Bridge at 29/X.17.B.2.6.	
LAUWE	15th		D.H.Q. moves to POTTELBERG, R.E. Hd. Qrs. to LAUWE. 210th & 223rd Fld. Coys. both move into LAUWE	
	16th		C.R.E. inspects bridge in course of construction by 211th Fld. Co. at X.17.B.2.6. Meeting held at D.H.Q. with a view to commencing competitions in football, boxing, cross country running etc. Capt. Ingham, 210th Fld. Co. attending as R.E. representative	
	17th		Special Thanksgiving Parade Service for Fld. Coys. and Pnr. Bn.: Held at LAUWE.	

Army Form C. 2118.

WAR DIARY
or
INTELLIGENCE SUMMARY.
(Erase heading not required.)

Instructions regarding War Diaries and Intelligence Summaries are contained in F.S. Regs., Part II. and the Staff Manual respectively. Title pages will be prepared in manuscript.

Place	Date	Hour	Summary of Events and Information	Remarks and references to Appendices
LAUWE.	19th		C.R.E.'s conference held, attended by all Fd. Co. Commanders. Programme of work discussed and preparations for ceremonial parade and inspection by G.O.C.	
	20th		211th Fd. Co. move from RENAIX to AVELGHEM area. C.R.E. attends conference at D.H.Q. Agenda Education Scheme & general programme of work.	
	21st		211th Fd. Co. move into LAUWE.	
	22nd		Divisional Education Officer relieved to all Fd. Coys on demobilisation. Warning order for move to St Omer area received.	
	23rd		223rd Fd. Co. move off with 93rd Bde. Group and proceed to MENIN area	
	24th		210th " " " " 94 " " " " " " "	
			93rd Bde. Group move on to YPRES.	
STOMER	25th		Dismounted portion of R.E. Hd. Qrs. move by lorry to STOMER. Road party and 211th Fd. Co. from 92nd Bde. Group & move to MENIN 94 to YPRES	
			93 KADEELE	
	26th		223 move into final billets in ARCQUES. 94 & 92 Bde. Groups still en route	
	29th		210th Fd. Co. move to ZUDANSQUES. 211 and road party of R.E.Hd. Qrs. into St Omer	

E.B. Blackburn Capt-?
for C.R.E. 31st Div.

31st Divisional Engineers Operation Order No 46.

MOVE of R.E. HD. QRS.

1. R.E. Hd. Qrs. will move on Monday, the 25th inst to the ST. OMER area.

2. For the purpose of the move, men will be divided into two groups :-

   (a) Those proceeding by road. This party will be in charge of R.S.M. HOLLOWAY, and will move with the remainder of D.H.Q. transport, and will be fed by the 92nd Bde. Group throughout.
   Further particulars regarding this party - its starting point and time of starting will be issued later separately to R.S.M. HOLLOWAY.

   (b) Those proceeding by lorry.

3. Parties are composed as follows :-

   (a) R.S.M. HOLLOWAY.   (b) Adjt.
       S/Cpl. MELLOR.   Stores Officer.
       Spr. WALDRON.   L/Cpl. LUNN.
       "   GRAHAM.   Spr. BILLCLIFFE.
       "   BRADLEY.   "   RHODES.
       "   INGRAM.   "   HARRIS.
       "   BAKER.   "   KERR.
       "   McMANUS.   Dvr. DODD.
       Pnr. CROWTHER.   "   BASHAM.
       Dvr. BELL.   Pte. SHEPHERD.
       Dvr. SIMPSON.
       Dvr. DICKENS.   Car - C.R.E.

          12   11

4. Rations will be drawn in accordance with the attached table.

23/11/18.

Lt.Col.R.E.
C.R.E. 31st Division.

Distribution :- Copy No 1. 31 Div. 'G'.
                       2. 31 Div. 'Q'.
                       3. 31 Div. Train.
                       4. Camp Commandant.
                       5. C.R.E.
                       6. Adjt.
                       7. R.S.M. HOLLOWAY.
                       8)
                       9) War Diary.
                      10. File.

Rations for consumption.	Drawn by.	From whom.	Where.	For whom.
24th.	C.R.E's Limber.	94th Bde. Group.	LAUWE.	R.E. Hd. Qrs.
25th.	Camp Commandant.	92nd Bde. Group.	MARKE.	(a) party.
25th.	Lorry.	" "	"	(b) party.
26th & 27th.				
26th.	Camp Commandant.	92nd Bde. Group.	YPRES Grand Place.	(a) party.
27th.	Camp Commandant.	92nd Bde. Group.	ABEELE.	(a) party.
28th.	Div. Train.	93rd " "	ARCQUES Square.	(b) party.
28th.	Camp Commandant.	92nd Bde. Group.	1½ miles S.W. of HAVINGHOVE Station, on the ARCQUES - CASSEL Road.	(a) party.
29th.	Div. Train.	93rd " "	ARCQUES Square.	(b) party.
29th.				
30th.	Camp Commandant.	92nd Bde. Group.	ARQUES Square.	(a) party.
30th.	Div. Train.	93rd Bde. "	ARQUES Square.	(b) party.
Dec.1st.	C.R.E's Limber.	93rd Bde. Group.	ARCQUES Square.	(a) & (b) parties.
30th.				

WAR DIARY

Copy No 9

R.E. INSTRUCTIONS No 71.

1. Following will be programme of working hours until after G.O.C's inspection on Thursday, 28th November.

   7-30 - 8.   Physical Drill and free gymnastics.
   8.   Breakfasts.
   9 - 10.   Ceremonial Drill.
   10-30 - 2-30. On works.
   2-45.   Dinners.

   No work on Sunday, and drill and clean-up Saturday morning with dinners at 1 p.m.

2. After G.O.C's inspection hours will be as follows :-

   7-30 - 8.   Physical Drill and free gymnastics.
   8.   Breakfasts.
   9 - 1.   On works.
   1-15.   Dinners.

   On Sundays Church Parade only.

F. Giles.
Lt.Col.R.E.
C.R.E. 31st Division.

HEADQUARTERS,
81st
DIVISIONAL ENGINEERS.
No.
Date 19/11/18.

Distribution:- Copy No 1. 210 Field Coy.
               2. 211 Field Coy.
               3. 223 Field Coy.
               4. 31 Div.'G'.
               5. 31 Div.'Q'.
               6. C.E. XIX Corps.
               7. C.R.E.
               8. Adjt.
               9.) War Diary.
               10.)
               11. File.

SECRET.   Copy No 7

R.E. INSTRUCTIONS No.70.

Work for 12/11/18.

1. 210th Field Company.R.E. and one Coy. K.O.Y.L.I. will move forward tomorrow to work in conjunction with one another on roads within the Divisional area East of QUATRE VENTS, S.11.a. Reconnaissance and reports should be made on all roads within the Divisional area with a view to selecting the best forward roads. Very steep gradients should be noted in the "Remarks" column.

2. Div. area is between lines running E and W through S.1.central and S.19.c.0.0.

3. 210th Field Coy. and the Coy. of K.O.Y.L.I. moving forward will arrange billets in conjunction with forward Brigade in the neighbourhood of EVERBECQ, U.9.a. Forward Brigade H.Q. are at EVERBECQ.

4. Remainder of R.E. and K.O.Y.L.I. will stand fast in their present billets.

5. Moves will not be commenced before 10 a.m.
   Owing to steep gradients it is recommended that Units concerned should move into forward area via. NEDERBRAKEL and PARICKE.

6. 210 Field Coy. at the conclusion of the move will send its bridging vehicles to be temporarily attached to 211 Field Coy. These can be used for taking up rations to 210 Field Coy. until they are sent to fetch bridging equipment from RUGGE.

7. ACKNOWLEDGE.(Field Coys. and K.O.Y.L.I. only.)

> HEADQUARTERS,
> 81ST
> DIVISIONAL ENGINEERS.
> 11/11/18.
> Date.........

                                                        Major.R.E.
                                          A/C.R.E. 81st Division.

Copies to :- No 1 210 Field Coy.
             2. 211 Field Coy.
             3. 222 Field Coy.
             4. 12 K.O.Y.L.I.
             5. C.R.E.
             6. Adjt.
             7.)
             8.) War Diary.
             9. File.

SECRET.
=========

Copy No 14

R.E. INSTRUCTIONS No. 69.

210th Field Company. R.E.

1. Move tomorrow, 11th inst. to RENAIX.

2. Keep in close touch with I.e. in the line and, if required, attach a section to them.

3. Reconnoitre, report on, and carry out necessary work on roads within Divisional Area East of S.11.a.4.3. (sheet 30) If any assistance is required in repairing roads apply direct to O.C. 12th K.O.Y.L.I. at RENAIX.

4. Send bridging vehicles to be at RUGGE Brudge at 1200 to collect light bridging materials.

5. Inform 211 Field Coy. of point at which you wish light bridging material to be dumped.

211th Field Company. R.E.

1. Move tomorrow, 11th inst. to neighbourhood of RENAIX.

2. Continue work in conjunction with 12th K.O.Y.L.I. on road AMOUGIES - RENAIX - S.11.a.4.3. (sheet 30)

3. Send bridging vehicles one journey to RUGGE Bridge (P.36.c.5.4. sheet 29) at 1200 to draw light bridging materials from 223 Field Coy. and take them forward to 210 Field Coy. billet in RENAIX.

223rd Field Company. R.E.

1. Collect and repair all light bridging materials within reach and dump them at P.36.c.5.4. (sheet 29) and hand them over to 210 and 211 Field Coys. tomorrow 11th inst. Report surplus not drawn to this office by 2 p.m.

2. Provide bridge guard for medium pontoon bridge and deviation at RUGGE.

3. Report progress of heavy bridge and deviation at RUGGE daily to this office by 4 p.m.

4. As soon as heavy bridge at RUGGE and deviation to it are complete, dismantle the medium bridge and its deviation and stack material at P.36.c.5.4.   *on the E side*

12th K.O.Y.L.I.

1. H.Q. and 3 Coys. move tomorrow, 11th inst. to RENAIX.

2. Work in conjunction with 211 Field Coy. on road AMOUGIES - RENAIX - S.11.a.4.3. (sheet 30)

3. Give assistance if asked for by 210 Field Coy. in work on roads East of S.11.a.4.3. (sheet 30)

4. Reconnoitre and report on roads within the Divisional area between AMOUGIES and S.11.a.4.3. excluding the main AMOUGIES - RENAIX - S.11.a.4.3. Road.

NOTE. Companies reporting on the main AMOUGIES - RENAIX - S.11.a.4.3. road and the best forward roads East of S.11.a.4.3. will send in a report daily on this road to reach this office by 4 p.m.

ACKNOWLEDGE. (Field Coys. and K.O.Y.L.I. only.)

10/11/18.

Capt. for Major. R.E.
A/C.R.E. 31st Division.

SECRET.

War Diary

Copy No 13

R.E. INSTRUCTIONS No 68.

210th Field Company.R.E. and 'C' Coy. 12th K.O.Y.L.I.

(1) Preparation and transport to forward positions of 2 light bridges each 120 feet long and 16 bivouac sheet boats for Right Battalion. All arrangements to be made in co-operation with 92 Bde. and Right Battalion.

(2) Reconnaissance and report on river in Right Battn. area.

(3) Reconnaissance of and report on roads within the Divisional area S.E. of line P.19.central - P.14.central, and of line P.14.a.0.0. - P.21.central - P.34.a.7.9.
Any urgent work on these roads to be carried out.

223rd Field Company.R.E. and 'B' Coy. 12th K.O.Y.L.I.

(1) Preparation and transport to forward positions of 2 light bridges each 120 feet long and 16 bivouac sheet boats for Left Battalion. All arrangements to be made in conjunction with 92 Bde. and Left Battalion.

(2) Reconnaissance and report on river in Left Battalion area.

(3) Reconnaissance of and report on roads within the Divisional area S.E. of line P.19.central - P.14.central and of the line P.14.a.0.0. - P.21.central - P.34.a.7.9.
Any urgent work on these roads to be carried out.

211th Field Company.R.E.

Preparation of materials for making plank roads at the STEENBRUGGE Dump.

'D' Coy. 12th K.O.Y.L.I.

Reconnaissance of and report on all roads within the Divisional area between the line P.19.central - P.14.central and the COURTRAI - BOSSUYT Canal.
Any urgent work on those roads to be carried out.

ACKNOWLEDGE. (Field Coys. and K.O.Y.L.I. only.)

HEADQUARTERS,
31ST
DIVISIONAL ENGINEERS.

No.
Date. 8/11/18.

R.A.Mansel
Major R.E.
C.R.E. 31st Division.

Distribution :- Copy No 1. C.E. XIX Corps.
2. 210 Field Coy.
3. 211 Field Coy.
4. 223 Field Coy.
5. 92 Inf. Bde.
6. 93 Inf. Bde.
7. 94 Inf. Bde.
8. 31 Div.'G'.
9. 31 Div.'Q'.
10. 12th K.O.Y.L.I.
11. C.R.E.
12. Adjt.
13.)
14.) War Diary.
15. File.

SECRET.   Copy No 8

51st Divisional Engineers Operation Order No 44.

1. Moves will be carried out as under :-

    (a) 210 Field Coy.R.E. will send forward one section tomorrow, 8th inst. to arrange with 88 Bde. for billets in the forward area. The 210 Field Coy. will move into these billets on the morning of the 9th inst.

    (b) 223 Field Coy.R.E. will send forward one section tomorrow, 8th inst. to arrange with 88 Bde. for billets in the forward area. The 223 Field Coy. will move into these billets on the morning of 9th inst.

    (c) 211 Field Coy. will send forward one section tomorrow 8th inst. to STACEGHEM to occupy billets now held by one section 223 Field Coy. On morning of 9th inst. 211 Field Coy. will occupy billets now held by 223 Field Coy. in STACEGHEM.

    (d) H.Q. R.E. will move tomorrow to STAVEGHEM. (probably about O.C.c.8.8.)

2. Pontoon equipment will be dealt with as under :-

    (a) Tomorrow, 8th inst. O.C. 211 Field Coy. will arrange to send 210th pontoon equipment and vehicles to be at 210th billets at N.32.a.0.8. by 1200 and to send 223rd pontoon equipment and vehicles to be at 223rd billets in STACEGHEM by 1500.

    (b) 210 and 223 Field Coys. will send on all their bridging vehicles tomorrow (8th inst.) afternoon to their new forward camps, where they will be unloaded and will become available for carting forward light bridging material.

3. Following arrangements will be made with regard to light bridging materials :-

    (a) 5 lorries will report to 210 Field Coy. at MARCKE Church, N.11.b.0.2. at 1200 tomorrow, 8th inst. These will load up light bridging materials at MARCKE and be taken on to the workshops at N.31.c.7.8.

    (b) 3 lorries will report to 210 Field Coy. at N.31.c.7.8. at 1500 tomorrow, 8th inst. These will be loaded with one bridge complete and 48 pieces of decking.

    (c) The 8 lorries as arranged in (a) and (b) will be sent to STEENBRUGGE Dump, where 24 pieces of decking will be handed over to 223 Field Coy. The lorries will be filled up with bivouac sheet boats and the whole lot sent on and unloaded at 210 Field Coy. forward billets. By this arrangement 210 Field Coy. should be able to get the greater part of the 2 bridges and 16 bivouac sheet boats for the Right Battn. to their forward billets.

    (d) Arrangements will be made for lorries on 9th inst. to move forward 223 Field Coy's light bridging stores from STEENBRUGGE Dump.

    (e) 210 Field Coy. and 223 Field Coy. will arrange to cart with their own transport one light bridge to forward position as arranged with Battn. Commanders on the evening of the 9th inst. The second bridge will be taken up on the evening of the 10th inst. Arrangements will be made with Bde. for getting forward the 16 boats for each Battalion.

4. 211 Field Coy. will work on STEENBRUGGE Dump on the 10th inst. preparing planks and runners for making plank roads.
    210th and 223rd Field Coys. will carry out reconnaissances of the river in their Battn. area, if possible in conjunction with officers from the 7.L.I. attached to them.
    223 Field Coy. will obtain all information possible about the road, bridge River South East of BRUGGE with a view to a pontoon bridge being constructed at this point.

Date 7.11.18

                                                                        Major.

Distribution :-

    Copy No 1. 210 Field Coy.
           2. 211 do   do
           3. 225 do   do
           4. 12 K.O.Y.L.I.
           5. C.R.E.
           6. Adjt.
           7.) War Diary.
           8.)
           9. File.

SECRET.

War Diary

Copy No 8

31st Divisional Engineers (Warning) Order No 43.

The following arrangements will be made with a view to crossing the River L'ESCAUT at an early date.

(1) 92 Bde. are attacking on a 2 Battalion front, and are endeavouring before this attack to push across the stream about 1,000 West of the main river, so as to establish posts on the main river as early as possible.

(2) 223 Field Coy.R.E. and one Coy.K.O.Y.LI. will work in conjunction and will assist the left Battalion in the line.
Work to be done :-

(a) Make any bridges required by Left Battalion over the small stream W of the main river.

(b) Supply to the Battn. 16 Bivouac Sheet Boats with necessary cordage (1 per platoon). These are now bwing made at STEENBRUGGE Dump.

(c) Put two light floating bridges across the canal in the Left Battalion area.

O.C. 223 Field Coy. will get into close touch with Left Battn. in the line as soon as they come in.(probably Friday,8th.)

(3) 210th Field Coy.R.E. and one Coy. K.O.Y.L.I. will work as in (2) for Right Battn. in the line.

(4) 211 Field Coy.R.E. and one Coy. K.O.Y.L.I. will stand by ready to put a pontoon bridge across the River L'ESCAUT as soon as the situation permits. Probable site P.36.C.

(5) 12th Battn. K.O.Y.L.I. are moving tomorrow, 7th inst to MARCKE where they will carry out light bridging practice with 92 Bde. 1 light bridge and 4 canvas boats are to be brought by lorry to MARCKE Church, M.11.b.8.3. at 1500.
On 8th inst, 12th Battn. K.O.Y.L.I. will move into area about KROTE, O.4.

(6) 210 and 223 Field Coys. will probably be moved into more forward positions on the 8th, and 211th Field Coy. into the KROTE area about the same date.

Sgd. R.A.S. MANSEL.,Major.R.E.
A/C.R.E. 31st Division.

6/11/18.

Distribution :- Copy No 1. 210 Field Coy.
2. 211   do   do
3. 223   do   do
4. 12 K.O.Y.L.I.
5. C.R.E.
6. Adjt.
7. File.
8) War Diary.
9)

SECRET.   War Diary   Copy No 8

31st Divisional Engineers (Warning) Order No 42.

1. The R.E. and 12th Bn. K.O.Y.L.I. will move tomorrow, 3rd inst into the area between HALLUIN and RONCQ.

2. Moves will be made as under :-

   210th Field Coy.R.E.)
   211th Field Coy.R.E.)
   2 Coys. K.O.Y.L.I.   )   March with 92 Bde. Group.
   now in I.30. & I.36.)

   223rd Field Coy.R.E.)
   H.Q. and 1 Coy. of   )
   K.O.Y.L.I. now at   )   March with 93 Bde. Group.
   STACEGHEM.   )

3. At the conclusion of the march the R.E. and 12th K.O.Y.L.I. will as far as possible be allotted billets in close proximity to one another.

4. Units will get into touch early with Bdes. in whose group they are marching, and will make necessary arrangements with them as regards time of start, billeting parties, etc.

2/11/18.

Sgd. R.A.S. MANSEL., Major.RE.
A/C.R.E. 31st Division.

Copies to:- No 1. 210 Field Coy.
           2. 211 do   do
           3. 223 do   do
           4. 12 K.O.Y.L.I.
           5. C.R.E.
           6. Adjt.
           7. File.
           8.)
           9.) War Diary.

ORIGINAL.

CONFIDENTIAL

WAR DIARY

of

Headquarters, 31st Divisional Engineers.

From Dec.1st to Dec.31st, 1918.

VOLUME XXXVI

Army Form C. 2118.

WAR DIARY
or
INTELLIGENCE SUMMARY.
(Erase heading not required.)

Month of December Sheet (1)

Instructions regarding War Diaries and Intelligence Summaries are contained in F. S. Regs., Part II. and the Staff Manual respectively. Title pages will be prepared in manuscript.

Place	Date	Hour	Summary of Events and Information	Remarks and references to Appendices
ST. OMER	1st		Course of instruction in horse and staff management commenced at No. 23 Veterinary Hospital St Omer. Capt. McKergin detailed to attend	
	2nd		211th Fd. Co. move from Gudanaques to St Omer. C.R.E. attends a demonstration at 2nd Army Infantry School Wisques	
	3rd		Conference of Field Company Commanders. Spade Kit supplied by Division allotted to Companies and cast iron bars of small papers etc. divided	
	4th		C.R.E. attends meeting of Mounted Sports Committee	
	7th		Rehearsal of Ceremonial parade on LONGUENESSE according to all Rue Fd. Coys. R.E.	
	9th		– Practice football match played to decide in selection of a Divisional R.E. team.	
	10th		"2nd Rehearsal Parade on LONGUENESSE Aerodrome	
	13th		Rugby Football Match 223 Fd Co. v 210 and 211 Fd Coys.	
	14th		Major R.O.S. Mansel M.C. 211th Fd. Co. R.E. proceeds to 32nd Division to take over duties as C.R.E. Lt. Partridge Staff Officer, goes on Special Leave.	

Army Form C. 2118.

Sheet ②

WAR DIARY
or
INTELLIGENCE SUMMARY.
(Erase heading not required.)

Instructions regarding War Diaries and Intelligence Summaries are contained in F. S. Regs., Part II. and the Staff Manual respectively. Title pages will be prepared in manuscript.

Place	Date	Hour	Summary of Events and Information	Remarks and references to Appendices
STOMER	18/12		Special performance of Div: Concert Party for R.E. Field Companies	
	20/12		Div: Race Meeting	
	21/12		Arrangements in progress to take over dump of C.R.E. Army Troops in Lumbres	
	26/12		C.R.E visits D.D.W. in BOULOGNE to arrange details of the handing over of Stores in the C.R.E STOMER's dump	
	28/12		Lt. Bashe, 211/R Fd. Co. R.E. assumes the duties of Stores Officer	
	30/12		Section of 223 Fd. Co. R.E. move out to Chateau d'Acad near THEROUANNE to superintend the dismantling of huts. Section of 210 Fd. Co: assisting 94 Bde clearing huts in LUMBRES.	
	31/12		Rugby football match between R.E. team and 93rd Bde.	

E.B. Elkington
Capt. R.E.
for Lt. Col. C.R.E. 31st Div.

Copy No 17

R.E. INSTRUCTIONS No 74.

Tomorrow being Christmas Day will be observed as a holiday.

No work will be undertaken by Field Companies, and the C.R.E's Office will be closed throughout the day except for messages of an urgent nature.

E.B.Eckington
Capt. R.E.
Adjt, for C.R.E. 31st Division.

24/12/18.

Copies to :- No 1. C.E. XIX Corps.
2. 31 Div. 'G'.
3. 31 Div. 'Q'.
4. 210 Field Coy.
5. 211 Field Coy.
6. 223 Field Coy.
7. 92 Inf. Bde.
8. 93 Inf. Bde.
9. 94 Inf. Bde.
10. 31 Div. Arty.
11. A.D.M.S.
12. 31 Div. Train.
13. 12 K.O.Y.L.I.
14. 31 Bn.M.G.C.
15. C.R.E.
16. Adjt.
17.) War Diary.
18.)
19. File.

War Diary

Copy No 16

R.E. INSTRUCTIONS No 73.

31st Divisional Engineers Headquarters Office will be closed, except for urgent services, as follows :-

    Weekdays - From 19.30 to 09.00

    Sundays. - From 13.00 to 09.00 on Mondays.

F. Giles.

Lt.Col.R.E.

13/12/18.   C.R.E. 31st Division.

Copies to :- No 1. C.E. XIX Corps.
- No 2. 31 Div.'G'.
- No 3. 31 Div.'Q'.
- No 4. 210 Field Coy.
- No 5. 211 Field Coy.
- No 6. 223 Field Coy.
- No 7. 92 Inf. Bde.
- No 8. 93 Inf. Bde.
- No 9. 94 Inf. Bde.
- No 10. A.D.M.S.
- No 11. 31 Div. Train.
- No 12. 12 K.O.Y.L.I.
- No 13. 31 M.G. Battn.
- No 14. C.R.E.
- No 15. Adjt.
- No 16.) War Diary.
- No 17.)
- No 18. File.

WAR DIARY

Copy No 16

R.E. INSTRUCTIONS No 72.

1. On and after Monday, 9th December, working hours for Field Companies will be from 8 a.m. to mid-day, except on Saturdays, which will be reserved for drill, route marches, etc. in the morning, and Sundays for Church Parade. Any services of an urgent nature will be dealt with specially as they arise.

2. Field Companies will cease to deal direct with their respective Brigade Groups in carrying out R.E. services. All orders for work must in future come through C.R.E's Office.

E.B. 72 Kingston
Capt. R.E.

8/12/18   Adjt. for C.R.E. 31st Division.

Copies to :- No 1. C.E. XIX Corps.
2. 31 Div. 'G'.
3. 31 Div. 'Q'.
4. 210 Field Coy.
5. 211 Field Coy.
6. 223 Field Coy.
7. 92 Inf. Bde.
8. 93 Inf. Bde.
9. 94 Inf. Bde.
10. A.D.M.S.
11. 31 Div. Train.
12. 12 K.O.Y.L.I.
13. 31 M.G. Battn.
14. C.R.E.
15. Adjt.
16) War Diary.
17)
18. File.

Vol 35

WAR DIARY.

of the

HEADQUARTERS, 31st.DIVISIONAL

ROYAL ENGINEERS.

for the month of JANUARY, 1919.

Army Form C. 2118.

WAR DIARY
or
INTELLIGENCE SUMMARY.
(Erase heading not required.)

Month of January 1919. Sheet 1

Instructions regarding War Diaries and Intelligence Summaries are contained in F.S. Regs., Part II. and the Staff Manual respectively. Title pages will be prepared in manuscript.

Place	Date	Hour	Summary of Events and Information	Remarks and references to Appendices
ST OMER.	1		Takeover from C.R.E. St Omer completed.	
	2		First new camp received of the Army. Horse coppe chiefly camp reguered to be built at the concrete factory ARQUES.	
	9		Major Major arrived and takes command of 211'tFd; Co; R.E.	
	10		Rugby Football match delivered 92 Bde — Div. R.E. Team. Drawn	
	11		Divisional Cross Country Run takes place	
	13		Match 92 Bde played again. R.E. lose	
	14		Letter sent to 19th Corps. Training proposals for administration of water and electricity in St Omer.	
	15		Horseshoeing dumming competition takes place. 2/6 Fd: Co: win	
	16		Div. R.E. play 113th at Association Football & lose	
	23		Finals of Div: Boxing Competition	
	24		Cable Football Finals for Fd Columns — R.E. Fd: One drawn up.	
	27		R. E. Mess commenced at 223 Fd; Co; Camp	
	29		Troops despatched to Calais to stop R.A.O.D. Strike. 92 Bde & section of 223 Fd; Co; leave at 7 a.m. 93 + 94 Bdes follow during day.	

E.B. D Kinghn Capt R E
for C.R.E. 31 Div.

WAR DIARY

Copy No 19

R.E. INSTRUCTIONS No 75.

1. The work of C.R.E. ST. OMER and his staff has been transferred to C.R.E. 31st Division.

2. The following arrangements will therefore take place from Monday, January 6th.

   (a) WORKSHOPS, ST. OMER.

   O.C. 223 Field Coy. will detail an officer and such sappers as may be necessary to take charge of these shops and all work in R.E. Yard. This Officer will take his orders direct from C.R.E's Office only.
   Field Coy. workshops will close down and all labour be concentrated in these workshops.

   (b) R.E. YARD & STORES, S. OMER.

   Becomes Divisional R.E. Dump and is directly under Stores Officer, R.E. Officer i/c Workshops can draw on his own authority, but must keep the Stores Officer informed.

   (c) PUMPING PLANT and ELECTRIC LIGHT INSTALLATIONS.

   These will be taken over from D.O. E.L. & M. by 354 E. & M. Coy. who will be responsible for maintenance and repair. Officer i/c Workshops, ST. OMER will afford men of this unit access to and use of fitters' shop whenever required on signed authority of an Officer of O.C. 354 E. & M. Coy.

   (d) HOSPITALS and CAMPS round ST. OMER.

   Maintenance and minor repairs to these will be undertaken in the same way as other Units of 31st Division, i.e. Os.C. concerned submit indents for work to this office which, if approved, will be detailed to Field Coys. as most convenient to other work.

   (e) LABOUR.

   P. of W. Labour will be indented for daily by D.O.R.E. ST. OMER as heretofore on O.C. 203 P. of W. Coy. The numbers asked for will include

   (i) Artizans for workshops and outside jobs.
   (ii) Unskilled labour for all work.

   Hours of work of P. of W. labour are

   07.30 - 12.00
   13.15 - 15.45

J Giles

Lt.Col.R.E.
C.R.E. 31st Division.

5/1/19.

P.T.O.

Distribution:- Copy No 1. C.E. XIX Corps.
2. 31 Div. 'G'.
3. 31 Div. 'Q'.
4. 210 Field Coy.
5. 211 Field Coy.
6. 223 Field Coy.
7. D.O.R.E. ST. OMER.
8. O i/c Det. 354 E & M Coy. HOULLE.
9. 203 P of W Coy.
10. 82 Labour Group.
11. Town Major, ST. OMER.
12. D.O. E.L.& M. ST. OMER.
13. O i/c R.E. Workshops, ST. OMER.
14. No 4 Stationary Hospital.
15. No 3 Canadian Hospital.
16. C.R.E.
17. Adjt.
18. File.
19) War Diary.
20)

WAR DIARY

Copy No 8

R.E. INSTRUCTIONS No 76.

Duties of Officer i/c R.E. Workshops, ST.OMER.

1. He will have complete charge of and be responsible for R.E. Workshops, ST.OMER and all personnel employed therein.

2. He will take orders for work from C.R.E's Office only.

3. He will keep a Works Book and enter up each order as received under the following headings :-

Item No.	C.R.E's No. of order.	Date of Receipt.	Nature of Order.	Date of commencing work.	Number of men employed.	Date of C.R.E. informed of completion.	Date of Issue.

The original order will be carefully filed for reference.

4. He is authorised to draw any stores he may require to carry out his work from R.E. Yard on his own signature, but must send a duplicate to Officer i/c R.E. Stores to enable latter to keep his stock sheets up to date.

5. Priority orders will always be specified as such by C.R.E. and must be begun immediately on receipt. The entry of a priority order will be marked with a red ✱ in the Works Book.

6. He will keep C.R.E. informed of the personnel he requires, both skilled and unskilled, to carry out his work's orders and will render a Daily Report shewing on what work each man, by trade, is employed, in accordance with pro-forma as under :-

Date _____

Rank & Name.	Unit.	Trade.	How employed.	Where Working

Unskilled labour will be shewn (in totals only) under column for "Rank & Name". The rest of the form applies as for skilled men.

H. Giles.
Lt.Col.R.E.
C.R.E. 31st Division.

5/1/19.

Copies to - No 1. Lieut. MITCHELL.
2. Officer i/c R.E. Stores.
3. N.C.O. i/c ST. OMER R.E. Dump.
4. Major LANGMAN.R.E.
5. C.R.E.
6. Adjt.
7. File.
8) War Diary.
9)

WAR DIARY.

HEADQUARTERS, 51st DIVISIONAL ENGINEERS,

FEBRUARY, 1919.

Army Form C. 2118.

WAR DIARY
or
INTELLIGENCE SUMMARY. Month of February 1919.
(Erase heading not required.)

Instructions regarding War Diaries and Intelligence Summaries are contained in F. S. Regs., Part II. and the Staff Manual respectively. Title pages will be prepared in manuscript.

Place	Date	Hour	Summary of Events and Information	Remarks and references to Appendices
ST OMER	3rd		Lt. Honnesen 12th ROYLI takes over duties of Stores officer at R.E. Hd. Qrs.	
	4th		O.C. 223rd Fd. Co. attends meeting of Recruiting Committee at 2nd Army H.Q. LILLE	
	5th		Colonel Giles proceeds on duty to Rouen to attend meeting of Recruiting Committee	
	10th		All Companies reduced to Cadre B Establishment	
	11th		Colonel Giles returns from England	
	12th		Conference of O.C. Coy. Commanders to discuss proposed concentration of units	
	14th		H.Q. R.E., 210 Fd. Co. + 211 Fd. Co. move into Camp occupied by 223 Fd. Co. R.E. in Rue du Giffern. Mounted Sections concentrated in Caserne d'Albret	
	22nd		R.A. Band visits ST OMER	
	23rd		Major Mason, 211 Fd. Co. R.E. returns from leave + proceeds on duty to Russia	
	24th		Gn. KRONA held on Rangemasse Aerodrome	

E. B Berkerry
Captain
for C.R.E. 31st Division

R.E. INSTRUCTIONS No. Ø 78.   Copy To

1. On the 14th inst. units of the 51st. Div. R.E. will be
   concentrated in the camp occupied by 223rd Field Coy. R.E.,
   Rue Francois Chifflart, ST.OMER.

2. H.Q.R.E., 210 and 211 Field Coys. R.E. will move into the
   above Camp under their own arrangements.

3. Mounted Sections of 210 and 211 Field Companies will remain
   temporarily at the College St.Joseph, in charge of Lt. Melille,
   210 Field Coy. R.E.

4. In order to economise Sappers as much as possible after the
   concentration has been effected, the following arrangements
   of internal economy will be brought into force :-

   210th Field Coy. will detail :

       1 N.C.O. to run mens' messing and cookhouse.
       1 assistant to Q.M.Stores.
       1 Cook (at present at H.Q.) for men's mess.

   211th Field Coy. will detail :

       1 N.C.O. to run Sgts Mess.
       1 Cook for Officer's Mess.
       1 Officers Mess waiter.

   223rd Field Coy. will detail :

       1 Cook for men's mess.
       1 Cook "   Sgts "
       1 asst Cook for Officer's Mess.
       1 Officer's Mess waiter

       and will draw rations for all from 15th inclusive.

                                                   Lt. Col.
   13/3/18.   C. R. E. 51st Div.

   Copies to:- No.1 - 210 Fld Coy.R.E.
              " 2 - 211   "   "   "
              " 3 - 223   "   "   "
              " 4 - C.R.E.
              " 5 - Adjt.
              " 6 - File
               7) War Diary.
               8)

WAR DIARY or INTELLIGENCE SUMMARY

Army Form C. 2118.

Month of March 1919.

Place	Date	Hour	Summary of Events and Information	Remarks and references to Appendices
ST OMER	1st		Ректор? of units to Corps A ordered	
	2.3.		I gave an orchestral concert in Palace Theatre at 6 p.m.	
	4th		Matinée and evening performance by R.E. Band	
	5th		R.E. Band leaves for Cassel.	
	13th		R.E. Band leaves for Cassel. Dined with Secretary over 15 Pk. Bttn 210 Fld. Coy.	
	15th		Cadres of N.C.Os. on to offices for the Army of New Belgrade.	
	16th		Cadres of units arrived.	
			16 RE and 16 Stn on 24k	
			to prepare billets for these postings have arrived	
	17th		Officers for cadre and [illeg] for these postings have arrived on leave	
			returns from leave	
	20th		Adjt. R.E. returns from leave.	
			H.Q. R.E. cadre Park down to 3 off. & 10 F.O.s., Coy R.E.	
	21st		Impressment and Evacuation of all men overdue to leave in England	
	22nd		[illeg] with of Black list strikes in Channel ports	
	23rd		Adj? R.E. leaves for 2 1/2 in Chavannes	
			and	

www.ingramcontent.com/pod-product-compliance
Lightning Source LLC
Chambersburg PA
CBHW080925230426
43668CB00014B/2196